MW00333911

Book Traces

MATERIAL TEXTS

Book Traces

Nineteenth-Century Readers and the Future of the Library

Andrew M. Stauffer

PENN

University of Pennsylvania Press

Philadelphia

Published by
University of Pennsylvania Press
Philadelphia, Pennsylvania 19104-4112
www.upenn.edu/pennpress

Printed in the United States of America on acid-free paper

10 9 8 7 6 5 4 3 2 1

Library of Congress Cataloging-in-Publication Control Number: 2020016928

ISBN 978-0-8122-5268-2

For my parents, my children, and Megan

DRUID. Take, if you must, this little bag of dreams;
Unloose the cord, and they will wrap you round.

FERGUS. . . . Ah! Druid, Druid, what great webs of sorrow
Lay hidden in the small, slate-coloured thing!
    —W. B. Yeats, "Fergus and the Druid" (1892)

Contents

Book Traces

Introduction

I

"This is not a book of history." So begins Michel Foucault's 1979 essay "Lives of Infamous Men," a preface to a planned collection of prisoners' micro-biographies that he found in the state papers at the Bibliothèque Nationale, which he called "brief lives, encountered by chance in books and documents": "The selection found here was guided by nothing more substantial than my taste, my pleasure, an emotion, laughter, surprise, a certain dread, or some other feeling whose intensity I might have trouble justifying, now that the first moment of discovery has passed."[1] As it was in much of Foucault's work, the impetus behind "Lives of Infamous Men" is reanimation, "to revivify, to bring something back that had been buried deep in oblivion," and to reflect on the paradoxical aspects of that critical thaumaturgy.[2] Foucault set for himself the task of creating an "emphatic theater of the quotidian" (165), one that might not only stage the lives of these eighteenth-century characters but also transmit his own sense of discovery and emotional engagement at the moment of their emergence from the archives. He aimed "to restore their intensity" (158).

It was crucial for Foucault, therefore, that his subjects be unknown and their records be only brief but evocative fragments, "that they would have belonged to those billions of existences destined to pass away without a trace; that in their misfortunes, their passions, in those loves and hatred there would be something gray and ordinary in comparison with what is usually deemed worthy of being recounted. . . . I had gone in search of these sorts of particles endowed with an energy all the greater for their being small and difficult to discern" (Foucault 161–62).

Several points relevant to the book you are reading can be drawn from these passages. First, Foucault's emphasis on "chance" and "discovery," on what Alan Liu has called the "serendipitous and adventitious" aspects of the new historicist project, frames the anecdotes as "always merely found, always merely picked up."[3]

Second, Foucault emphasizes the counter-historical force of this material ("This is not a book of history"), its apparent escape from the orders of historical knowledge along two vectors, its idiosyncratic-yet-quotidian nature (i.e., it is not that which is "usually deemed worthy of being recounted"), and the emphatic affective response of the interpreter to it. Finally, as the essay moves forward, a paradoxical dialectic between order and disorder structures Foucault's representation of fragments from the archive. As Catherine Gallagher and Stephen Greenblatt argue, the counter-historical anecdote has a dark obverse: the entropic disorder of "thought in ruins," wherein "everything is in shreds and there is no possibility of repair" (72). The critic wants to drive an anecdote like a wedge into some settled historical narrative ordering, breaking it open to new possibilities; but this can also produce what seem mere piles of rubble, an anecdotal anti-order so profound in its deracination that it approaches the sublime, like the atomized "lone and level sands" that conclude that quintessentially anecdotal Romantic sonnet "Ozymandias" or the "wreckage upon wreckage" piled at the feet of Walter Benjamin's angel of history.[4]

"Brief lives, encountered by chance in books." Foucault's statement describes the foundational material and method of *Book Traces*, a project that began when I started listening to unnoticed voices in the stacks, the voices of unknown nineteenth-century readers who left marks in their books: inscriptions, marginalia, flowers, drawings, locks of hair, and other things that altered the volumes in subtle, far-reaching ways. Donated to academic institutions, these books had been on open library shelves for generations, yet their unique features were invisible to all forms of search but one: going book by book, turning every page, eyes open for traces. That was the method, and it has involved the hands of many students, librarians, and colleagues at multiple institutions.[5] This is their book, too, its argument grounded in marked books that required a community of searchers to detect and interpret. It also belongs to those past readers whose shades we summoned to help map an underlying affective economy in nineteenth-century American society that shaped, and was shaped by, book use. Finally, it belongs to you, the reader, who may find in it a partial road map for the future of our academic library collections and, by extension, for the work of the humanities.

Foucault's prisoner records were not only contingent traces in their own right; their preservation and discovery depended also on chance: "it had to be just this document, among so many others scattered and lost, which came down to us and be rediscovered and read" (163). Caught in the archival apparatus of state power like flies in amber, the brief notices of the lives of his prisoners (many of them condemned men) get transmitted at the moment of their deaths; their records survive thanks to the institutions of power that condemned them—and that also paradoxically enable the disciplinary procedures of the critic. The books and readers presented here have more varied histories and have left more traces than Foucault's examples, yet their relationship to the institutions of cultural memory that produced and sustain them is part of the story I have to tell. In framing it, I have tried to choose examples, resonant with particular energy and emotion, that might serve as touchstones of nineteenth-century reading practices, rather than attempting to give a synoptic view of readers writing in books. I have gravitated toward examples that help me get conceptual purchase on several questions: what were nineteenth-century books of poetry, and what are they now? And in what sense can the individual book—as an instance of a specific, case-bound case history—speak within a larger framework of cultural analysis?

Book Traces adopts guided serendipity as a tactic in pursuit of two goals: first, to read nineteenth-century poetry through the traces left by ordinary nineteenth-century readers in their books; and second, to defend the value of the physical, circulating collections of nineteenth-century volumes in academic libraries.[6] The vulnerability of those printed books—both their material fragility and their institutional precarity in the digital age—underlies the contributions I hope to make to the history of reading and to library policy conversations. In addition, I engage debates about the relative value of close and distant reading, primarily by grounding my argument in a method that might be called intimate or micro-reading: paying close attention to what a poem in a particular material vehicle meant to a specific individual. Sentimental attachment is part of both my subject and my method. For a number of reasons that this book explores, the examples I have chosen tend toward narratives of loss. In almost every case presented here, I start from a particular book of poetry pulled by hand (and, in a sense, by chance) from a shelf in the open stacks of a college or university library, uncatalogued except as a copy of that edition and available to be checked out by patrons. In these books I found inscriptions, annotations, and insertions made by their original owners, and, using these as exemplary cases, I have turned to rare-book rooms, special collections, and online resources to unpack their histories. The marks in question were not made by library patrons; rather, they can be definitively traced to specific nineteenth-century readers who transformed their own books by marking them. In so doing, the readers have illuminated the braided significance of poems and particular books as sites of sociability and reverie, of love and melancholy.

Sentimentality is integral to these books and how they were marked, in two ways. First, most of them contain verse by poets whom we tend to classify, at least in part, under the heading of the sentimental: Thomas Moore, Felicia Hemans, Jean Ingelow, Henry Wadsworth Longfellow, John Greenleaf Whittier, James Whitcomb Riley, and other popular authors of the century on both sides of the Atlantic. Second, the inscriptions themselves are charged with emotion—mourning lost beloveds and dead children, recording moments of recognition, and using poetry to build a language for the self in episodes of passion. And if we think we can resist the emotional appeals of sentimental nineteenth-century verse, the marginalia can surprise us. When we as modern critics encounter these old books with their handwritten traces of former lives, we are drawn toward a fresh encounter with the poetry, reawakened by affect. We read the poetry through the eyes of someone for whom it was personal. In this way, we arrive at a clearer understanding of the value of our inherited library of nineteenth-century books. Not only do they give us direct evidence of what poetry and books meant to the culture that is our object of study, but they reorient our perspective on literary value by channeling the sympathy and sentiment of the past. Further, these marked copies elevate the individual, the specimen, the example, and the case—they counter the views of copies as duplicates and lives as reducible to the mass data of demography. In that way, they amount to a defense of the humanities.

An example by way of orientation: an 1881 book titled *Geraldine: A Souvenir of the St. Lawrence*, from the circulating collection at the University of Louisville, once owned by Esther Annie Brown (1863–1936) of Cloverport, Kentucky.[7] This is the first edition of Alphonso Alva Hopkins's long narrative poem of romance, *Geraldine*, written in anapestic couplets and bearing close similarities to Owen Meredith's wildly popular verse novel *Lucile* (1860). Sometime before 1887, when she married Arthur Younger Ford, Brown wrote on the flyleaf, "Esther A. Brown's / Geraldine / Handle with care & / return promptly."[8] The imperative nature of that inscription points to the fact that this book circulated among a group of readers, at least four of whom (including Brown herself) annotated it heavily in pencil. Beyond making these orthographic marks, someone also inserted several honeysuckle blossoms between the pages. Many passages were marked as worthy of special attention with brackets, underlining, and X's, and, in the margins of 80 of the book's 321 pages, Brown and her friends wrote verbal remarks on the poem, frequently in dialogue with one another. Marginalia like these offer a detailed view of readers' responses to poetry while also revealing the sociability of the reading and interpretation that occurred on the pages of a shared volume. A little world is encoded there.[9]

The amount of marginalia in this volume of *Geraldine*, and the interactive character of that marginalia, establishes the book as an object of special interest for the historian of reading. As one examines the penciled commentaries, each in a recognizably different hand, a community of readers begins to emerge. Next to lines in the poem describing life as a "battle-field wide," one reader has written, "A true but sad story of life's struggle" (171). But after an inset lyric about life as the "Valley of Tears," a different reader has commented, "I do not take such a 'tearful' view of life. Its valleys of tears are not quite dark & we do not have to remain in them long" (197). In this copy, the poem frequently prompts such med-itations when its readers react to passages as texts that stand alone, apart from their dramatic context. For example, next to the lines "Woman lost Eden to man; / But he finds it again in her love," one reader has written, "A happy hit, if true," and a second has replied (perhaps with irony), "it must be true from the <u>many</u> happy homes" (84). Near a passage regretting that men do not bear "the respect that they ought for all women," one reader has remarked, "True & it is to man's shame" (55). It is fascinatingly possible in a book like this to observe nineteenth-century poetry as readerly practice, its strategies worked out collaboratively over time by means of marginal annotations. Next to the poem's supposition "if poetry means / to bewil-der the senses with fanciful scenes," Brown has penciled "not my idea of poetry," and directly beneath that, a second reader has written "nor mine" (8).

The marginalia in Brown's book display a range of responses, including those that spot connections to other poems.[10] But the majority of the annotations in this copy focus on the characters of the poem and their behavior in the romance plot—with special attention to the manipulative Isabel Lee, whom these readers love to hate. Throughout the volume, less is written by the annotators about the saintly heroine, Geraldine, whom one reader calls in her marginal notes only "a noble character" and "a lovely woman" (200, 253). But of Isabel, one writes, "I do not like her" (213), and another writes elsewhere, "I have no patience with Mrs. Lee" (111). Annotating Isabel's proclamation of love's power—"Such a love as a man gives one woman in life"—one reader writes, "Beautiful," but another takes a dimmer view: "The thought is beautiful but it came not from her heart so I think this deceit destroys" (98). Brown's comment on the same passage puts a fine point on it: "She talks well but I detest her" (98). On one particular pair of pages (see Figures 1a and 1b), we see at least four different hands commenting on Isabel's character; one writes, "It is hard to tell whether she is simply acting a part or showing her real heart & its language," and another, "I doubt her sincerity and rather suspect that she is a trained 'flirt'" (99).

If we pay close attention to the various kinds of handwriting in this copy of *Geraldine*, personalities start to emerge. On a passage describing the "lingering kisses" between the hero, Percy Trent, and Isabel, one wry reader remarks in the margin, "They are a little fond of that pastime," and another follows that with "Who blames them?" (113). Later, that sardonic first reader writes after Isabel's submissive praise of Trent's genius as a poet, "enough to make a man forget him-self" (211). Of Isabel's lament that she is haunted by the ghost of Trent in his ab-sence, this same reader comments, "She is making this 'ghost' of hers a cause for frequent appeals. It's a troublesome ghost" (234). And she responds to Isabel's epistolary question to Trent, "Am I writing / Unreason?" with the salty retort, "I think so—and forgetting that it would have been nobler to help Trent be true to

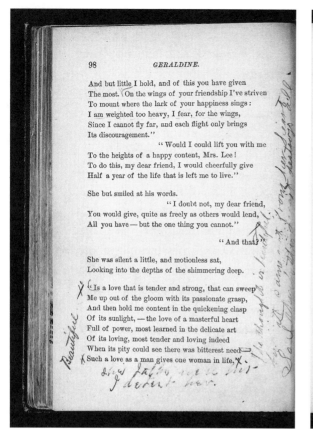
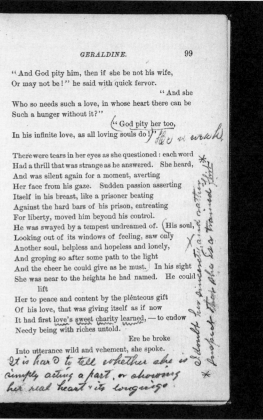

Figure 1a and b. Marginalia in Alphonso Alva Hopkins, *Geraldine: A Souvenir of the St. Lawrence* (Boston: James R. Osgood, 1881), 98–99. Esther Annie Brown's copy. Donated by Arthur Y. Ford, University of Louisville Library. PS 1999 .H415G3 1881.

his duty in forgetting her, than to be making his burden harder to bear by telling of such love" (240). At the end of that section of the poem, she adds the annotation "Take warning friends, and be sure of your affections before your committal." But another reader takes a different view, following this remark with an opinion written just beneath it: "Miss Lee spoke only in fun; he was a fool for being so easily duped" (146).

These annotations evince a culture of reading and book use whose features both recall our current social media exchanges (e.g., sharing, texting, liking, commenting on comments) and also seem part of a lost world, given their penciled form on the pages of a long narrative poem in anapestic couplets.[11] That is, the marginalians' use of the poem involves strategies we recognize, such as spotting allusions and close reading for character, and ones that are less familiar, like the decontextualized commentary on poetic phrases as philosophical propositions, a kind of aphoristic reading practice by which people incorporated poetry into the operating systems of their lives.[12] As I will emphasize in the chapters that follow, another, less familiar type of annotation used by nineteenth-century readers of poetry appears in Brown's volume, a type that involves personalization and memorialization. Midway through *Geraldine*, the narrator laments the end of a day of sweet happiness: "If it take / Of our heart's-ease, and cruelly leave but the ache / Of disquietude, hunger, and longing, what need / That we wonder and grieve?" In her copy, Esther has bracketed these lines and written a date in the margin, "Jan. 19th, '82" (193). Drawing a quiet analogy between the words of the poem and remembered events, she reads the lines as an expression of her own fate, adopting their words as the language of emotion. A little more light is shed later in the book, where Esther comments on a passage in which Trent parts from Isabel, saying, "I am going away. . . . We must follow the line / Of our separate fates" (237). In the margin, Brown writes, "Leaves from rose room to hear Faust, Jan. 1882," a miniature vignette of romantic parting in the rose room, when a beloved headed to the opera without her. Date-stamping her copy this way, Brown turns *Geraldine* into a souvenir—not of the "St. Lawrence" of its subtitle, but of her own emotional life. Finding this particular book on a library shelf, the modern critic engages with Hopkins's *Geraldine* according to neglected modes of personal reading that made poetry crucial to identity in the nineteenth century.

Through its marginalia, Brown's copy of *Geraldine* has been transfigured in ways that help us see what books and poems were to nineteenth-century readers—how they functioned as social objects, remembrancers, and fields upon which those readers developed their identities. In taking this annotated copy as a primary source, I am working within a robust tradition of reading history that has demonstrated the evidentiary value of marginalia and other physical traces left in books, from the doodled snails decorating medieval manuscripts, to the classical and biblical commentaries crowding around early printed texts, to the scholarly annotation of copies of Erasmus, to the running marginal skirmishes between Blake and Reynolds, and beyond. Most of the critical and historical work on these traces has focused on medieval and early modern readers and their books, including Kathryn M. Rudy's *Postcards on Parchment: The Social Lives of Medieval Books*, William Sherman's *Used Books: Marking Readers in Renaissance England*, Stephen Orgel's *The Reader in the Book*, the essay collection *Women's Bookscapes in Early Modern Britain*, and Abigail Williams's *The Social Life of Books: Reading Together in the Eighteenth-Century Home*.[13] Heather Jackson's seminal work *Marginalia* exposed and taxonomized a great number of examples of the practice of readers writing in books in the period before 1830, after which, as she argued in a later work, she sees the practice of book annotation as "in retreat."[14] After the Romantic era, Jackson writes, "What seems to have happened is that by and large readers retreated into themselves, and annotation became predominantly a private affair, a matter of self-expression. Annotating readers went underground" (*Romantic Readers* 73). But a book like Brown's *Geraldine* challenges that assumption, suggesting that more work needs to be done on the readers of the long nineteenth century.[15] The rise of middle-class reading and book culture in the Victorian era has been an oft-told history, but personal copies have so far played a minor role.[16]

Part of the problem has been the great quantity and dispersal of nineteenth-century volumes, their medium-rare status making them more available for casual reading but, in some ways, less suitable for scholarly study than earlier materials held, well catalogued and preserved, in rare-book rooms. Many academic libraries in North America built their general collections primarily through donations and bequests of family libraries, particularly before World War II. Usually the rarer and older books would receive high levels of care and descriptive record keeping, but the vast range of nineteenth- and early twentieth-century imprints were conscripted to fill the shelves of the general research libraries. Such books were meant to circulate as mere copies rather than to abide as permanent artifacts. Their browsable discoverability has been foundational for the Book Traces project, which uses many hands and eyes to discover and help catalogue the inscribed and annotated books from library shelves. Yet those shelves—a tiny percentage of which we have been able to traverse thus far—are also places of vulnerability, especially now.

The fact that many nineteenth-century books are currently in circulating collections rather than rare book rooms amplifies concerns regarding their future. In many academic libraries, plans to decrease the size of physical collections are well under way. Nineteenth-century print volumes are particularly vulnerable to downsizing, for a number of reasons. Most books printed before 1800 have been moved to special collections, and most books printed after 1923 remain in copyright in the United States and thus cannot be shared freely online. In addition, many nineteenth-century books are in bad condition, due not only to the cheaper materials used in their making as the century went forward but also to the sheer length of time they have spent in the circulating collections of libraries. This is even more true of books printed after 1860, when wood-pulp paper—now often tan and brittle from the acids used in its making—came into general use in the publishing trade.[17] In addition, many of these books are not valuable first editions but rather reprints, collections, and later printings that typically have not been given much attention by collectors or scholars.[18] The result is a neglected set of materials, increasingly housed in offsite storage warehouses and represented by online surrogates offered by Google, HathiTrust, and others.

Yet we need the lessons these books have to teach, the stories they have to tell. The great age of print produced our reading habits and the academic institutions within which we now operate.[19] That is, it reflected and elaborated the legacies of Romanticism that continue to shape our understanding of time and memory and of the humanities and their materials of study. If we want to make good decisions regarding the disposition and preservation of these books, we need to look at them afresh, as bibliographic interfaces that encouraged various forms of interaction, as affective souvenirs and platforms for self-development, and as literary objects that for a time helped make poetry a household word. Emerging from many hours and from hands moving through the library stacks, what follows is an attempt to gather examples, anecdotal but evocative and evidentiary, left by the ordinary readers of the great age of mass literacy and industrial printing (roughly 1830 to the early twentieth century)—the age when books were king.

Two important recent studies have unfolded and elucidated the bibliographically inflected imaginations of readers in the nineteenth century.[20] In *How to Do Things with Books in Victorian Britain*, Leah Price explores "representations and perceptions of, and fantasies and illusions about, the circulation of books" during this period (36). She reveals the operative tensions among the reading, handling, and circulating of books across the Victorian era and conducts a rich survey of its book culture by looking at episodes of what she calls nonreading and excessive reading. Her stated aim is to "reconstruct nineteenth-century understandings of, and feelings toward, the uses of printed matter" (5). Like me, she is interested in the ways books get turned by their users into operational objects: go-betweens, shields, agents—ultimately, carriers of relationships. Similarly, in *Dreaming in Books: The Making of the Bibliographic Imagination in the Romantic Age*, Andrew Piper asks "how we became bookish at the turn of the nineteenth century" and demonstrates "how the printed book was a far more richly imagined and a far more diversely used media object than we have traditionally assumed" (3, 4).

Both Price and Piper expand our historical conceptions of reading by thinking bibliographically, or rather by examining intersections of literary content and book form as cultural nodes. As Piper writes, "It was through Romantic literature where individuals came to understand their books, and it was through their books where they came to understand themselves" (*Dreaming* 4). For Piper, the "bibliographic surplus" of the nineteenth century gave rise to a proliferation of book formats and genres, and this diversity opened up new networks of expression that enlivened thinking about the relationship of the individual to the social and the material to the cultural (5). Nineteenth-century books were explicitly open, unfinished, and interrelational: their cultural roles emerged out of ongoing negotiations among authors, publishers, printers, illustrators, and readers.[21] Piper offers a vision of books as primarily social objects, whose details of production and reception left traces that are key to their significance and meaning. Moreover, whereas Price depends primarily on textual (i.e., linguistic) evidence for discerning the Victorians' attitudes toward print, Piper "insists upon a hands-on encounter with books as the central means of understanding our bibliographic heritage" (8). His work takes us back to specific editions, and in some cases specific copies, to meditate on the meanings of their interlocking verbal and bibliographic codes.

Book Traces is an experiment based on the book in the hand, a return to the specific material objects once held and used by nineteenth-century readers. At the same time, my study attends to the hand in the book: the marks left behind in those individual copies by their owners. Witness a traced hand on the rear free endpaper of an 1853 copy of the *Works of William Shakespeare*, with the schoolgirl Miriam Trowbridge's teasing inscription, "Ruthie Whitehead's ugly hand—Oh! No, I mean beautiful one—" (see Plate 1). Made circa 1855 when the girls were classmates at Madame Chegary's fashionable boarding school in New York, these hand tracings make visible the somatic, haptic processes of reading, calling us to attend to historical books as physical and social interfaces and suggesting the presence of past lives that accumulate in books as they move through time.[22] Price proceeds toward such phenomena by way of metaphor, first recalling *The Mill on the Floss* and Maggie Tulliver's encounter with an old book with its "corners turned down in many places," in which "some hand, now forever quiet, had made at certain passages strong pen and ink marks, long since browned by time."[23] Maggie follows those brown marginal notations—were they manicules?—toward a conversion experience, a "thrill of awe" and "ecstasy" brought about by her guided reading (G. Eliot 310). Recalling this scene, Price sets her agenda: "the most interesting question to ask of these hands now quiet may be not what they felt about the book but why they felt so much. To grope our way back into their intellectual and emotional and ethical investments in paper . . ." (*How to Do Things* 18). Amplifying Price's metaphor, I have grounded this book in the examination of individual copies of nineteenth-century volumes—primarily of poetry—that have been marked by their original owners and readers. Handling a great many of these books, I have made uncertain contact with the hands of the dead, like Swinburne with his book of Baudelaire's poems: "These I salute, these touch, these clasp and fold / As though a hand were in my hand to hold."[24] Or perhaps like Whitman: "This is no book, / Who touches this, touches a man, / (Is it night? Are we here alone?) / It is I you hold, and who holds you, / I spring from the pages into your arms."[25]

In emphasizing my contact with the past, I am following Gillian Silverman's recent work on nineteenth-century reading and "the fantasy of communion."[26] And we both follow the work of Stephen Greenblatt, who wrote famously in his 1988 *Shakespearian Negotiations*, "I began with the desire to speak with the dead. . . . [T]he dead had contrived to leave textual traces of themselves, and those traces make themselves heard in the voices of the living. Many of the traces have little resonance, though every one, even the most trivial or tedious, contains some fragment of lost life; others seem uncannily full of the will to be heard."[27] Like Greenblatt, I am interested in "trying to track what can only be glimpsed, as it were, at the margins of the text" and in so doing, explicate "a poetics of culture" (4, 5). For him, the "textual traces" left by the dead resolve to "voices." Working from Shakespeare and focusing on the discursive exchanges of that era, he finds his metaphor of contact in sound: "speak," "resonance," "heard." My own method is more bibliographically minded and materially based, depending not only on verbal content but also on the material formats of books and the physical traces left in them by past readers: the marks, lines, notations, and other modifications made to their personal volumes. I am invested in the detailed, pathos-driven anecdote as the primary mode of engagement with the past, Greenblatt's "speak[ing] with the dead" by employing "some fragment of lost life." As Alan Liu has argued, New Historicist criticism finds its center in "its passion for constructing microworlds each . . . intricately detailed, yet also . . . expansive in mythic possibility."[28] Liu identifies a legacy of Romanticism and its pursuit of "transcendental release" via fragments and "minute particulars" (76): the idiosyncratic local detail of past lives and "lost life-worlds" (86). The result here is what Foucault describes as "an anthology of existences: singular lives, transformed into strange poems[,] . . . that . . . I decided to gather into a kind of herbarium" (157).

I turn to printed books of nineteenth-century poems as sites of uncertain memory, a phenomenon visible not only in the personalizing, appropriative, revisited marks left by everyday readers but also in the reveries that encounters with books inspired and continue to evoke. As Silverman puts it, books were "recognized by nineteenth-century readers as deeply personal communications, the touch of which could conjure up the hand of the long-dead author"; at times "the reader recognizes in the used book the traces of another (the stranger, the friend, even the very reader herself at an earlier moment), and the book becomes revered as a material record of a human past" (79). Such marks and reveries help us understand the place of books as domestic and social objects, as scenes for imaginative projection that transformed personal volumes into souvenirs, diaries, love letters, and memorial sites—into bargains with mortality. They also reveal how poems were integrated into, and in some sense were the occasion for, the emotional lives of their readers. But marked copies not only show us the lives of the long dead; they also allow us to trace the roots of our own emotionally charged attitudes toward the book as both a platform and an interface, attitudes inherited from the nineteenth century and now perhaps changing in response to new forms of media. How did we learn to love the secular book with an intimacy, even a ferocity, beyond the scope of its contents? What did it mean for modern, middle-class readers to involve their lives with books and poems beyond holy scriptures, and what gains and losses were enjoined upon them with that bargain? How can a richer understanding of that history help inform our collective decisions about the future of print collections in the digital age?

Answering such questions means confronting the limits of our standard models of close and distant reading, both of which depend on asserting an objective stance toward linguistic structures and textual information. It is clear that, following the modernist rejection of nineteenth-century mushiness, many literary critics are still wary of sentimental literary works and emotional responses to them. W. K. Wimsatt's doctrine of the affective fallacy still holds an uneven sway.[29] For the close reader, a poem generates its meanings in networks of language; for the distant reader, large networks of language can be organized according to statistical, evolutionary models of culture.[30] But neither mode has much to say about what a particular poem meant to a particular reader or about the larger importance of personal, human reading habits for literary history. Yet for nineteenth-century readers of poetry, sentiment was a crucial category, as it remains for historians of reading.[31] Robyn R. Warhol writes that, although feminist academics have "rehabilitated" sentimentality "particularly in nineteenth-century U.S. women's literature, . . . [t]races of distaste for being made to cry still surface . . . in what even the most progressive critics say—or don't say—about sentimentality."[32] My attraction to sentiment involves its origins in both impulse and reflection, the doubled or mediated reaction that James Chandler takes as his subject in *An Archaeology of Sympathy*.[33] As he puts it, "Sentiments . . . are the result of a projective imagination across a network or relay of regard" (12)—precisely the marginalian's mode of reaction, in which emotion is rendered into marks legible (at least in part) to other readers in a real or envisioned network.

In writing about my own emotional reactions to the books I present here, I am similarly in search of a sentimental idiom that might carry us through to a rediscovered mode of critical engagement. Recently, Rita Felski has made the case for the affective phenomenology of reading: she argues that we literary critics have been too skeptical, demystifying and diagnosing literary texts while excluding readers' "emphatic experiences" of literature, including our own.[34] In responding to Felski's call, I want to emphasize that those interactions are embodied and embedded not only within language (by which they move from affect to sentiment), but also within media that have a cultural history of their own. What follows is an attempt to see my way into those emphatic experiences of previous readers and book users, making room for the legacy of sentiment, attachment, and emotional experience transmitted by nineteenth-century volumes. I am tracing empathic moments often communicated by means of emphatic traces: underlining, brackets, check marks, and handwritten pointers of various kinds.

Under such conditions, reading becomes vertiginous. On the table is the specific physical book, itself a layered construction; on its pages, the verbal text, printed and perhaps marked or annotated; above the text, the reader, shaped by the past; around the reader, the institutions that inform the scene of reading. At every level, not only has the evidence been determined by multiple cultural forces that could be adduced and analyzed, but also every attempt to read such evidence has been structured by the larger phenomenon under investigation—that is, by the dynamics of modern memory and its relation to the codex. As Pierre Nora has characterized it, memory in "our hopelessly forgetful modern societies" is vestigial, mediated, "nothing more in fact than sifted and sorted historical traces."[35] He writes, "Modern memory is, above all, archival. It relies entirely on the materiality of the trace," which enables the "thaumaturgical operation" of the interpreter (13, 18). Like Felski, and like Greenblatt speaking with the dead, Nora in effect calls for a personally inflected critical method, one that admits the interpreter into the frame, "an art of implementation, practiced in the fragile happiness derived from relating to rehabilitated objects and from the involvement of the historian in his or her subject" (24). So, book, text, and reader are in a layered field of analysis and enchantment, an affective biblio-critical method that can move among the words of a poem, its material embodiments and markings, and the interpretive scene itself, redeeming for a moment the vanished past and revealing the heterochronic, eventful nature of books as constellations of encounters.[36]

A reader's traces elevate to visibility and even legibility some fragment of a book's past. That fragment might serve as evidence in a historical narrative of reading practices, even as we acknowledge that, as Michael C. Cohen has written, "given that so much reading goes unmarked, any reader who has left behind a trace of his or her readings is no longer a representative reader."[37] Price writes in a similar vein, "The most impassioned reading destroys its own traces. The greater a reader's engagement with the text, the less likely he or she is to pause long enough to leave a record: if an uncut page signals withdrawal, a blank margin just as often betrays an absorption too rapt for note taking. Can a book mark us if we mark it?"[38] The short answer is yes, a claim I attempt to make good on with the examples presented here. Although their presence is anomalous, marginalia make at least partially visible that which is normally lost: the reader's encounter with pages as interfaces, as individual sites of engagement within the larger bundle called the book and within the larger culture of book use in which that encounter took place. We find evidence not merely of reading but also of the navigation, interaction, and modification of bibliographic media from various impulses and toward various ends. Marks in books transform our own experience of the book, tilting it toward an artifactual encounter, a way out of the fierce presentism of our personal and professional lives. Unique marks in printed books remind us forcefully of the individuality of every copy, which in turn evokes the individual who owned or borrowed the book and made those marks in the first place. Set against the sameness of the mass-produced book, and asserting the lived experience of individual persons against the wash of time, marginalia and inscriptions transform the codex from a container of verbal content into a memorial, time capsule, or message in a bottle. The future of books is predicated on the futures evoked by their individual, heterochronic pasts. Personal markings alter our reception of books in ways both intellectual and institutional, and both of these influences shape the future of the nineteenth-century book.[39]

In her study of the history of the document as such, Lisa Gitelman pays close attention to specific subgenres of text objects in an attempt "to adjust the focus of media studies away from grand catchall categories like 'manuscript' and 'print' and toward an embarrassment of material forms that have together supported such a varied and evolving scriptural economy."[40] Gitelman unfolds the history of things like the movie ticket, the library card, and the application form, revealing the underlying material economies of documentary production and use in American society from 1870 to the present. Gitelman's habits of attention provide a crucial supplement to the abstract theoretical frameworks of book history, and my own work moves even further toward that "embarrassment of material forms" by attending to specific books—that is, singular, individual copies, each with its own history. As Benjamin adapts the Latin tag *habent sua fata libelli*, "not only books but also copies of books have their fates" (*Illuminations*, 61). Copy-level attention takes us beneath genre for a moment, revealing the layered and variable quality of books whose category we thought we knew. Looking at individual volumes, we find traces—we could call them hypodata—that challenge the certainties of metadata and of our assumptions about the sameness of books printed in the industrial era. Personal inscriptions, dates, annotations, and records of lives interact with the ostensible content of the printed books. Yet such books also strike one as eccentric, partial, even private: they remain stubbornly anecdotal in a world of big data, wherein the verbal contents of hundreds or thousands of books are available for computational analysis. Under the wide-angle lens of the distant reader, the single copy—unless we are talking about the medieval or early modern book, long recognized as sites of evidentiary import, or the book owned and marked by someone famous—fades to insignificance. This is a different order of "the great unread": the millions of copies of nineteenth-century books now held by academic libraries but passed over for the sake of modern editions, including digital ones. How can we begin to integrate this massive, distributed archive into our histories of nineteenth-century reading?

Quantitative analysis might help. Networked archives can be searched and manipulated in ways that produce new objects for analysis: lists, graphs, statistical reports, topic clusters, and the like, which provide new perspectives on nineteenth-century reading outside the book-reader relation. Indeed, digital technology seems to offer ways to exploit the virtual to make the past operational, beyond the materiality of the trace and the embodied reading practices engendered thereby. But in these chapters, I model a kind of intimate micro-reading. I proceed by way of a small-scale, associative method, investing in biographical detail and giving space to a range of subjective responses. That is, I have chosen a qualitative over a quantitative approach, avoiding any attempt at statistical significance (except, perhaps, in my final chapter) and choosing resonant examples emblematic of larger practices of book use in the nineteenth century and evocative of our abidingly Romantic attitudes toward the historical book. I am persuaded by Theodore M. Porter, who has argued that "quantification is a technology of distance," the whole ethos of which is "the exclusion of judgment, the struggle against subjectivity."[41] Distant reading proceeds from an assumption that distance brings an empirical clarity unavailable at close range, avoiding the partiality of the lovingly curated anecdote and responding to John Plotz's concern "that those who claim too close a proximity to their material often end up telling stories of their own lives and minds, not of those they set out to map."[42] I suppose humanistic interpretation always takes that risk, submerging currents of personal investment in scholarly argument or diverting them through channels of intellectual rigor, but in either case implanting some portion of the evidence that interpretation purports to discover. This I deem a risk worth running: a liability, if it is one, that remains inextricable from certain sorts of reward—witness Emerson's "alienated majesty" of selfhood on detour—that humanist scholarship seeks.[43] Given the nature of the material I am presenting (individual personal copies of books) and of the questions I am pursuing (what did books mean, and what do they mean now?), doubling down on subjectivities within networks, and even committing to sentiment, seems appropriate. As Nicholas Dames speculates, "What if you didn't resist nostalgia, face it with political suspicion, or mask it with sophistication, but immersed yourself in it so directly that you ended up coming out the other side? You'd risk sentimentality and obviousness, but you'd have taken a stab at clarity."[44]

Svetlana Boym helps us move in this direction, offering a renewed vision of nostalgia in which "longing and critical thinking are not opposed to one another."[45] For Boym, nostalgia is a "rebellion against the modern idea of time," a mental state that "can present an ethical and creative challenge, not merely a pretext for midnight melancholias" (xv, xvii). She defines nostalgia as "the mourning of displacement and temporal irreversibility," and she places it "at the very core of the modern condition," "a historical emotion that came of age at the time of Romanticism and is coeval with the birth of mass culture" (xvi, 16). In other words, it is an emotion bound up with the history of the modern book. Part of this involvement has to do with the fragmentation and deracination of the archive. Boym writes, "Reflective nostalgia cherishes shattered fragments of memory . . . the incompleteness, the fossil, the ruin, the miniature, the souvenir, not the total recreation of a past" (49, 16). The surplus of paper that haunted the nineteenth-century imagination also fed it, providing ready materials for longing after immemorial traces.[46] At the same time, modern ideas of reading significantly overlap the nostalgic reverie: the escape from time's current, a move that Christina Lupton explores as reading's "irregularity and the dream of revolt against . . . regimens of productivity."[47] In Boym's description, one could easily replace "longing" with "reading": "There is, after all, something pleasantly outmoded about the very idea of longing. We long to prolong our time, to make it free, to daydream, against all odds resisting external pressures and flickering computer screens. . . . Nostalgic time is that time-out-of-time of daydreaming and longing that jeopardizes one's timetables" (xix). The contrast here between the dream time of nostalgia and the "pressures" associated with the "flickering computer screen" is telling in its resemblance to laments over the end of deep reading in the digital age.[48] In other words, the charge of nostalgia leveled against the sentimental attachment to old books is completely overdetermined. Within a literary horizon, it cannot be evaded, if only because post-Enlightenment ideas of books and identity, and of reading and longing, have always been entangled. Moreover, poetry in the long Romantic tradition made its business the elaboration of these entanglements. From Keats with his Chapman's Homer (or even Crabbe with his parish register) onward, much of the enduring verse of the nineteenth century uses this kind of reverie—a synthesis of reading and longing meant to evoke its sympathetic double in the reader—as its driving engine. As Lupton says, "It's reading poetry that gets you out of time" (*Reading* 13).[49]

Marginalia, sentimentality, nostalgia, and poetry seem wound inextricably together in the nineteenth century. Throughout the Romantic and Victorian eras, poetry in particular inspired readers to become annotators. Books were growing cheaper and more commonplace, literacy was rising precipitously, and printed poetry was permeating middle-class life in the form of gift books, albums, periodicals, collected editions, scrapbooks, and other media of transmission. In addition, poetry on the page was often surrounded by white space for annotation.[50] For some who were critical of what they saw as poetry's decline toward the domestic and the conventional, the cheapness of the books and the cheapness of the sentiments went hand in hand, both prompts to the annotating reader. Volumes of nineteenth-century poetry implicitly ask us to confront the claims of nostalgia in nuanced ways, as we recognize the deep engagement of that era's book culture with commonplace affect and the rhetoric of the full catastrophe of our human compulsions, triumphs, and bereavements. Our analysis of nineteenth-century books cannot be merely sentimental, but neither can it remain wholly disengaged from the sentiment that forms part of the historical record. We need to approach the nineteenth-century book in a spirit of rigorous nostalgia: an essentially homeopathic method whereby our nostalgia for the nineteenth century can run interference, make an opening through that century's nostalgia for the many traditions that its own industrial modernity had estranged it from, and in the process bring us closer to a doubled truth, its own and ours.

II

Since the mid-twentieth century, academic libraries in the United States have usually divided their print collections into two categories: special and circulating. Books in special or rare collections are counted as unique objects, meriting augmented cataloguing, extra security, preservation in the form of custom-made housings and regulated storage conditions, rules for careful handling, and conservation efforts to repair wear and damage. This attention is predicated on the idea that researchers, now and in the future, will need ongoing access to a particular artifact, not merely a copy of a work (e.g., Henry David Thoreau's *A Week on the Concord and Merrimack Rivers*) or even an instance of an edition (e.g., the 1849 Boston edition of *A Week on the Concord and Merrimack Rivers*) but a physical item with its own history and individual features (e.g., Walt Whitman's annotated copy of the 1849 edition of *A Week on the Concord and Merrimack Rivers*, now in the Library of Congress).[51] It almost goes without saying that most of these books are valuable assets in their own right; they are collectors' items and would fetch significant sums if sold. Circulating books, on the other hand, receive comparatively low levels of support. The assumption is that they are indeed copies, not especially rare, and replaceable as needed. Instances of circulating books fall easily into the category of duplicates, imagined as identical for the purposes of scholarship. Humanities research in fact depends on the duplicate nature of the scholarly record, the idea that the physical copy or digital version of this book you are reading is, in essence, the same as the one currently being read by someone else across the country. Hence libraries' reliance on interlibrary loans or Google book scans (created mostly from books found in the circulating stacks) for many nineteenth-century circulating materials. Put simply, circulating collections supply access to content in replaceable copies, whereas special collections supply access to unique bibliographic objects that have acquired value either for sheer rarity or insofar as they are differentiated from other instances of their type.

I rehearse these matters for the obvious reason: most of the books discussed in this study were found in the circulating collections of academic libraries.

Discovered by students, faculty members, and librarians during hands-on searches, these books challenge the distinction between special and circulating collections in their emphatic singularity, in their marks of individual history, in their visible traces of provenance and use. All used books bear such traces to some degree. The question becomes, what can we make of such evidence? Or perhaps, what types and levels of marking are sufficient to draw attention (and resources) to a singular physical book? A single scuff mark on a binding is not going to be enough, but an elaborate set of annotations might be—especially if they were made by an original owner of the book, a historical reader whose re-actions we have come to value because of the passage of time. Do markings need to be made by a Coleridge to matter, or, as the nineteenth century recedes, do the everyday readers of that era merit our attention? This book is an attempt to demonstrate the dividends of attention paid to a specific subset of such materials: books of poetry found on library shelves.

Like all archives, this one has a broader social history unique to the American context. John Higham reminds us, "In 1860, there was no American university fully worthy of the name. The United States had no libraries of national or international renown."[52] Most academic libraries either were departmental affairs or, as the century wore on, consisted of a single room and a few thousand volumes at most. But, according to the library historian Phyllis Dain, as American colleges and universities grew and professionalized in the early twentieth century, library collections began "a steep move upward in holdings," which were in many cases built up by donations of books by alumni, professors, literary societies, trustees, and local families—often the descendants of the books' original nineteenth-century owners and readers.[53] As Dain says, at many academic institutions, "not until well into the twentieth century did reliance upon gifts . . . give way to substantial regular general appropriations" (15). So large numbers of nineteenth-century volumes came into academic libraries from private donors during this period, roughly until the transformative academic growth of the post–World War II era.[54] Unless these books were in fine condition, rare and valuable, or were associated with a well-known historical personage, they went onto the circulating shelves, where they formed a substantial but unevenly relevant (and casually preserved) component of the research collections.[55] In fact, according to Neil Harris, "before the 1930s . . . few universities had well-established rare book or special collections departments," so the stacks may have been the only option for some donated books.[56] This arrangement worked out well anyway, because libraries at that time wanted large print collections to enhance their status. And at many colleges and universities, those books still occupy the same open shelves, having mostly failed as circulating materials and never been reclas-sified as "special," because of the relative plenitude of books from the age of industrial printing.[57] The result is that one of the greatest archives of American middle-class reading remains hidden in plain sight, uncatalogued as such and distributed across the library shelves of academic institutions—and now endangered, as readers prefer modern or digital editions, and libraries are moving away from commitments to their local print collections.

In this distributed archive, it appears that approximately 10 percent of the books printed before 1923 contain inscriptions, annotations, and other marks made by their owners and readers.[58] Such traces are even more common in books of poetry, in which female readers feature prominently—as they do in the examples I present here. By the end of this book, you will have encountered Esther Brown and Miriam Trowbridge (again), Ellen Pierrepont, Charlotte Cocke, Deborah Adams, Annie Deering, Henrietta Partridge, Elsie Barlow, Mary Cosby, Juliana Shields, Jane Slaughter, Sallie Meredith, Emily Clark, and others. They all are nineteenth-century readers of poetry whose books contain evidence of their interactions, opinions, and experiences. I did not set out to write a history of women's reading, but their books emerged to provide terms and examples that had a compelling unity and force. Part of my impetus was to get outside traditional library protocols that privilege famous (typically male) writers and readers, to start paying attention to other orders of the archive. Of course, these orders have their own exclusions, because most—though not all—of the nineteenth-century books donated to academic libraries came from white, wealthy families of that era.[59] But at least this is a beginning—a first look at the marks in books on the shelves. What were the communities of readers that contributed to the collections, and what did books and poems mean for those communities? In order to pursue these questions, we need the books to remain available at their institutions.

To us now, printed books are a technology of patience; old books seem heavy with time. In the following chapters, I attempt to reinhabit some of the volumes on the shelves and draw out a poetics of reading that might enlarge our sense of the nineteenth-century book. As the books and their layered marks dictate, my four primary chapters are heuristic and thematic, with considerable overlap among them. The chapter titles relate to nineteenth-century literary works whose titles offer provisional answers to my earlier questions: what were nineteenth-century books of poetry then, and what are they now? Each of these answers— "Images in Lava," "Gardens of Verse," "Time Machines," and "Velveteen Rabbits"—is meant to evoke a cluster of relations among poets, publishers, and readers, visible chronically in the poems, the books, and the traces left in individual copies. My final chapter, "Postcard from the Volcano," turns to issues of academic library policy and the future of the print collections on which my research has depended. Far from offering a comprehensive survey, this book is resolutely meant as a series of braided case studies involving a prevalent strain of poetic reading among a primarily female, middle-class, American audience. I am carving a relatively narrow swath through the archive in pursuit of evidence of a distinctive nineteenth-century mode: the personal appropriation of poetry, which depends in part on the rise of Romantic reading practices and the sociocultural developments that brought printed books into everyday domestic life in nineteenth-century Britain and America. Taken as a whole, these chapters suggest several larger themes governing the use of poetry and poetic volumes in the long nineteenth century, including personalization, adoption, revisitation, memorialization, and interpersonal exchange—a range of activities and experiences that fall under the larger heading of interacting with print. At the same time, I mean to point out the ways in which our own critical methods are productively involved with the affective dynamics that these examples model. *Book Traces* is a contribution to, and a brief on behalf of, the new sentimentalism in book history.[60]

Chapter 1, "Images in Lava: Felicia Hemans, Sentiment, and Annotation," presents the origin story of the Book Traces project in the University of Virginia library stacks, and it uses nineteenth-century copies of Felicia Hemans's poetry to address a paradox in her reception history. Modern critics have often attempted to rescue Hemans from the terms of her own popularity; what if instead we immersed ourselves in the dynamics of sentiment that propelled her to fame, and allowed ourselves to read her work unencumbered by the prejudices of later reactions against it? Beginning with an annotated copy of Hemans's works discovered in the library by my students, I examine marginalia of longing and bereavement by female readers of Hemans, by means of which their books come to recall Hemans's poem "The Image in Lava": a "thing of years departed" upon which "woman's heart hath left a trace."[61] Such books help make a case for the importance of affect and personal emotion in our apprehension of nineteenth-century poetry, which its readers valued as a collaborative, intimate language for the heart. Specific historical copies allow us to apprehend the evidence of such personal application, bringing to view what Hemans, and what books of poetry more generally, offered to readers. We need to find ways to integrate such books into our accounts of nineteenth-century literary history, and to do this we need them to remain in our library collections. As Hemans puts it in the last line of her poem (using italics as if it were a marginalian's emphatic underlining), "It must, it *must* be so!"

My second chapter, "Gardens of Verse: Botanical Souvenirs and Lyric Reading," focuses on poetry books that have flowers and leaves pressed between their pages. Using examples found in the University of Miami library stacks and elsewhere, I show how botanical material was pervasively and complexly involved with poetry as it was written, published, and read in this era. Poets such as Letitia Landon, Elizabeth Barrett Browning, John Greenleaf Whittier, and Jean Ingelow wrote knowing that floral, botanical practices were part of the field of reception; publishers and illustrators designed books that called them forth and echoed them; and readers engaged in this layered scene of reception as they inserted blossoms and buds between the leaves. Emblems of ephemerality and resurrection, of memory and its fading, the pressed flowers come to incarnate the lyric reading moment. Botanical insertions in books of poems create souvenirs of Romantic reading, involved with nature and ideas about the self in time. Further, I argue that readers' alterations of their books by means of such insertions amount to interpretive deformations of the page, formal experiments in design and meaning making that anticipate modernist aesthetics. I show how illustrators alluded to those practices in later Victorian editions of both Wordsworth and Ingelow, depicting inserted flowers in a trompe l'oeil mode, and I connect these books to anxieties over the fate of individuality in modern culture. What does it mean to be a copy, a specimen, an instance? A flower in a personalized book of sentimental poetry is an incarnate meditation on the question.

In Chapter 3, "Time Machines: Poetry, Memory, and the Date-Marked Book," I examine the readerly practice of affixing specific dates to poems, anchoring them along one's personal timeline and within an ethos of rereading. The two prime Romantic modes of poetic reading—sublime discovery and nostalgic revisitation—converge in books marked with dates, which preserve multiple reading moments in their marginalia. Thomas Hardy's "Her Initials" and W. B. Yeats's "When You Are Old" model poetic reading as a process of recognition and nostalgia, epiphany and longing. Four books of poetry (found in the stacks at Virginia, Columbia, and Louisville) form the heart of the chapter. Each one contains annotations by a different pair of nineteenth-century lovers, written next to poems and revisited and re-annotated later; those marks enhance and make visible the multiple temporal layers of the book. The poems presented in these books—by Winthrop Mackworth Praed, James Wright Simmons, Thomas Moore, and Henry Wadsworth Longfellow—provide our reading couples with occasions for flirtation, personalization, disagreement, affinity, longing, and loss. In turn, the books demonstrate poetry's integration into the emotional and romantic lives of its readers over time. These books suggest the origins of our own attitudes toward nineteenth-century books as objects in (and out of) time, instinct with the passions of the dead. They remind us of the complex temporality and affective overloading of the historical book.

Chapter 4, "Velveteen Rabbits: Sentiment and the Transfiguration of Books," takes the Margery Williams story about a plush rabbit becoming real as a parable of the balance between investment and damage that can transform books into artifacts and heirlooms, objects in relation to the bodies of their owners and readers. Well-loved volumes seem to conjure past readers and past selves with the marks and scars they bear, as bibliophilic poetry of the nineteenth century reflects. Worn copies, like the locks of hair they sometimes contain, remind us of the embodied nature of reading even as they inspire reveries of lost time, of childhood, of the ghosts of readings past. In this chapter, I present a series of poems—by Barrett Browning, Walter Learned, Frank L. Stanton, Eliza Cook, Hemans, Tennyson, and others—in individually marked nineteenth-century volumes that reflect readers' oscillation between looking at books as material remains and viewing poems in terms of transcendent memory. Our phenomenologies of reading need to account for the material book itself as a sentimental, transitional object that is fundamental to the affective processing of its contents. Its evolution from pristine copy to marked and worn relic is driven by multiple readerly engagements, its defacement a kind of transfiguration.

My final chapter, "Postcard from the Volcano: On the Future of Library Print Collections," presents a defense of library print collections in the digital age, a call to action on the part of scholars, students, and librarians to reengage with the granular bibliographic history embedded in those collections. Proponents of shared print networks and the downsizing of print have, in general, overestimated the extent to which one copy of any book can truly serve as a duplicate for another. Libraries are now contending with the preservation and access issues surrounding their legacy print collections even as they are experiencing almost irresistible pressures to make room for more study space, more digital resources, and more-flexible research environments. All of that means fewer books on the open shelves. If they would like to resist the warehousing and deduplication of little-used multiple copies, scholars of the nineteenth century must demonstrate now, in their research and teaching, that those copies still matter, that individual physical volumes are necessary as part of an alternative conception of the content of books. I close with a defense of the book-filled academic library as a laboratory and research site crucial to the humanities disciplines, one that also serves as an archive of each institution, community, and region that built its collections over time. Housed and preserved in spaces of collective discovery, these battered, enhanced volumes are envoys to a future that will need them.

CHAPTER 1

Images in Lava

Felicia Hemans, Sentiment, and Annotation

I

In the fall semester of 2009, I asked the students in my graduate seminar on nineteenth-century British poetry at the University of Virginia to go into the stacks of our research library and find a nineteenth-century copy of Felicia Hemans's poetry to bring to class. The idea was to leave behind the modern anthologies and see what Hemans's poetry looked like in its original formats. After all, Hemans was one of the most popular poets of that era, and I wanted us to consider that fact at the level of media, examining books as they had appeared to her readerships across the century.[1] I knew that our library—like many academic libraries—had a large number of Victorian editions in the circulating collection. Neither rare nor up-to-date, these books exist in a kind of institutional shadowland, somewhere between the valuable first editions and the efficient modern ones. I had a sense they might have things to tell us about Hemans that were otherwise occluded. But the assignment was a mere impulse, not well theorized. And it ran athwart standard bibliographical practice in its embrace of randomness and its leveling of editions: the students were being asked to follow their noses, not seek out specific volumes to describe and assemble into genealogies. Any Hemans volume printed before 1900 would do. More exceptionally, they were being asked to do their research in the circulating collection, the open stacks. The vast majority of scholars interested in bibliography and book history do their work in special collections and rare-book rooms. In those contexts, one encounters volumes already recognized as important in any number of ways: rare, early, valuable, owned by the famous. Indeed, if I had thought more clearly, or planned ahead, we undoubtedly would have looked at the Hemans books in our special collections instead, comparing early editions, looking at well-curated, carefully preserved copies. But then we would not have made the discoveries that underlie this chapter and, ultimately, this book.

As the students talked about the books in front of them, they gravitated to the bookplates, library stamps, pen and pencil markings, and written inscriptions, most of which I was ready to dismiss as irrelevant afterformations, even damage. After all, these were circulating library books, vulnerable for decades to the shocks and scars of shelf life at a busy university. But one of the volumes brought us up short: a battered 1843 edition of *The Poetical Works of Mrs. Felicia Hemans*, published in Philadelphia by Grigg & Elliot. A student pointed to a poem written in pencil on the rear free endpaper and asked, "What's this?" (Figure 2):

> Sing mournfully, sing mournfully
> Our dearly loved is gone.
> The gifted and the beautiful
> Is from our sight withdrawn.
> Then let us sing her requiem now
> In this our parting hour
> And softly breathe her name, who was
> Our fairest, loveliest flower
>   Mary, Mary, Mary

It was a poem in Hemans's own style (adapting lines from "The Nightingale's Death-Song" and "Burial of an Emigrant's Child in the Forests"), written in pencil in nineteenth-century cursive and clearly the work of the book's original owner: she had inscribed her name in the same hand on the title page, "Ellen Pierrepont / 1846."[2] Our first thought was that it might be a transcription of an obscure poem by Hemans or another poet, but online searches turned up nothing. More searching led us to family genealogies, and we determined that Ellen Pierrepont had married James Monroe Minor in 1847 and had had a daughter Mary (her third), who was born in 1855 and died at the age of seven.[3] The poem was an elegy for her. As this story emerged, I think all of us in that classroom knew we had made contact with a life, had glimpsed a moment in the history of reading, the import of which we felt but had yet to understand. We had touched the edge of something, being ourselves touched by a fragment of a much larger archive that had been occluded by the protocols of our discipline and institutions.

The discovery of this volume and its inscriptions was necessarily accidental: marks in books in the circulating stacks are uncatalogued and often thought of as damage or graffiti. Further, the conditions for our explication of the volume's history had only just emerged in 2009. On the one hand, we needed the plenitude of physical books in the open stacks: the multiple, historically layered

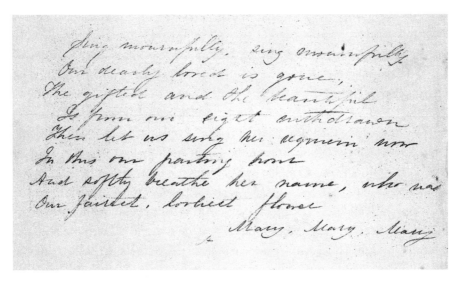

Figure 2. Inscription on rear endpaper of *The Poetical Works of Mrs. Felicia Hemans* (Philadelphia: Grigg & Elliot, 1843). Ellen Pierrepont Minor's copy. Alderman Library, University of Virginia. PR 4780 .A1 1843.

copies of the same content (Hemans's poetical works) available for browsing, cross-comparison, and serendipitous discovery. On the other, in order to determine the originality of the elegy for Mary Minor and to discover the details of the Pierrepont and Minor families, we needed Google Books, HathiTrust, and large-scale genealogical sites like Ancestry.com, which did not exist even five years earlier. If we had found the book then, we would have been uncertain how to proceed: the task of unearthing the histories of both poem and family would have been too daunting. Yet we were able to do that research on the fly, in the classroom, from our laptops. It was the synthesis of two types of searching—one among the books in the stacks and another among massive text repositories and databases online—that brought this volume to life. And if we had waited much longer, the books might not have been there: older print collections across the nation's academic libraries are currently being moved off-site, consolidated, and downsized, particularly in the wake of the large-scale digitization projects that have made nineteenth-century content so readily available online.[4]

But what is "nineteenth-century content" after all? My students' discovery made very clear the difference among copies as well as the importance of these books as individual scenes of evidence in the history of reading and book use. Marked copies offer rich data for literary historians, but their work has mostly stopped short of the nineteenth century.[5] Yet readers continued to write in books, many of which are now held in circulating library collections. As library patrons increasingly turn to online surrogates for nineteenth-century texts, and as libraries reconfigure their collections as distributed, collective networks of content rather than copy-specific collections, these unique books are under a general threat of loss. In a related way, as scholars write literary histories based on the reading of abstracted printed texts—whether in modern anthologies or large digital data sets—they elide the individual bibliographic features fundamental to literature as a cultural activity. In this chapter and those that follow, I mean to give a copy-specific inflection to the study of reader response and affect, and to make the case for intimate micro-reading as a counterweight to both New Critical modes of close reading that assume an objective stance and to the distant reading of the nineteenth century now well under way in the digital humanities. In the background, you should hear an implicit call for the retention of physical books in libraries, not out of mere sentiment but predicated on a renewed attention to them as objects and interfaces with sentimental histories of their own. As we will see, Hemans turns out to be an ideal author with whom to pursue such a project.

A number of the other Hemans volumes we looked at that day had names, dates, inscriptions, and marginalia clearly placed there by nineteenth-century readers. But the elegy for Mary Minor haunted us, in part because we had just read Hemans's poem "The Image in Lava," with which it seemed to resonate heavily. In a note, Hemans describes its subject: "The impression of a woman's form, with an infant clasped to the bosom, found at the uncovering of Herculaneum"—that is, a concave imprint of the ancient bodies of a mother and child preserved in rock after the eruption of Mount Vesuvius:

> Thou thing of years departed!
>   What ages have gone by,
> Since here the mournful seal was set
>   By love and agony!
>
> Temple and tower have mouldered,
>   Empires from earth have passed
> And woman's heart hath left a trace
>   Those glories to outlast!
>
> And childhood's fragile image
>   Thus fearfully enshrined,
> Survives the proud memorials reared
>   By conquerors of mankind.[6]

In the context of Ellen Pierrepont Minor's copy of Hemans, "The Image in Lava" seemed to be about that book itself, a "thing of years departed" set with "the mournful seal" of the elegy, Mary Minor's "fragile image / Thus fearfully en-shrined." "Woman's heart" had "left a trace" in this book, which we encountered in a spirit of sympathetic and even sentimental awe. This inscribed book had sur-prised us and drawn us into the imaginative field of Hemans's poetics, a field far wider and deeper than we had imagined.[7]

"The Image in Lava" models a certain kind of encounter with material from the past. We might call it sympathetic reading—part evocation, part projection— of the kind we now were practicing with a mother's handwritten elegy for her daughter. As Brian P. Elliott has written of the poem, "The poet creates a space for the speaker's elegiac personal mourning by 'emptying' the central objects of meaning. . . . Hemans creates objects of contemplation that are ciphers . . . whose impersonal nature opens up the possibility of intensely personal investment."[8] Hemans's mother had died in 1827, the year in which she wrote "The Image in Lava." Reading about the impression of the mother and child, Hemans fills in the gaps, expanding the reference by investing it with personal emotion drawn from her recent experience. In so doing, she makes the "print upon the dust" re-fer to her own biography and feelings. As a matter of disciplinary expertise, we typically discourage this mode of reading by our students, who often want liter-ature to be relatable, to refer to their own emotional experiences.[9] We urge in-stead objectivity and hermeneutical rigor, leading them from alienation to tentative mastery by means of careful reading, theorizing, and research. But now we were outside those protocols, in the midst of a layered scene of identification and sentiment: Hemans with her ancient monument, Pierrepont with Hemans's poetry, and our class with Pierrepont's book.

Recent theoretical work has addressed the relation between such responses and the enterprise of literary criticism. In *Theory of the Lyric* (2017), Jonathan Culler urges us to question "the presumption that poems exist to be interpreted," and to develop new—or rediscover old—models of reading lyrics: we might "take them to illuminate the world" rather than using them as occasions for hermeneutic elabo-ration.[10] Mary Louise Kete's work on sentimental collaboration, in which she re-jects the idea that sentimentality involves merely "a sham display of emotion," provides another framework here.[11] Reading a different mourning poem written by a nineteenth-century mother for her dead child, Kete finds that "the distinguishing function of the poetics of sentimentality is . . . to reattach symbolic connections that have been severed by the contingencies of human existence" (6). Pierrepont's plural pronouns—"let us sing her requiem now / In this our parting hour"— partake of this collaborative sentimental dynamic, evoking a community of mourners (call it a family) that may sing aloud and together the very poem now being read silently and alone. Marks in books of poetry cross this divide of private and public affective response. Karen Sánchez-Eppler writes that while "the loss of a child must be one of the most intimate of griefs, . . . the myriad of nineteenth-century child elegies suggests that the death of a child serves a public function as well," articulating "anxieties over the commodification of affect" in that culture.[12] The mid-nineteenth century, she writes elsewhere, saw the rise of various cultural practices involving poetry (such as making scrapbooks and sending greeting cards) predicated on the idea that "someone else's words . . . might provide the best expression of private feeling."[13] For me and my students, this copy of Hemans authorized our own sentimental collaborations in the classroom.

Pierrepont's book also exposes a tension in Hemans criticism, since modern literary historians have at times been disdainful of Hemans's nineteenth-century readers. Susan J. Wolfson writes that the recovery of Hemans "has been a project of rescuing her from the terms of her nineteenth-century popularity."[14] Stephen C. Behrendt similarly identifies "the central problem in 'Hemans studies': the split between the famous sentimentalized poet, 'Mrs. Hemans,' and the largely unappreciated interrogator of cultural practices [and] cultural assumptions."[15] Beginning with Tricia Lootens's article in 1994, several influential studies have stressed the fierce complexities of Hemans's imagination, presenting her as a subtle critic of patriarchal violence and the costs of empire, even amid her ostensible domestic commitments that her Victorian reviewers praised.[16] David E. Latané has pointed out the contradiction in our implicit dismissal of the readers that made her one of the most popular poets of the century: "If we are going to teach Hemans against the grain, demonstrating how her poetry may be seen to be socially progressive, feminist, or more ironic than presumed, then raising the issue of popularity causes problems of intentionality because we must then assume . . . Hemans's readers did not know how to read her."[17] Now, confronted with a book owned, read, and marked by one of those readers, we realized we might be in a better position to produce a sympathetic account of Hemans's popularity and to get a purchase on the affective dynamics of her work—a project begun by Marlon Ross but never much pursued according to the responses of individual readers.[18]

But we needed to know more. A little research revealed that Pierrepont's collected edition of Hemans, produced by the Philadelphia publisher Grigg & Elliot, was a very common book: first stereotyped in 1836 and augmented and reprinted almost annually for several decades, Grigg & Elliot editions became perhaps the most common and affordable editions of Hemans's collected work for nineteenth-century Americans.[19] We also discovered that the University of Virginia holds another copy, in special collections, published in 1839 and inscribed "To Charlotte M. Cocke . . . from a friend, Xmas 1840."[20] Charlotte Cocke annotated it lightly, marking about a dozen poems with signs of emphasis. But on one page, the level of attention increases radically: underlining, brackets, check marks, and exclamation points erupt across the text of "The Graves of a Household," especially around the third stanza (see Plate 2): "One, 'midst the forests of the West, / By a dark stream is laid—/ The Indian knows his place of rest, / Far in the cedar shade" (lines 9–12). Next to these lines, Cocke (now Mrs. Charlotte Gordon) has written, "My darling William / died Dec 29th / 1879." For Hemans as a British poet, that "Indian" in the "cedar shade" was likely meant to evoke a colonial scene in western India (as in Tennyson's "Locksley Hall": "Where in wild Mahratta-battle fell my father evil-starred"), but Cocke has relocated the reference to Fort Concho, in western Texas, and made the Indian presiding over her son's grave into a Native American.[21] And at the bottom of the page, she has written one word, apparently in response to Hemans's conclusion, "Alas! For love, if thou wert all, / And nought beyond, O earth!" (lines 31–32). That one word is "No": a denial of Hemans's conditional lament that earthly existence and mortal love might be, in fact, all she wrote. Like Pierrepont, Charlotte Mary Cocke (1818–81) received her copy of Hemans when she was young (Cocke was twenty-two years old) and unmarried, and she turned to it much later as a mother to mourn the loss of a child: William Fitzhugh Gordon died at the age of twenty-eight in Texas, by the dark streams of "the West," exactly thirty-nine Christmases after Cocke first received her Hemans book as a gift.[22] As it has in Pierrepont's copy, Hemans's poetry has become a touchstone for maternal loss, and the book has taken on a quasimemorial character, marked and revisited across the years.

One more example, with a difference: another copy of the Grigg & Elliot edition of Hemans (this one published in 1836), which I bought after these initial discoveries. According to the gift inscription, it was given "To Miss Catherine Taylord with fatherly affection and esteem," in Charleston, South Carolina, on November 1, 1837. Its reader has marked the book extensively in pencil, placing brackets around lines, underlining passages throughout the entire volume, and turning down the corners of several pages. But that is all: there are no other identifying marks or dates or marginalia. Furthermore, I have been unable to find out anything more about Miss Taylord and her family. As is the case for most old books, its human history—its journey from the press to readers and owners to ourselves—is encrypted, traceable only in the most general ways. Yet some themes emerge from her marking of various passages in the book. She registers nostalgia for a lost childhood home (the "My home of youth!" stanza from "The Forest Sanctuary," on page 15); a desire for love ("Oh give me . . . a human heart where my own may lean!" from "Fairy Favours," on page 318); the promise of reunions in heaven ("There is a land where those who loved, when here, / Shall meet to love again" from "The Troubadour and Richard Coeur de Lion," on page 145); fond memories of her mother ("the eyes of the mother shine soft" from "The Land of Dreams," on page 245); affection for a sister (e.g., "Sister, sweet Sister!

let me weep a while" from "The Sisters of Scio," on page 238); faith in the Christian God ("Heaven hath balm for every wound it makes" from "Stanzas to the Memory of the late King," on page 155); and a lament for a dead child ("No bitter tears for thee be shed / Blossom of being!," from "Dirge of a Child," on page 267). These are commonplaces for a nineteenth-century reader—indeed, they resemble extracts in a commonplace book, reflecting typical experiences of the generally white, middle-class, and often female audience for Hemans's poetry. But in Taylord's penciled lines and markings, we are catching the traces of a single life, of a hand in motion, a mind at work, a heart yearning, a soul aching or comforted. Her home, her mother, her sister, her beloved—these belonged to her, and her thoughts of them were brought to bear powerfully upon her reading of Hemans's poetry. In turn, they instantiate a wider practice of adoptive and adaptive reading that was a key feature of nineteenth-century poetic consumption.

Annotations like Taylord's allow us to witness this layering of common and individual experience—so fundamental to Hemans's poetic procedures—on the page itself. The printed words (ostensibly public) and penciled underlining (ostensibly private) produce a third space, a field of encounter that might in fact *be* sentimental poetry as a completed circuit and is likely the closest thing we have to pure evidence of reading. We do not know the exact import of the marks: she may have been admiring the poems generally or recognizing them as applying pointedly to her own experiences. Moreover, for all we know, she may have left unmarked the poems that struck her most poignantly, transfixing the annotator. But, because Taylord marked her copy of Hemans sporadically throughout (and thus across a period of reading and revisiting the book), we can construct a tentative persona that emerges from the themes and subjects that attracted her attention. Are they Hemans's themes? Or Taylord's? Or are they, now, our own? The field of encounter is not limited to the book and its annotator; it also includes readers in the present, whose sympathetic imagination of their predecessors (Hemans and Taylord) folds back upon their own experiences. You cannot read this copy of Hemans without the emphases Taylord has added to the passages she selected; your eye is drawn to the underlined passages and bracketed stanzas. And so it becomes a different kind of media object, a collaborative record that calls for doubled engagement with the poems and with this past reader.

Such engagement has risks, in that this book plainly offers to expose readers' hearts, luring them away from a distanced, objective perspective and into emotional crosscurrents of sympathy and recognition—not just with Hemans's poetry but with the reader who made it her own and left marks to dream on. In fact, a kind of fear comes over me each time I begin to read parts of it, since I already know that Hemans has the power to shatter if I allow myself to be taken inside her poetry and sympathize with its rhetoric and themes, as Taylord's marks

essentially require me to do. Her nonverbal marks encourage me to supplement them with details from my own experiences: my childhood home, my beloved, my mother. And suddenly I am in a palimpsest of longing and grief,
absorbing and projecting sentiment alongside Hemans and Taylord according to
the dynamics they have modeled. "The Image in Lava" is a parable of those dynamics, as I have said, and Hemans's readers followed them as they read, volunteering their own hearts and leaving traces of their own projections in their
copies of her poems, their own often "mournful seal[s] of love and agony."[23] The
book exposes this sentimental theater of meaning by drawing me into its operations directly—in short, by making me cry.

II

Thus far I have discussed three copies of the Grigg & Elliot edition of *The Poetical Works of Mrs. Felicia Hemans*, published from stereotype plates in Philadelphia in 1836 (Taylord's copy), 1839 (Cocke's copy), and 1843 (Pierrepont's
copy). Led by accident to examine the markings within them, I have come to see
them as case studies in a mode of reading that runs athwart the priorities of
much literary-critical practice, particularly with regard to Hemans's poetry. Individual copies with their marks of reading can be powerful sources of evidence
for the literary historian, yet, in general, nineteenth-century marginalia have
not been given much attention, in part because book annotation was such a common practice. Virtually ubiquitous, the marks of everyday reading in nonrare
books remain uncatalogued and thus largely unavailable for analysis. We
know, however, that such marks were seen by nineteenth-century commentators
as proof of a poet's influence. In the preface to the 1836 Grigg & Elliot edition of
Hemans, the anonymous editor writes that an author's true fame

> is seen not in the diamond editions that glitter on the centre-tables of gen-
> teel society, or crowd, with everything else, the bibliopole's multifarious
> collections of rarities; but in the ragged volumes of every circulating li-
> brary, grown old and illegible before their time by dint of reading—and
> the thumbed copies that lie on the window-ledge of the poor man's cot-
> tage, with the leaves turned down by the good woman "to keep the
> place." . . . [T]hese are the quick pulses that prove the existence of an au-
> thor in his fame. Such has been already the success of Mrs. Hemans.[24]

With this homely vignette of book use and book marking as key measures of
Hemans's fame, the editor emphasizes the involvement of literary history with

material book history while also evoking the centrality of the domestic scene of reading in and for Hemans. Evidence of use—the "ragged" library volumes and the personal "thumbed copies" with "leaves turned down"—provides the index of a reception history that the editor imagines for the volume in the reader's hands, its pages ready for thumbing, turning, and marking. It seems that commentators have long noted that what is generally true for all poets is intensely so for Hemans: reading her sympathetically and historically depends on the material record of what was read, and how. And as Rachel Ablow has reminded us, emotions were key to the experience: "in the mid- to late nineteenth century, reading was commonly regarded as at least as valuable as an affective experience as it was as a way to convey information or increasing understanding."[25]

In his 1822 essay "Detached Thoughts on Books and Reading," Charles Lamb professes a preference for "sullied leaves" that lead to reveries of former readers:

> Thomson's *Seasons*, again, looks best (I maintain it) a little torn, and dog's-eared. How beautiful to a genuine lover of reading are the sullied leaves, and worn out appearance, nay, the very odour . . . of an old "Circulating Library" Tom Jones, or Vicar of Wakefield! How they speak of the thousand thumbs, that have turned over their pages with delight!—of the lone sempstress, whom they may have cheered . . . after her long day's needle-toil, running far into midnight, when she has snatched an hour, ill spared from sleep, to steep her cares, as in some Lethean cup, in spelling out their enchanting contents! Who would have them a whit less soiled? What better condition could we desire to see them in?[26]

Like the "good woman" in the "poor man's cottage" who has enthusiastically thumbed the leaves of her Hemans, Lamb's "lone sempstress" is summoned by the speculative imagination of an inheritor. Examining the worn book with its traces of use, Lamb uses them to work an enchantment of his own, a spell of evocation that brings the sempstress-reader before him as a figure of lonely reading at midnight, not without a hint of the erotic. I will have more to say about this potent cocktail of nostalgia and desire that often drives engagements with old books, but for now I want only to register the fact that Hemans's contemporaries were already engaged with the processes of imaginative reception history. The corollary point is that much nineteenth-century poetry was written in expectation, and even elicitation, of readers' traces.

Jerome McGann has written that "the dynamic of [sentimental] poetry gets clarified by one of its most characteristic answering forms—the personal reading, and in particular the private response articulated in marginalia. . . . Most useful are the marginalia generated by ordinary people in volumes of sentimental poets from their personal libraries," what he calls elsewhere "fragile gestures toward communion" that offer to expose the limits of typical, professional ways of reading meaning in poems.[27] McGann cites a copy of Letitia Landon's poetry—another artifact of the 1840s—to illustrate this point:

> I have in my library an interesting book, *The Poetical Works of Miss Landon*, published in Boston in 1841, in one volume. On the front flyleaf is a signature in ink, "C.R. Stenson," . . . [and] near the end of the book is a poem titled, "Can You Forget Me." These are its last five lines:
>
>> The happy hours that I have pass'd while kneeling
>>> Half slave, half child, to gaze upon thy face.
>> —But what to thee this passionate appealing—
>>> Let my heart break—it is a common case.
>>>> You have forgotten me.
>
> The marginal note here, placed next to the first line I have quoted, is a date: "1846 & 1847." ("Private Enigmas" 459–60)

For McGann, this marked copy evokes "a sympathetic injunction to enter into and share this transatlantic mid-Victorian exchange on the subject of frustrated desire" (461). He uses this copy of Landon's poetry as a prompt to think past our critical paradigms of reading, beyond, as Rita Felski puts it, "the limits of critique." Those limits or rules of engagement, within which such private sentimental reactions are found inconsequential or even dangerously soft-minded, were the reason my students and I could find and read these marked books only by chance, as part of a series of blind moves that led us outside the perimeter of standard critical practice. Once there, it became clear that we had to approach these annotations programmatically and even rigorously, even as we held a space open for sentiment and for the rush of sympathetic feeling that underlay their making and our reception of them.

After reading Taylord's copy, I returned to the Hemans books owned by Cocke and Pierrepont, with eyes freshly open to the aggregated effect of nonverbal marks of emphasis across the volumes. Cocke's rather minimal underlining and bracketing (on about a dozen passages in the whole book) revealed at first only a general piety—for example, various passages in "The Sceptic" dealing with Christian faith (148–53), and the last three stanzas of "The Nightingale," which are essentially a prayer for mercy and protection from "Father in Heaven" (252). Yet, given the importance she placed on the passage "One midst the forests of the West" from "The Graves of a Household," two other marked passages stood out. The first is from "Edith: A Tale of the Woods," in which Cocke has underlined a passage that reads in part,

> solemn are the boundless woods
> Of the great Western World, when day declines,
> And louder sounds the roll of distant floods
>
> ·
>
> Awful it is for human heart to bear
> The might and burden of the solitude!
>
> ·
>
> Of him alone she thought, whose languid head
> Faintly upon her wedded bosom fell;
> Memory of aught but him on earth was fled,
> While heavily she felt his life-blood well
> Fast o'er her garments forth (211, lines 1–3, 7–8, 25–29)

Although the date of this underlining is unknown, one is tempted to make the connection: a mother's imagining of the scene of her distant son's death, a mournfully envisioned *pietà* with his dying head on her bosom, in those "forests of the West," "the boundless woods / Of the great Western World." The second passage comes a bit later in the volume: in "The Release of Tasso," Cocke underlines a single sentence in the midst of a long column of verse: "Was the deep forest lonely unto him / With all its whispering leaves?" (279). Both passages seem to prompt a grieving mother's emphasis, reading Hemans in fearful sympathy with her son's experiences and end in the forests of Texas. One of the last poems Cocke underlines in the volume is "The Angels' Call": the whole is double-bracketed, and the penultimate stanza has a check mark next to it, as Cocke doubles down on Hemans's own emphasizing italics: "Come to thy father!—it is finished now; / *Thy tears have all been shed* " (406). She died two years after losing her son, in 1881.

When I returned to Pierrepont's copy, the elegy for Mary Minor written in that book led me to predict what the annotations would emphasize. I expected marks on poems such as "Dirge of a Child," "Burial of an Emigrant's Child in the Forests," and "The Nightingale's Death-Song"—we know she read these last two closely because she echoes them in her poem for Mary. Instead, a different story tentatively emerges, one that I had not noticed in my first pass through the volume. I should note here the difficulty of navigating these editions of Hemans. Each has 556 pages of double-columned text with no index. Small, lightly penciled marks appear in the margins and text, and many of these books are in poor condition (Pierrepont's copy has a broken binding, its first gathering of pages is detached, and its spine has been repaired with brown duct tape). If you want to find a particular poem, you have to search the table of contents, which is not particularly helpful. The poems are grouped according to Hemans's published volumes, with large swaths of unordered "Miscellaneous Poems."[28] This aspect of the book makes annotation a strategy of orientation if nothing else, and Pierrepont does mark a number of titles in the table of contents as apparent favorites.

Two poems in the book receive particular attention from Pierrepont, in that they are accompanied by verbal marginalia. I will say more about the mute brackets and check marks that appear throughout the volume, but these two with marginalia are key: "The Italian Girl's Hymn to the Virgin" and "To the Memory of Bishop Heber." Both attest to Hemans's strength as a poet of post-Romantic hymns and prayers such as "A Prayer of Affection," "The Prayer in the Wilderness," and "Evening Prayer at a Girls' School," all of which have been marked with emphasis by either Taylord or Pierrepont. Although Hemans is known as an admirer primarily of Byron's and Wordsworth's poetry, Shelley's also provides her with a model for the rhetoric of supplication and desire that she so consistently and movingly voices in her lyrics.[29] Working in a Christian framework, and poised on the edge of the dramatic monologue, Hemans takes up positions charged with need and shapes a language of endless longing and appeal directed toward a variously named divine order: God, heaven, the virgin, departed spirits, mother, home, and love. In this poetry, her readers found a language for their own baffled hearts, an almost ritualized unpacking of emotion like a chant or spell, whereby the book becomes a source of expression when one's own words fail. Such a dynamic partly accounts for this annotative practice of emphasis and adoption by Hemans's readers who, parted from a loved person through death or absence, find themselves in prayer amid her lyrics.

"The Italian Girl's Hymn to the Virgin" can be read as an allegory of this relation between Hemans and her female readers. It begins, "In the deep hour of dreams . . . Mother of Sorrows! lo, I come to thee" (lines 1, 4), an invocation that mirrors the moment of reading: "Thou know'st the grief, the love, / The fear of woman's soul;—to thee I come" (lines 111–12). Opening a book of Hemans's poetry, readers like Taylord and Pierrepont find both listener and voice: Hemans is both the "Mother of Sorrows" who seems to know their souls and the author of this prayer that they can underline, bracket, and internalize "in the deep hour of dreams," which may well be the hour of reading. The poem encourages a similar sympathetic conflation of Virgin and supplicant, expressing the commonality of woman's lot: "Many, and sad, and deep, / Were the thoughts folded in thy silent breast; / Thou, too, coulds't watch and weep—/ Hear, gentlest mother! hear a heart opprest!" (lines 13–15). The double oscillation between speaker and addressee, and between poet and reader, makes the poem into an allegory of its own reception, a spell of readerly communion with the folded thoughts of the book.

Pierrepont has bracketed stanzas 5 through 8 of "Italian Girl's Hymn," and above stanza 5 has written a date in a tiny cursive hand: "March 5, 1846."[30] The marked stanzas are worth quoting in full:

> There is a wandering bark
> Bearing one from me o'er the restless waves;
>   Oh! let thy soft eye mark
> His course;—Be with him, Holiest, guide and save!
>
>   My soul is on that way;
> My thoughts are travelers o'er the waters dim
>   Through the long weary day
> I walk, o'ershadowed by vain dreams of him.
>
>   Aid him,—and me, too, aid!
> Oh! 'tis not well, this earthly love's excess!
>   On thy weak child is laid
> The burden of too deep a tenderness.
>
>   Too much o'er *him* is poured
> My being's hope—scarce leaving Heaven a part;
>   Too fearfully adored,
> Oh! make not him the chastener of my heart! (233, lines 17–32)

Hemans's "wandering bark" is also Shakespeare's, evoking the "love" of sonnet 116 that "is the star to every wandering bark." And the Italian girl's hymn centers on her beloved, away at sea "o'er the restless waves": it is a prayer at once for his protection ("guide and save!") and for her own heart, filled with "love's excess" for "*him*," a man "[t]oo fearfully adored," who she worries will become "the chastener of [her] heart!" The poem seems already haunted by marginalia: in the tenderly enjambed plea to "let thy soft eye mark / His course," which calls forth pencil marks from Pierrepont, and in the italicized pronoun already marked with feeling and specificity: "*him*." The typography of Hemans's poetry often evokes marking, highlighting, and emphasizing; she frequently bears down on certain words and phrases through the use of italics, dashes, and exclamation points. To annotate Hemans's poems with marks of emphasis is to collaborate with its own procedures. That "*him*" has already been prepped to refer to one's own beloved; and, as Pierrepont marks the "wandering bark" stanza with bracket, check mark, and particular date, she fulfills this logic by making this hymn all about her *him*.

"March 5, 1846": Pierrepont was seventeen years old then and unmarried. It was the same year she had acquired the book, and it seems to be the year in which she made most of the annotations therein. The elegy for her daughter Mary, written in the early 1860s, turns out to be a late addition, made when the grieving mother reached for her old Hemans volume, a sourcebook of feeling already laden with her marks of emotional response, to draft a fragment of grief. But here, it seems, was evidence of an earlier moment of passionate encounter with Hemans's poetry, a specific date of reading when her mind was on a beloved away at sea, "wandering . . . o'er the restless waves," and when she was troubled by the intensity of her feelings, by "too deep a tenderness" for one "[t]oo fearfully adored." What could one do but read poetry—and especially a type of poetry that gave printed voice to the "thoughts folded" in a "silent breast," thoughts that blended religious devotion with romantic love? Intensely private in its associations for readers and yet offering more public communion than keeping a journal or diary, Hemans's poetry became indispensable to so many nineteenth-century readers because it provided a way out of the yearning self's mute prison. It offered a ritual and a rhetoric of loss.

The other poem that Pierrepont annotated with more than just marks of emphasis, "To the Memory of Bishop Heber," is not one that might be expected to receive her attention: a eulogy written to honor Reginald Heber, the English bishop of Calcutta for many years and a friend and mentor of Hemans. But the poem has been repurposed by brackets and check marks placed next to the first two stanzas and by another penciled date in Pierrepont's hand next to them: "April 19, 1846" (Figure 3):

> If it be sad to speak of treasures gone,
>   Of sainted genius called too soon away,
> Of light from this world taken, while it shone
>   Yet kindling onward to the perfect day;—
> How shall our griefs, if these things mournful be,
> Flow forth, oh! thou of many gifts, for thee?
>
> Hath not thy voice been here amongst us heard?
>   And that deep soul of gentleness and power,
> Have we not felt its breath in every word,
>   Wont from thy lip, as Hermon's dew, to shower?
> —Yes! In our hearts thy fervent thoughts have burned—
> Of Heaven they were, and thither have returned. (lines 1–12)

Six weeks after the date written next to the "Italian Girl's Hymn," which offered a prayer for the safety of a beloved at sea, comes this laconic register of loss, perhaps even of that prayer's unfulfillment: a specific date next to plangent lines such as "How shall our griefs flow forth . . . for thee?" Then, in faded, almost illegible letters above the poem, Pierrepont has also written three initials: "A" and (I think) "HJ." She would marry another man, James Minor, eighteen months hence.

But let the sound roll on!
It hath no tone of dread
For those that from their toils are gone;
   — *There* slumber England's dead.

Loud rush the torrent-floods
The western wilds among,
And free, in green Columbia's woods,
   The hunter's bow is strung.

But let the floods rush on!
Let the arrow's flight be sped!
Why should *they* reck whose task is done?
   There slumber England's dead!

The mountain-storms rise high
In the snowy Pyrenees,
And toss the pine-boughs through the sky,
   Like rose-leaves on the breeze.

But let the storm rage on!
Let the forest-wreaths be shed!
For the Roncesvalles' field is won,
   There slumber England's dead.

On the frozen deep's repose
'T is a dark and dreadful hour,
When round the ship the ice-fields close,
   To chain her with their power.

But let the ice drift on!
Let the cold-blue desert spread!
Their course with mast and flag is done,
   There slumber England's dead.

The warlike of the isles,
The men of field and wave!
Are not the rocks their funeral piles,
   The seas and shores their grave?

Go, stranger! track the deep,
Free, free the white sail spread!
Wave may not foam, nor wild wind sweep,
   Where rest not England's dead.

TO THE MEMORY OF BISHOP HEBER.

IF it be sad to speak of treasures gone,
   Of sainted genius called too soon away,
Of light from this world taken, while it shone
   Yet kindling onward to the perfect day;—
How shall our griefs, if these things mournful be,
Flow forth, oh! thou of many gifts, for thee?

Hath not thy voice been here amongst us heard?
   And that deep soul of gentleness and power,
Have we not felt its breath in every word,
   Wont from thy lip, as Hermon's dew, to shower?
—Yes! in our hearts thy fervent thoughts have
   burned—
Of Heaven they were, and thither have returned.

How shall we mourn thee?—With a lofty trust,
   Our life's immortal birthright from above!
With a glad faith, whose eye, to track the just,
   Through shades and mysteries lifts a glance of
     love,
And yet can weep!—for nature thus deplores
The friend that leaves us, though for happier
   shores.

And one high tone of triumph o'er thy bier,
   One strain of solemn rapture be allowed—
Thou, that rejoicing on thy mid career,
   Not to decay, but unto death, hast bowed:
In those bright regions of the rising sun,
Where victory ne'er a crown like thine had won.

Praise! for yet one more name with power en
   dowed,
   To cheer and guide us, onward as we press;
Yet one more image, on the heart bestowed,
   To dwell there, beautiful in holiness!
Thine, Heber, thine! whose memory from the
   dead,
Shines as the star which to the Saviour led.

THE HOUR OF PRAYER.

CHILD, amidst the flowers at play,
While the red light fades away;
Mother, with thine earnest eye
Ever following silently;
Father, by the breeze of eve
Called thy harvest-work to leave;
Pray!—ere yet the dark hours be,
Lift the heart and bend the knee!

Traveller, in the stranger's land
Far from thine own household band;
Mourner, haunted by the tone
Of a voice from this world gone;
Captive, in whose narrow cell
Sunshine hath not leave to dwell;
Sailor, on the darkening sea—
Lift the heart and bend the knee!

Warrior, that from battle won
Breathest now at set of sun!
Woman, o'er the lowly slain
Weeping on his burial plain:
Ye that triumph, ye that sigh,
Kindred by one holy tie,
Heaven's first star alike ye see—
Lift the heart and bend the knee!

THE VOICE OF SPRING.

I COME, I come! ye have called me long,
I come o'er the mountains with light and song;
Ye may trace my step o'er the wakening earth,
By the winds which tell of the violet's birth,

Seen through this lens, the whole book reveals a hidden pattern of grief associated not with the death of daughter Mary, but with the earlier death of Pierrepont's beloved *him*, prompting extensive marking of her copy of Hemans. The evidence is circumstantial, but the pattern is remarkably coherent. The first marked poem in the volume is "Annabella Stuart": "never more . . . let sorrowing love on earth / Trust fondly . . . the hope is crushed / That lit my life" (201). She also highlights lines in "The Fountain of Oblivion": "there are, there are, / Voices whose music I have loved too well . . . but they are far—/ Never! oh—never in my home to dwell!" (247). This lament for a lost voice is a common thread to some of the passages Pierrepont marks, not only in the poem to Bishop Heber ("Have we not felt its breath in every word") and in "The Fountain of Oblivion," but others as well. She brackets and checks a passage from "A Spirit's Return" that reads, in part, "The world held nought / Save the *one* Being to my centered thought. / There was no music but his voice to hear, / No joy but such as with *his* step drew near" (227). Again we see Hemans's own italics preparing the way for readerly identification: "*one* Being," "*his* step." Encountering the poem "Breathings of Spring," Pierrepont brackets a passage that reads, in part, "How we are haunted, in thy wind's low tone, / By voices that are gone!" (315). Almost all of the marked passages in this edition have something to do with the loss of a beloved—not a child, but a romantic partner—and the darkened mind of a grief-stricken survivor. In "Juana" she marks the epigraph "This love, / This wild and passionate idolatry, / What doth it in the shadow of the grave? / Gather it back within thy lonely heart" (219). Only at the end of the volume, in the last poem she annotates, does she turn toward another "*him*," again prompted by Hemans's italics, bracketing a passage from "The Home of Love" that reads, in part, "Oh! pray to be forgiven / Thy fond idolatry, thy blind excess, / And seek with *Him* that bower of blessedness" (416). Pierrepont's marking of the book ends there—except for the later elegy for her daughter on the rear free endpaper.

There are uncertainties here, and we are right to be skeptical of any decisive narrative: we know only that Pierrepont mourned someone with the first initial "A" several weeks after sympathizing with a prayer for the safety of a romantic beloved at sea. Those specific date-stamps tell us that her response to those poems was more than mere general sympathy or aesthetic approval; rather, they spoke to her situation and emotional state (first anxious, then mournful) with reference to those dates in her early life (the spring of 1846). The annotations on the poem to Bishop Heber could register a lament for anyone; but the remaining pattern of underlining and emphasis in Pierrepont's copy confirms a fixation on the death of a lover. If I am right, the man (call him "A") was loved intensely, even fearfully, and then lost. Pierrepont married late the following year, so there was no interval for a second beloved: virtually all her penciled marks would have been made with "A" in mind. After his death, the book seems to have become a consolatory handbook, which she proceeded to mark according to the state of her heart in that heartrending year—the dates (March 5, April 19) entered retrospectively.

We do know that several months later, in late July 1846, Ellen and her mother took their last leave of the old Pierrepont family mansion in Brooklyn Heights, which had been sold to settle her father Hezekiah's estate and make way for the construction of the Montague Street Ferry from Brooklyn to Wall Street.[31] Ellen's mother, Anna, records in a memoir her reaction to the news from her son, Henry, that the house where they had lived for over forty years, and where twelve of her thirteen children had been born, was to be sold and torn down: "I answered, if so my son, do not think of me. I cannot aid you but by prayer and that I shall not cease to do. I am a stranger & a pilgrim. I have long ago crucified pride and had my worldly attachments weakened. . . . I said no more. I walked quietly away & went to prayer . . . and now at 62 am to begin a new life; every old association with the home of my youth to be broken up" (Moffat 35). One can imagine Pierrepont, the youngest child, mourning the loss of "A" that lonely summer amid the packing and moving and praying and farewells. Retreating to a private chair, she was poring over her Hemans book, then brand new but rapidly acquiring the check marks, brackets, and annotations that it still bears. A few of her marks register the end of the family's years in the old family home: she checks or brackets stanzas in "The Bride's Farewell" ("I leave my sunny childhood here, / Oh therefore let me weep!" [204]), "The Two Homes" ("And what is home, and where, but with the loving?" [243]), and "Things That Change" ("Thy pensive eye but ranges / O'er ruin'd fane and hall, / Oh! the deep *soul* has changes / More sorrowful than all" [425]). *Plus ça change*: the mansion was demolished, but the Hemans book survives.

Because this copy of Hemans had been classified as nonrare and was kept in the circulating collection, my students and I had been able to find it by browsing the open stacks. But now, I turned to the special collections library to fill in the gaps in our knowledge of its history. Online searching had already exposed certain features of Pierrepont's genealogy, including the presence of some family papers at the University of Virginia. Among those papers are two more marked books: large Bibles, both dating from midcentury, with preprinted "Family Record" pages for "Births," "Marriages," and "Deaths" that have been extensively filled in by members of the family, especially Pierrepont herself. One Bible belonged to her husband, James, given to him by his mother in late September 1847, just before the wedding, and the second was Pierrepont's own, given to her in 1854 by her brother-in-law. In both, she records her marriage, the births of her eight children, and family deaths, a task taken up later by others. In her own Bible, under "Deaths," she first records the passing of her "beloved mother" in 1859, and then this (Figure 4):

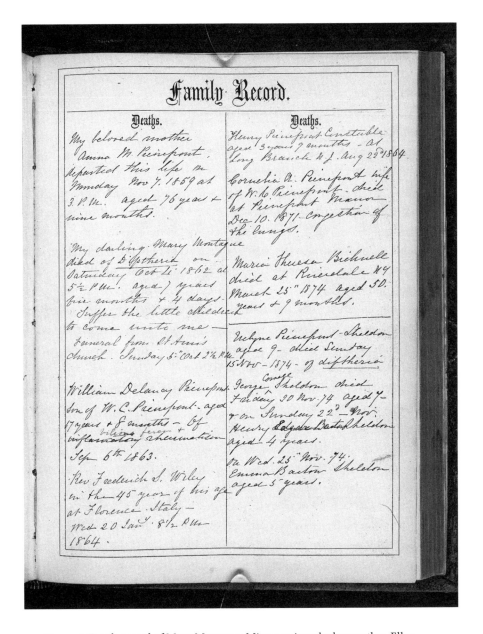

Figure 4. Death record of Mary Montague Minor, written by her mother, Ellen Pierrepont Minor, in *The Holy Bible* (Philadelphia: E. H. Butler and Co., 1853). Papers of the Pierrepont and Minor families, 7286-c, Albert and Shirley Small Special Collections Library, University of Virginia.

My darling Mary Montague
died of <u>Diptheria</u> on
Saturday Oct. 4, 1862 at
5 ½ p.m. aged 7 years
five months & 4 days.
Suffer the little children
to come unto me—
funeral from St. Anne's
Church Sunday 5th Oct. 2 ½ p.m.

So there it was. Another rude monument, more print upon the dust. From that little elegy for "Mary, Mary, Mary" in the copy of Hemans in the library stacks, I had found my way to this spare register of the event of her death, both written by Pierrepont in one of her books.[32] Like her poem that speaks of "this, our parting hour," the Bible entry offers the piteous detail that Mary died at 5:30 p.m., and, in the enumeration of her lifespan that follows, we feel the mother reaching plaintively for just a little more time: seven years, five months, four days. And in her underlining of the disease that killed her daughter—diphtheria—we see her habit of textual emphasis in a raw and terrible form.[33] What more to be said—except to quote from the book at hand in consolation: "Suffer the little children to come unto me" (Luke 18:16).[34]

III

In this chapter I have argued that we might see more clearly Hemans's place in nineteenth-century culture when we attend in detail to the traces left by her original readers. Or, rather, the limits of current critical approaches might become apparent when we examine personal encounters with her poetry and the specific bibliographic forms in which it circulated, some of which contain revealing evidence of use. We might also begin to see nineteenth-century sentimental poetry through the eyes of those to whom it most frequently mattered, those ordinary readers whose reactions shaped the ways poetry was written and used throughout this bookish century.[35] As I have pursued it, such an argument runs counter to at least six trends or forces that have shaped the study of nineteenth-century poetry. First, the pervasive demotion of sentimental verse in favor of difficult and complex lyric explorations of subjectivity. Second, a general (and often gendered) suspicion of personal, appropriative responses to literary works wherein literature is valued for being relatable. Third, if bibliographic and book-historical approaches are deemed relevant, the assumption that later collected editions (posthumous, pirated, transatlantic, and cheap) have little of importance to tell us. Fourth, the rarity of copy-specific attention to nineteenth-century books, unless they are particularly rare or were owned by famous people. Fifth, the difficulty of studying ordinary readers (particularly women), and a concomitant suspicion of any evidence of their reading as anecdotal and eccentric. Sixth, the organizing principle of library collections that has left books like Pierrepont's unprotected and uncatalogued as unique copies, their special features discoverable only by accident.

Rather than spend paragraphs documenting these trends, I offer them to my reader's general recognition. More important is what we might apprehend in resisting them, by moving in the direction marked out by Catherine Taylord, Charlotte Cocke Gordon, and Ellen Pierrepont Minor—all of whom, it should be said, were white, middle- or upper-middle-class, Protestant women living in the eastern United States in the middle years of the nineteenth century. Their reading habits form only a small part of the many reading cultures of their era, and I do not mean to present them as universal guides to the consumption of poetry and the use of books. Nor can I claim that the patterns I have analyzed here represent a statistically significant portion of the archive of the Hemans books we have inherited from the nineteenth century. However, an important interpretive lens is recovered by examining both individual and aggregated interactions between readers and their volumes. Moreover, this lens exposes more than just the dynamics of Hemans's popularity. It also allows us to see new topographies in the landscape of nineteenth-century poetry. By presenting evidence of what books of poetry were for, and by taking seriously how original readers used the contents and physical formats of those books, I hope to offer notes toward an alternative literary history of the era in which poetry was both printed and read on an industrial scale. To pursue this project, we need the books to remain on the library shelves, catalogued and preserved according to their unique value as evidentiary objects produced, sold, handled, read, and marked by the network of nineteenth-century actors that constituted the literary culture of this era.

Reading Hemans through the eyes of Pierrepont or Cocke or Taylord means confronting the interlocking significations of poetry and books in the nineteenth century. The careful inscription of the owner's name in the front of each copy suggests a kind of ownership that the personal markings in its pages confirm. Contemporary readers picked up their copies of Hemans to customize them according to their own preoccupations, desires, fears, and bereavements. Much of this occurred without leaving any evidence behind; but the evidence we do have points toward a mode of reading as personal application, a volunteering of the heart, like a gift outright, to the poem. Hemans's popularity was essentially dependent on this mode of active, invested, adoptive reading. Furthermore, the affordability of books in the middle of the nineteenth century meant that home libraries swelled with volumes valuable enough to be saved across the decades (and then passed on as legacies to children and grandchildren, and eventually to university libraries), but not so precious as to forbid personal annotation that was also nonscholarly and nonprofessional. As Christina Lupton writes of this historical change, which began in the eighteenth century, "Books came into view as everyday property, things that could actually be read and not just observed from a distance, and reading them became closely associated with the development of subjectivity."[36] In the 1820s, the decade in which Hemans rose to fame, Herbert Tucker perceives "a constellation of developments that include the commodification of poetry, the routinization of its manufacture, and the professionalization of its makers."[37] To this might be added the expansion and enfranchisement of its readerships. As the century progressed, readers could purchase those commodified, manufactured volumes of verse and buy into selected sentiments conveyed therein, making books of poetry their own.

In Tucker's language of poetry books as commodities, we might choose to hear a rebuke, as if nineteenth-century readers were in the grip of ideologies that induced them to trade high art and authentic emotion for the cheap falsities of the mass market. That itself is a Romantic idea, something close to Wordsworth's chiding in the preface to *Lyrical Ballads* that bad literature is corrupting public taste and reducing readers to "a state of almost savage torpor" (*Poetry and Prose*, 80). Yet as Kete, Sánchez-Eppler, and others have argued, it rests on two questionable assumptions: first, that middle-class poetry of sentiment has an inferior role to play in the history of culture; and second, that everyday readers are essentially passive consumers with inner lives impoverished by insufficiently nuanced books. But if we take seriously the active reading visible in nineteenth-century marginal notations, we see that poets like Hemans allowed readers to shape their identities through improvised, braided selections of lines and passages, something like what Walter Pater calls "that strange perpetual weaving and unweaving of ourselves."[38] Individual copies with annotations and marginalia show nineteenth-century poetry embodied in physical books, each with its own history, revealing completed circuits of decoding, recognition, and application—the reception of the signal. Taking these moments seriously means reencountering the poem "The Graves of a Household" from the inner standing point of Charlotte Cocke Gordon grieving over the news of her son's death in Texas, or "The Italian Girl's Hymn to the Virgin" as Ellen Pierrepont Minor's prayer for her beloved "*him*" at sea. It means seeing nineteenth-century books of poems as lived collections of words, not merely available to personal application but rather only knowable to readers (including, in some sense, ourselves) in that way. It means reimagining poetry's value in lives we might call ordinary, traced and touched across the years and through their books, and gathering into literary history's account of nineteenth-century verse the far-off interest of tears.

Coda: Grace Under Pressure

The governing force of "The Image in Lava" is that of downward pressure: the fixing of a seal, the pressing of the body, the imprinting of flesh in rock—and, implicitly, the marking of paper, with the inked type of a press or with a pen or pencil. This force is both literal (the weight of lava bearing on the mother and child) and figurative (the "mournful seal . . . set / By love and agony" [lines 3–4]). The poem is driven by layered oscillations between these two registers. Lava and love, love and lava: both work on these human bodies and press them into service. Hemans imagines the "Babe . . . slumbering / Upon thy mother's breast" (lines 13–14)—here, her physical body—and then goes on to say, "Haply of that fond bosom / On ashes here impressed, / Thou wert the only treasure, child! / Whereon a hope might rest" (lines 21–24).

Consider that "fond bosom," the child's resting place, which is both the literal flesh and bone of the mother's breast and a metaphoric organ of feeling, an engine of fondness. As with its equally divided resident, the "loving heart" (line 18), the bodily organ can be pressed into the ashy substrate, but the metonymic one slips into a mode of signification that is, in this poem, Hemans's true ground. The physical heart and breasts are crushed, and the child is slumbering on that foundational bosom—and on that child "a hope might rest." We can see the stanza working to build up its stratified image from the flat materiality of the ashes, through the bodily form of breasts to bosom, upward to the ideality of a conditional "hope." The muscle and tissue of these ancient bodies become symbols under the transfiguring weight of "love and agony" (line 4) and under the imaginative pressure of Hemans's poetics. Love sets her seal upon these bodies, just as Hemans presses pen to paper, pushing downward toward meaning, reversing the direction of her upward-soaring male Romantic precursors like Shelley and Keats. Yet under this weight, the bodies paradoxically rise toward the "holiness" of the symbolic order: an expression of feeling that nourishes meaning.

Though physically vanished, the body weirdly abides in Hemans's poem, haunting the scene as a trace or because of one. There are no bodies in this divot of rock: but there is meaning in the physical trace that "[s]urvives" as a "rude monument" (line 35) and "[o]utlives . . . cities of renown" (line 39). The "fond bosom" of stanzas six through eight seems to have become purely figurative of the mother's emotional identity, but Hemans tells us it was "[f]ar better" for that bosom "to perish, / Thy form within its clasp, / Than live and lose thee, precious one" (lines 29–31). The key term here is "clasp," by means of which the doubled breasts return to nestle the infant between them. And as the poem moves between flesh and image, warm breasts to fond bosom and back again, we see a metaemblem for the emblematizing work of Hemans's poem. Confronting these ancient figures (in fact, imagining them), Hemans bears down on them in order to make them signify, culminating in the poem's last line, "It must, it *must* be so!" (line 44). Those italics, like the annotations of nineteenth-century readers, bear witness to this poetics of impression, of pushing meaning outward and upward via the downward pressure of marked emphasis. "Print upon the dust" attests to the immortality of "human love" (lines 37–38), yet that signification depends entirely on the material traces on which it is predicated, just as love requires human bodies in this world, with all their scars. Poems need readers and they need forms of embodiment, too: the books in which they flourished, and the marks they bear.

CHAPTER 2

Gardens of Verse

Botanical Souvenirs and Lyric Reading

I

In an unpublished essay described by Hermione Lee, Virginia Woolf mocks an imagined nineteenth-century female reader "who draws 'thick lachrymose lines' in books of poetry 'beside all the stanzas which deal with early deaths, & hopes of immortality,' and sends the books back to the library with 'a whole botanical collection' pressed between the leaves."[1] Woolf's vignette contains some revealing ambiguities. The phrase "lachrymose lines" evokes both the reader's underlining and the poet's verses, a reciprocal scene of sentimental engagement, even as it suggests something like teardrops staining a page. The mention of botanicals "pressed between the leaves" also seems to blur the boundaries between the book and its insertions: lines under lines, leaves within leaves, pressings within products of the press. All of this is to the purpose, as Woolf means to scorn both Victorian readers and the poets who wrote the books that they read, marked, and altered according to sympathetic or sentimental protocols that the modernists held in contempt. In Chapter 1, I argued that by giving more attention and respect to those "lachrymose lines," marks, and annotations, we might reorient our perspective on nineteenth-century poetry and what it meant to its contemporary readers. Now I want to lead you down the garden path, toward a consideration of pressed botanicals in books of poems and their relationship to nineteenth-century Anglo-American verse. As with marginalia writing and other social practices surrounding poetry in the nineteenth century (memorization, reading aloud, scrapbooking, commonplacing), putting flowers in books shaped the writing, publishing, and reading of verse as parts of a continuous network of interaction. Poets wrote knowing that these practices were part of the field of reception; publishers and illustrators designed books that called them forth and echoed them;

and readers engaged this layered scene of reception as they read and marked those books. Of course, people were sometimes just pressing flowers and leaves in between the pages of a heavy book to flatten and dry them for botanical or decorative purposes.[2] But that is far from the whole story, particularly when it comes to books of nineteenth-century poems—and our encounters with them.

Poetry has been perennially involved with flowers and other botanical material, and was so emphatically in the century after Erasmus Darwin's *The Botanic Garden* (1791), the era that saw the *Forget-Me-Not* and other illustrated annuals,[3] a general luxuriance of flowers in Romantic and post-Romantic nature lyrics (vide Wordsworth's daffodils, Emerson's rhodora, Christina Rossetti's broad-faced asters, and Emily Dickinson's virtual lyric herbarium), and the hothouse aesthetics of the decadent movement à la Baudelaire's *Fleurs*. As Dahlia Porter writes, "Botanical metaphors for the poetic collection have a very long history, . . . [and] the field of nineteenth-century literary annuals was lush with these figures."[4] For more examples, one can also wander among the century's many Anglo-American sentimental flower books, such as *Flora's Interpreter, or The American Book of Flowers and Sentiments* (1832); *Flora and Thalia, or Gems of Flowers and Poetry* (1835); *The Poetry of Flowers and the Flowers of Poetry* (1841); *The Bouquet: Containing the Poetry and Language of Flowers* (1846); *Drops from Flora's Cup, or The Poetry of Flowers* (1848); *The Ladies' Vase of Wild Flowers* (1850); *The Lady's Book of Flowers and Poetry* (1859); *Flora Symbolica* (1869); *The Language and Poetry of Flowers* (1871); *Bards and Blossoms* (1877); and *The Poetry of the Flowers* (1885), all of which contain scores of floral-themed verses, most of them by nineteenth-century authors.[5] At the same time, the long-standing association of pages with leaves was made freshly dynamic in the century that saw the rise to ubiquity of machine-made paper, enabling the modern global network of publication prophetically trumpeted by Shelley in 1819 in "Ode to the West Wind": "Drive my dead thoughts over the universe / Like withered leaves to quicken a new birth!" (lines 63–64). Of course, linen paper was also made out of organic material, and experimentalists had attempted to make paper from flax, straw, and other plant-based materials for centuries—to say nothing of the long history of papyrus.[6] But as the technologies and materials of papermaking evolved after midcentury, wood pulp increasingly took the place of linen rags as the primary stuff of paper, instantiating the fundamental connection between books and trees henceforth.[7] For evidence of a general arboreal-poetic spirit of the age, we might point to such signal volumes as Coleridge's *Sibylline Leaves* (1817), Whitman's *Leaves of Grass* (1855), Edith Nesbit's *Leaves of Life* (1888), Amy Levy's *A London Plane-Tree* (1889), Michael Field's *Underneath the Boughs* (1893), and even perhaps, as the Great War put an end to the long Edwardian summer, Joyce Kilmer's *Trees* (1914).[8]

Flowers and leaves made their way into books of poetry in the nineteenth century; the poets, publishers, and readers of the era all collaborated in making this happen.[9] The anthological, florilegial aspect of Victorian verse and its consumption forms a large part of the common texture of the nineteenth-century poetic imagination. Both Wordsworth's daffodils flashing upon the "inward eye / Which is the bliss of solitude" and Tennyson's "flower in the crannied wall" evoke not only moments of botanical possession but also bibliographic spaces: the flash of the preserved flower between the inward, folded gatherings of pages of a book, and the apparition of a little flower in the crannied wall of a cleft and open codex.[10] In pursuing this theme, we might start at the end of Elizabeth Barrett Browning's *Sonnets from the Portuguese*. Readers tend to linger on the famous accounting of sonnet 43 ("How do I love thee? Let me count the ways"), but if they continue to the next and final poem in the sequence, they find a retrospective envoi that casts the whole collection in floral terms:

Beloved, thou hast brought me many flowers
Plucked in the garden, all the summer through
And winter, and it seemed as if they grew
In this close room, nor missed the sun and showers.
So, in the like name of that love of ours,
Take back these thoughts which here unfolded too,
And which on warm and cold days I withdrew
From my heart's ground. Indeed, those beds and bowers
Be overgrown with bitter weeds and rue,
And wait thy weeding; yet here's eglantine,
Here's ivy!—take them, as I used to do
Thy flowers, and keep them where they shall not pine.
Instruct thine eyes to keep their colours true,
And tell thy soul, their roots are left in mine. (sonnet 44, lines 1–14)

Barrett Browning writes that the sonnets "unfolded" in the same room that hosted the "many flowers / Plucked in the garden" that Robert brought her through the year. Now she offers them, drawn from her own "heart's ground" and from her soul where they have left their roots. Her choice of specific flowers—"here's eglantine, / Here's ivy!"—is precise. According to *The Language and Poetry of Flowers* (1860), eglantine stands for poetry and ivy for marriage.[11] And her final directives—"keep them where they shall not pine" and "keep their colours true"— might well be instructions to press them carefully in a book, preserved as emblems and souvenirs as a true anthology. Plucking, giving, gathering, saving, folding, and unfolding: as Barrett Browning presents them, poetry and flowers become dream versions of each other, merging as related objects of nineteenth-century social and material practices.[12] Such figuration was plainly central to the era: a complex poetic language of flowers that went far beyond allegory (e.g., ivy equals marriage) and into a layered cognitive, social, and creative network of meaning making.

Troubling the distinction between the content and contents of a book, inserted botanical material conveys "nature" or "the natural" into the heart of a text-based cultural object, even as its faded, desiccated state attests to its preservation as an ambiguous relic from a time gone by. Indeed, the pressed flower assumes an emblematic, lyrical status in its own right, in dialogue with the poetry on the printed page and with the structure of the book in which it was placed. As both evidence of a moment of sentimental reading and a prompt to later readings of the object according to the protocols of personal sentiment, flowers in a book of nineteenth-century poems both enfold and predict the subjective, affective, lyric self that was central to the cultural value of poetry in the post-Romantic era. At the same time, those flowers transformed the page into an experimental scene of design in ways—despite Woolf's scorn—that anticipate modernist manipulations of layout and the *mise-en-page*, including Mallarmé's *Un coup de dés*, Pound's *Cantos*, and the pages of the avant-garde periodical *BLAST*. As they are pressed into service as tokens and figures (of love, of loss, of memory) in books of verse, such flowers and leaves escape into art, avoiding the general mulching of the turning year and finding an emblematic suspension in the unturned pages of a book. Where have all the flowers gone? Most to a general biological recycling, but a few turned into abiding objects of culture—some specimens, some embedded souvenirs—by virtue of their uneasy marriages to particular printed books.[13]

The speaker of Robert Browning's "The Flower's Name" roams through a garden recently visited by his lady, examining blossoms and leaves for signs of her, for mementos of her visit and her interactions: "Come, bud, show me the least of her traces," he demands, asking, "Is not the dear mark" of her handling "still to be seen?" (lines 45, 40). He fondly remembers her giving the plant "its soft meandering Spanish name," but his interest centers on the sound of her voice, "speech half-asleep or song half-awake," rather than on the flower as such, which has become an erotic souvenir (lines 20–22). What kind of reading can be done regarding these objects—I am not sure they can be called flowers or leaves anymore, given the way they have been transfigured by human actions, by their bibliographical contexts of signification, and by time—these *leavings* that emerge out of nineteenth-century books? For Susan Stewart, they are now "objects generated by means of narrative," subsumed or incorporated into a personal and private search for origins.[14] For Browning's speaker in "The Flower's Name," that search must fail, since the energy driving our relation to the souvenir emerges from loss, a "partiality which is the very source of its power" (136). Hence the nostalgic's loop and the reverie that goes along with it. As Stewart writes, "The realization of re-union [with the past] imagined by the nostalgic is a narrative utopia that works only by virtue of its partiality, its lack of fixity and closure: nostalgia is the desire for desire" (23).

The dynamics of discovery and the unclosed loop of nostalgia associated with flowers in books were well-known to Victorian readers, as evidenced by a short poem entitled "The Dead Flower," published in *Chambers's Journal* in 1866:

> In an old and musty volume, of strange and curious lore,
> A relic found I, dried and withered, of some happy days of yore.
> By whose hand had it been placed there—why or wherefore,
>   when or where?—
> Of true love perhaps a token, stored away by maiden fair!
> Haply gathered from God's-acre, dear memento of a friend
> Gone before, yet in the memory ever living to the end!
> There it lay, its pristine beauty faded—gone; but to the eyes
> Of the one who there concealed it, dearer than any prize!
> As I found it, so remains it, undisturbed, but not forgot.
> Ever sacred I preserve it, for it says: Forget-me-not![15]

Emerging from "an old and musty volume," the flower-as-relic prompts a series of speculations as to its significance: perhaps a souvenir of "happy days," or a "memento" from the grave of a friend, or a love-token "stored away by a maiden fair." In the end, the poem rests on the idea of preservation for its own sake, a strangely contentless memory embodied in the injunction that is also the name of the flower itself: forget-me-not. One thinks also of Barrett Browning's poem "A Dead Rose," which asks of a flower kept seven years in a drawer, "who dares to name thee" rose? The poem ends by affirming that "the heart doth recognize thee / Alone, alone!" That is, the dead rose's existence as a souvenir defines it and brings it to life: "the heart doth smell thee sweet, / Doth view thee fair," despite the flower's desiccation. Memory of the affections keeps the flower fresh in its keeper's mind. As Letitia Landon puts it in one of her lyrics,

>   —oh, only those
> Whose souls have felt this one idolatry,
> Can tell how precious is the slightest thing
> Affection gives and hallows! A dead flower
> Will long be kept, remembrancer of looks
> That made each leaf a treasure.[16]

Similarly, we have Julia Ward Howe addressing a dying rose in a lyric from her volume *Passion Flowers* (1854):

> Thou hast so smiled upon my heart,
> That I can scarcely from thee part,
>   Without a tear of sorrow,
> For I shall come thy cup to kiss,
> And my beloved companion miss,
>   Forever gone, to-morrow.[17]

Invested with memory and feeling, the dead flower is hallowed into a remembrancer and idol, a doubled fetish of love and its enemy, time. In Barrett Browning's poem, the rose's metaphorical similarity to the speaker's heart, and thus its extrabotanical existence as a symbol of desire, depends on the narrative of blighted love that the poem evokes at its conclusion: "Lie still upon this heart which breaks below thee."[18] In Stewart's terms, the narrative of the possessor incorporates the dead flower into a private nostalgic reverie, transfiguring it into a souvenir. Further, the aleatory dispersal of these books and their botanical additions across the library shelves of the nation puts them into what Stewart calls contexts "away from the business and engagement of everyday life, . . . tied to the temporality of the past." Thus "lost," these books obtain the souvenir's power to "'surprise' and capture [the] viewer into reverie" (150).

Experiencing reveries and memories seems to have been the aim for Victorian readers, who used flowers to encode the past by means of associative thinking. In an 1841 essay for *Ladies' Companion*, Mary A. Coffin writes of her own collection of pressed flowers in books, "Flowers are my associates. I never receive any particular pleasure, without instantly memorializing it with a flower; and there is hardly a book in my possession, whose leaves do not bear the impress of several of the 'fairies sweet tenements.' There is a volume now before me filled with such fair mementos of joys departed! As I turn its pages over, many a vision of past delight rises up before me, and had each sweet blossom the gift of speech, it would take more than one volume to hold the tales 'they could unfold.'"[19] Coffin turns the pages of her book, but rather than reading text she is dreaming over its pressed botanical contents as "many a vision of past delight rises up" to entrance her. She goes on to tell four "tales" evoked by four separate gatherings of flowers she has preserved, each linked to the moment of its acquisition. First, a "bunch of pressed violets" recalls for her a Wordsworthian walk in the woods when she was healed of her melancholy by communing with the "invisible spirit of Nature" and her own heart. Second, she describes a bouquet presented to her by a young man as part of a fortune-telling game with friends in a garden, on a day she remembers with exquisite pleasure. Third, a lily of the valley recalls her earliest friend Lizzy, who presented it to her. And finally, a bunch of "wild wood flowers" brings back a springtime nature walk with her friend Nannie, during which they

> could not help repeating to each other, many a sweet lay of the poets, re-calling, as it were, in poetry, the beautiful scenes before us. Then, too, we encountered, frequently—
> "A violet by a mossy stone,
>   Half hidden from the eye,
> Fair as a star, when only one
>   Is shining in the sky."
> bringing those sweet lines of Wordsworth continually to our lips. (204)

Note how inescapable Wordsworth is for these antebellum American wanderers through nature. They are gathering flowers that have already been associated with his poetic representation of them, and they seem to be stumbling over poems as frequently as blossoms. Coffin's earlier experience of "communing . . . within Nature's temple" similarly follows a script laid down by Wordsworth, and she duly memorializes it with a "bunch of violets . . . half covered with lifeless forest leaves," like his "half hidden from the eye" (203). Her quoted allusion to the ghost in *Hamlet*—"they could unfold"—provides further confirmation of the entanglement of personal experience with literary quotation, of interiority and affect with poetic language. Where else should such relics be placed but within the leaves of a book of poems, whence they may speak of their braided existence as signifiers of the poetry of life and its paradoxical ephemerality and permanence? Coffin concludes her essay with "time has followed swiftly since that pleasant time, and my delicate blossoms of remembrance have quite lost their sweet hues; but their forms, faded and frail though they be, will ever express most distinctly the fair scenes with which they are associated" (205).

Found (and plucked) as flowers, saved (and then lost) as souvenirs, found again through chance encounters, and speaking primarily of loss (of the past, and of one's own mortality) when found—these bookish flowers signal both preservation and absence, their *fort-da* alternations seemingly overcharging them with nostalgia's recursive narratives. Pressed flowers transform or supplement the lyric spaces of the book, augmenting the poetry on the printed page even as they partially efface or damage it (and are in turn damaged—crushed, flattened, faded, dried—by it). In books of poems, flowers become traces of lyrical reading: a collaboration with the language of verse and the material spaces of the book, a shaping of one's inner life according to brief flashes of personalized resonance found there. Romantic ideas of soul making and epiphanic recognition underwrite the process. In *Dickinson's Misery*, Virginia Jackson discusses a leaf that Emily Dickinson pinned to a note to her brother Austin in 1851, which reads, "We'll meet again and heretofore some summer 'morning.'" Jackson calls the note "a bit of ephemera that tempts while it also resists lyric reading," writing that we latecomers "will understand [the leaf] . . . as a reminder of what you cannot share with Dickinson's first readers, an overlooked object lyrically suspended in time. What may seem lyrical about it is the apparent immediacy of our encounter with it. . . . Yet Dickinson's message pinned to the leaf asks its intended reader to understand that a leaf taken out of context is not self-defining."[20] Marked unintentionally with the postmaster's stamp, the leaf evokes a "pathos of transmission" and becomes a different kind of emblem. "Let it stand . . . for the institutions that exceed even as they deliver literature," Jackson remarks, adding that "Dickinson could not have foreseen that the faded leaf would end up in a college library" (13). Dickinson's token of a summer "morning" accrues other meanings as it moves through space and time, serving now, for Jackson, as a figure of its own refiguration by transmission and archiving. Like the books surveyed in this chapter, themselves also "overlooked object[s] lyrically suspended in time," it "tempts while it also resists lyric reading."

Even more to my purpose is Dickinson's 1859 poem "Whose cheek is this?" To the manuscript version of the poem, Dickinson attached a small flower (now gone) and sent it to her sister-in-law Susan:

> Whose cheek is this?
> What rosy face
> Has lost a blush today?
> I found her—'pleiad'—in the woods
> And bore her safe away—
>
> Robins, in the tradition
> Did cover such with leaves,
> But which the cheek—
> And which the pall
> My scrutiny deceives—[21]

Jackson discusses this poem in terms of the figure of the poetess, one that Dickinson repeatedly both deploys and empties out in her lyrics; the "pleiad" flower is both a "feminine figure of lyric personification" and "a thing . . . neither alive or dead, neither figurative 'cheek' nor effaced 'pall,'" (228, 233) which escapes personification by means of the poem's final uncertainties. And the material absence of the flower seems to incarnate this escape: a "cheek" gone "pall," both shroud and lost blush that has faded to stain and devolved to stem on Dickinson's pale sheet of paper. To deepen this analysis, I want to press harder on that strange interruptive in the first stanza—"pleiad"—which Jackson associates with La Pléiade, Pierre de Ronsard's circle of Renaissance poets, which named itself after the Alexandrian Pleiad of the third century BC (231). But a contemporary allusion is more likely. Letitia Elizabeth Landon's poem "The Lost Pleiad" speaks of her heroine's doing a star turn in similar terms: "o'er Cyrene's cheek the rose, / Like moon-touch'd water, ebbs and flows; / And eyes that droop like Summer flowers / Told they could change with shine and showers."[22] After all, Dickinson's "cheek" or "rosy face" has been "lost"; and it seems likely that the (lost) flower once attached to the manuscript was an aster (from the Greek word for "star"), also called starwort or Michaelmas daisy, a later variety of which was the "Pleiad."[23] The fact that Dickinson sent her flower early in 1859 suggests she found the fallen bloom sometime in the late fall or early winter, not long after asters begin to fade in New England (and when the Pleiades constellation becomes prominent in the sky there as well). The aster-star-pleiad pun is characteristic of Dickinson and in turn evokes another of Landon's poems, one of her earliest, published in the *Literary Gazette* in 1820, entitled "The Michaelmas Daisy":

> Last smile of the departing year,
>   Thy sister sweets are flown;
> Thy pensive wreath is still more dear,
>   From blooming thus alone.
> Thy tender blush, thy simple frame,
>   Unnoticed might have past;
> But now thou com'st with softer claim,
>   The loveliest and the last.
> Sweet are the charms in thee we find,
>   Emblem of Hope's gay wing;
> 'Tis thine to call past bloom to mind,
>   To promise future spring.[24]

The "blush" and "smile" of the late-blooming aster recall Dickinson's "rosy face" that "lost a blush"—another feminine personification. For Landon, this lost pleiad, "loveliest and last" of the season, becomes an "Emblem of Hope's gay wing," a Shelleyan reminder that if winter comes, spring cannot be far behind. Thus the allusion to the "pleiad" in Dickinson's lyric points to both the attached flower and the poetess tradition as represented (and resisted) by Landon's work. "The Lost Pleiad" speaks of "the gather'd flower, which is to bear / Some gentle secret whisper'd there," and these concepts, of flowers as emblems and flowers as messengers, inform Dickinson's floral and poetic missive to Susan, itself a meditation on what is lost and saved.

II

Dickinson's singular, handmade poetic texts have the virtue of clarifying protocols of reading that are hard to trace across the vast reaches of nineteenth-century printed books. Her manuscripts are now treasures and have received correspondent levels of preservation, curation, and scholarly attention for decades. Further, her methods are assumed to be a function of her genius. Her insertions of flowers into her manuscripts are canny and theoretically interesting, avant-garde moves that deploy nineteenth-century conventions in order to subvert or extend their significance. But Dickinson's imaginative practice is taken largely as an exception that proves the rule. We tend to assume that middle-class readers were merely inhabited by conventions and that they placed botanical objects in books as a matter of unself-conscious fashion or accident. Further, the printed books of poetry from the second half of the nineteenth century, especially editions meant for a mass market, have been relatively unsponsored by bibliographers, librarians, and collectors. Many have been kept in circulating library collections, and many more have ended up in used bookstores, when they have not fallen apart or been discarded altogether. Whole gardens-full of lost pleiads—a bibliographic Goldengrove unleaving, to employ Hopkins's phrase, where "worlds of wanwood leafmeal lie."[25] Flowers and leaves inserted in such volumes remain there mostly by chance and as a function of neglect, since unturned pages and shut volumes lead to a kind of fortuitous preservation. Yet if those pages remain unturned, the insertions are effectively lost, and, in the context of academic libraries, their invisibility makes the books that contain them vulnerable to deduplication, particularly given the current enthusiasm for downsizing print collections. Even when they are discovered, botanical insertions are typically left uncatalogued and may be removed, either on purpose (because they are staining the pages or otherwise obscuring the text) or by accident (they may fall out as the book is handled). As a result, each flower found in a book has an aleatory, synecdochic relation to a numberless library of similar flowers and to the set of cultural practices that put them where they ended up. It was a souvenir for its former owner of an individual reading experience, and it has become for us now an object evocative of that owner, of other readers, and of the world they inhabited. All books from past eras share in this phenomenon. We have, and can manage, only a remnant of the total number of volumes that were produced and read, and thus each must stand as both representative case and herald of loss, what Du Bois calls, in the final phrase of "The After-Thought" that concludes *The Souls of Black Folk* (1903), "these crooked marks on a fragile leaf."[26] Books containing flowers raise the memorial aspect of the historical codex to vivid, allegorical levels: they become emblems of the souveniring of the past's remainders.

Consider, as an example of this process and as a kind of commonplace counterpart to Dickinson's manuscript letter with its lost pleiad, a copy of *The Waif,* published in Cambridge, Massachusetts, in 1845 and now held by the University of Miami, discovered in the open stacks during a Book Traces event held there in 2015. Compiled by Henry Wadsworth Longfellow, *The Waif* is a miscellaneous anthology of short, fugitive poems by various authors.[27] An inscription on the flyleaf of this particular copy tells us it was presented to "Deborah F. Adams, from her brother William, Feb. 17, 1845," and several botanical samples were inserted into it. On a page containing Horace Smith's "Hymn to the Flowers," one can see the shadowy stain of a two-stemmed blossom, now gone, that had been inserted into a small slit in the page on which Smith calls flowers "Ephemeral sages! . . . Posthumous glories! angel-like collection! / . . . Ye are to me a type of resurrection / And second birth" (Figure 5).[28] Like Dickinson's manuscript, this page seems both an illustration of and an allegory for the content of the poem it contains. At the same time, the inserted flower has effectively printed itself, transforming the page from a mass-produced copy into a serendipitous, one-of-a-kind art object. As did Dickinson, Smith presents flowers as simultaneously lost and saved: for Dickinson, "lost" and "bore . . . safe away," and for Smith, "ephemeral" and "a type of resurrection." The floral additions made by Dickinson (as a poet) and by Adams (as a reader) have disappeared but left their traces, so that the pages themselves instantiate the dialectical relation between presence and erasure. Each serves not only as a static, material illustration of a poem's themes, but also as a dynamic witness to the larger processes of reception (transmission, marking, preservation, loss) that have constituted the document's history. The flower in *The Waif* is almost a book inside the book and a distillation of its cultural poetics, a waif in its own right. Our emblematic reading of the (missing) flower is prefigured by Smith's declaration that each fading blossom is "a *memento mori* / Yet fount of hope," recalling Landon, for whom the late-blooming Michaelmas daisy becomes an "Emblem of Hope's gay wing."[29] In his poem, Smith calls "every leaf a book," and exclaims, "Oh may I deeply learn and ne'er surrender / Your lore sublime!" For Smith, the dying flower suggests not only the cycle of the seasons

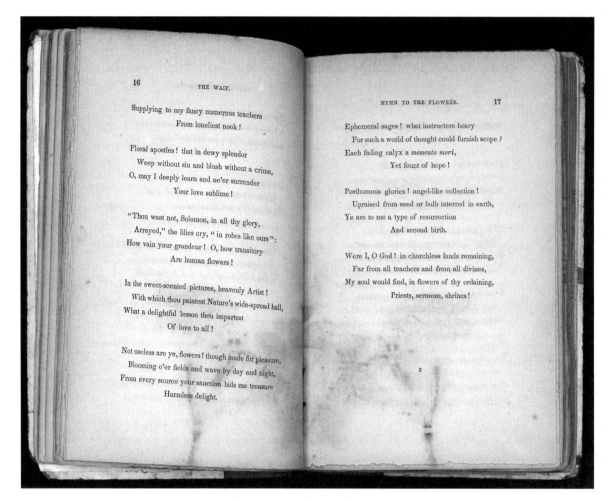

Figure 5. Flower stains in *The Waif: A Collection of Poems*, ed. Henry Wadsworth Longfellow (Cambridge, MA: J. Owen, 1845), 16–17. Adams family copy. Richter Library, University of Miami.

but also the Christian narrative of death and resurrection. Adams, who plucked a flower and affixed it to this page, presumably saw something similar in the turning over of the year. For us, surveying only slits, stains, and a few stray petals in the book's gutter, this *Waif*'s lesson becomes Ozymandian: nothing beside remains—except the book as perhaps an emblem of hope after all. Its owner has penciled in a sketch of a small garland of flowers just beneath the title of the poem.

Adams's copy of *The Waif* has two more botanical samples attached to its pages, one next to the second stanza of Felicia Hemans's "No More"; the stem is still there but the bloom is gone, leaving only a slight halo, a print of loss (Figure 6). The reader—presumably Adams herself—has bracketed the stanza in pencil. It reads,

To dwell in peace with home affections bound
   To know the sweetness of a mother's voice,
To feel the spirit of her love around,
   And in the blessing of her age rejoice,—
            No more! (111)

Genealogical databases indicate that the book's owner was Deborah Foster Adams (née Chickering; 1813–79) from Dedham, Massachusetts, who had a brother, William (ca. 1814–73), and a mother who had died in 1843, at age fifty-four. Two years later, Deborah received this book and proceeded to mark it according to that loss, and then another. The second sample—a green sprig of leaves—has been inserted in a slit in the page at the end of John Pierpont's "My Child" (titled in this volume "Death of a Child"), after pencil-bracketed stanzas that read in part,

   He lives!—in all the past
   He lives ; nor, to the last,
Of seeing him again will I despair;
   In dreams I see him now ;
   And, on his angel brow
I see it written, "Thou shalt see me there!" (96; Plate 3)

Adams had lost two of her children by the time she acquired this copy of *The Waif*: her first son, William, at age seven in 1841, and her first daughter, Lucy, at age two in 1843. Placed with a primary reference to William (since the poem mourns a male child) but with thoughts of Lucy, too, the green sprig becomes a memorializing annotation to the Pierpont poem, as does the flower placed next to Hemans's "No More" as a mourning commemoration of her mother. At the same time, in Smith's terms, each is a "fount of hope," an emblem of the eternal rebirth that will allow mothers and children to be reunited after death, promised in the message the poet Pierpont imagines inscribed on the child's forehead as if it were a sublime annotation of a page: "Thou shalt see me there!" Given their careful attachment to the pages, the flowers may have been gathered from the graves of the departed: in other words, actual physical relics and small reincarnations of those they mourn.

    Another example, also from the Miami stacks: a copy of an anthology of Christian poetry called *The Changed Cross*, published in New York in 1872 (Plate 4). On the flyleaf is a presentation inscription from Charles Deering (1852–1927) to an aunt or cousin, Mary E. Deering, giving the book to her "with much love" on November 3, 1876.[30] Below this, a death notice has been pasted in, and below

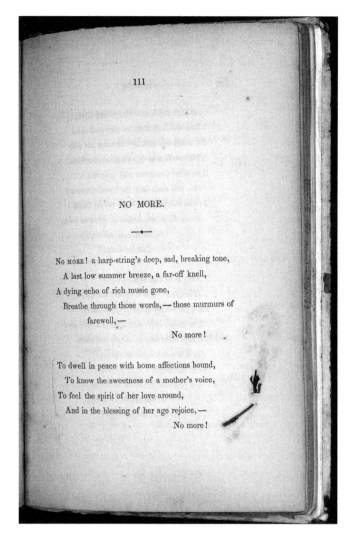

Figure 6. Flower stem inserted in *The Waif: A Collection of Poems*, ed. Henry Wadsworth Longfellow (Cambridge, MA: J. Owen, 1845), 111. Adams family copy. Richter Library, University of Miami.

that, a small red flower has been affixed with glued paper staples. By means of these additions and others, the book has been transformed into a memorial for Annie Case Deering (1848–76), Charles's wife. Annie died in Maine in late October 1876, two weeks after giving birth to their first child, a son, just one year into their marriage.[31] Soon thereafter, Charles inscribed the book to a relative, and it remained in the family until it was donated to the University of Miami as part of the Charles Deering bequest. Deering was a member of the family that built the John Deere corporation. He was a renowned art collector who moved to southern Florida in the early twentieth century. His family's book ended up in the circulating stacks, catalogued simply as a copy of *The Changed Cross* rather than a part of the Deering papers. Like all the examples discussed here, it required essentially random discovery to reveal its special features.

In addition to the inscription, pasted notice, and inserted flower, two things set this volume apart. First, the flower itself has been annotated via a small slip of paper, on which someone has written "Annie. Dec. 20, 1877," possibly a record of a visit to her grave at Christmastime, a souvenir from a bouquet or wreath left in her memory. Second, the book also contains marginal annotations that refer specifically to Annie's deathbed scene. At the top of page 166, above the poem "Coming," by Barbara Miller MacAndrew, is the following note in Charles's hand: "A short time before her death Annie asked her mother to read this poem, saying that she often thought of it. Mrs. Case read it in the presence of those gathered about the deathbed." On the next page, at the midpoint of the poem, Charles's annotation continues: "Annie tried to read here, but her sight failed. 'I guess I can't read it,' she said, smiling." The lines she attempted to read are about the long watches of the night, a time when God might come:

> . . . when the midnight
>   Is heavy upon the land
> And the black waves lying dumbly
>   Along the sand;
> When the moonless night draws close,
> And the lights are out in the house;
> When the fires burn low and red,
> And the watch is ticking loudly
>   Beside the bed. (116–17)

In this moment, the words of the poem—spoken by Annie's mother and then swimming before Annie's eyes as she tried to read them herself before failing, confessing her blindness, and smiling—would have resonated with uncanny force, as the night drew close and darkness fell upon those "[b]eside the bed" and in it. Facing her death at a young age, this new wife and mother turned for solace to a poem that "she often thought of," more evidence of the intertwining of poetry and lived experience in this era. Her husband's annotation describing the scene soon after it happened marks the impact the poem made on him and the other observers-turned-mourners. I claimed earlier that dried flowers inserted, pinned, or otherwise affixed into books can hardly be called flowers anymore, having been transformed into almost pure emblems or souvenirs. A similar point can be made regarding the poem "Coming" as it exists in this particular copy of *The*

Changed Cross: it has been so transfigured (changed, like the Cross) by the ways it was read and marked that it is not really a poem anymore—at least, not a poem like those we normally approach and analyze. As Patricia Crain writes of a poem marked with an inscription about the death of a child, "the poem is transformed—by the inscription, and by the news it conveys—into a stark cry of loss" (139). This copy has become a singular human document and monument, the meanings of which depend on overlays of handwritten marks on printed literary pages.

Deborah Adams's *Waif* and Annie Deering's *Changed Cross* both bear evidence of complex acts of reception, in which reading becomes visible as a layered set of private and social responses (remembering, recognizing, altering, personalizing, giving). Those marks and augmentations help us understand the nineteenth-century poetry book as a media object, both in the individual histories such books record and in the aggregate patterns of use they suggest. These two books, discovered on a single day of searching the stacks in a university library, attest to readers' memorial attachment of flowers to pages of printed verse—and readers' attachments to flowers, not only as souvenirs of the dead but as nonverbal yet richly signifying commentaries on the poems and what they meant. My use of the past tense here is deliberate, because we sometimes proceed as if poems contain networks of meanings within them, as if they did not require specific acts of reception to exist. We often construct critical readings according to semiotic unpackings that assume linguistic ambiguity and cultural specificity, but we are rarely able to ask what a poem meant to a particular reader, in the moment and across a life, someone outside the canon of famous readers and reviewers. Looking at individual copies brings local scenes of collaborative meaning making to the fore, defamiliarizing nineteenth-century poetry for us by showing how familiarity played itself out in the books of that era.

One final example of this kind is an 1881 copy of John Greenleaf Whittier's collected poetry that carries a gift inscription from Charles Leo Partridge (1872–1908) to his older sister Henrietta (1860–1947), dated March 25, 1890.[32] When I discovered this book in the stacks at the University of Virginia, it contained a dried maple leaf between two pages of the poem "Snow-Bound," next to some lines marked in pencil and a marginal annotation: "July '90" (353). Emily Partridge, a sister of Charles and Henrietta, died on June 17, 1890 (at the age of thirty-two), and several passages from "Snow-Bound" related to her loss are marked, such as the following:

> Look where we may, the wide earth o'er,
> Those lighted faces smile no more.

We tread the paths their feet have worn,
>   We sit beneath their orchard trees,
>   We hear, like them, the hum of bees
And rustle of the bladed corn;
We turn the pages that they read,
>   Their written words we linger o'er (353)

In these lines, Whittier's poem connects trees, books, and mourning, depicting memorial acts of communion embodied in documents and leaves that are materially instantiated in this copy: "We sit beneath their orchard trees" and gather maple leaves; we "turn the pages that they read" and feel a connection to those shared leaves as well. Like the flowers in the volumes belonging to Adams and Deering, the inserted leaf is an augmentation of and commentary on the poem (or was). I recently went back to the library to have another look at Partridge's book. I found it in the stacks, but when I turned to the page, which I had photographed quickly when I first saw it, the leaf was gone.

III

Vitality and death, preservation and loss, beauty and decay: botanical material plucked or gathered and then placed in books by readers incarnates some of the same contradictory impulses that organized nineteenth-century poetry in the Romantic tradition. Wordsworth's talking flower from the Intimations Ode may be taken as an early progenitor and representative: "The pansy at my feet / Doth the same tale repeat: / Whither is fled the visionary gleam? / Where is it now, the glory and the dream?" (lines 55–58).

That pansy tells tales and speaks volumes, as a shadow of its former self that was brought into existence by the former self of the poet. For Wordsworth, flowers and trees "speak of something that is gone" (54) because of the loss of the "celestial light" (4) that once covered them, a light whose source was the transfiguring power of the poet's imagination. Nowadays, the rose is still "Lovely," but "there hath passed away a glory from the earth" (18). On this May morning, "children are pulling / On every side . . . fresh flowers" (46–48), but the days of "splendour in the grass, of glory in the flower" are past for the adult poet (183). Throughout this foundational Romantic lyric, the poet's responses to botanical material form the index of his internal state (an attitude that Byron will satirize in *Don Juan*, wherein his lovelorn, adolescent hero is seen poring moodily "upon the leaves, and on the flowers" until he realizes that he has missed his dinner).[33] Wordsworth concludes the poem with a return to floral communion, or more accurately to the poet's own thoughts upon observing the lowly blossoms at his feet: "To me the meanest flower that blows can give / Thoughts that do often lie too deep for tears" (207–8). This little flower that gives deep thoughts— apparently, the poem we have just read—recalls the earlier "pansy at my feet," so named from the French *pensée*; as Ophelia says, "There's pansies, that's for thoughts." For the Romantic poet, flowers prompt reveries of the self measured along a temporal axis (who was I, who am I, who will I be?). Taking their cue, readers of those poems pulled flowers and used them to personalize and make souvenirs of their books according to their own thoughts and memories.[34] The post-Romantic self was organized around moments of achieved sensibility and remembered recognition, lyrical moments that found both their prompt and echo in poetry. The plucked and preserved flower figures forth those moments of selective claiming and self-definition, which are central to lyric reading.

In addition to providing evidence of such topical and figural engagements by poets and readers, nineteenth-century poetry books frequently displayed images of floral material, as illustrations, ornaments, and decorated publishers' bindings be-came common in the landscape of print culture. To stay with Wordsworth's pansy for a moment, consider the 1885 illustrated gift-book edition of the Intimations Ode and "Tintern Abbey," published by Cassell and Company.[35] By this point in the century, the practice of attaching flowers to books (which we have seen in the case of *The Waif*) had become so common as to inspire the illustrator to produce a trompe l'oeil version of a pansy next to Wordsworth's lines about "the pansy at my feet" (Figure 7). A flower has been virtually inserted and saved in the page, a pre-printed scrapbooking effect that recalls the practice of generations of readers. The flower depicted here is a cultivated pansy, first introduced in the United Kingdom around 1839, whereas Wordsworth would have been thinking of (and with) the *viola tricolor*—the wild pansy or violet-pansy, also called heartsease or love-in-idleness (the same one that Puck uses to cause trouble in *A Midsummer Night's Dream*). The difference between the wild and the cultivated flower underscores this book's status as a horticultural and bibliographic latecomer; and like Wordsworth's flower, the illustration speaks of something that is gone—in this case, primary access to Romantic categories of feeling. The Victorians had to take their raptures in nature, along with the fading of those raptures, at second hand.

Cassell's edition of Wordsworth displays throughout its pages this style of lay-ered trompe l'oeil illustration—recognizably an 1880s mode—in which flowers occupy a closer representational plane than the depicted images of natural scenes from the poem.[36] On one of the pages of "Tintern Abbey" (Figure 8), images depicting Wordsworth's lines, "the sounding cataract . . . tall rock, / The mountain, and the deep and gloomy wood," are stacked up as if they were paintings or photographs, each partially obscured by the others on top.[37] The top-layer image

And the babe
leaps up on
his mother's
arm :—
I hear, I hear,
with joy I
hear !
But there's a
tree, of many
one,
A single field which I
have look'd upon,
Both of them speak of something that is gone :
The pansy at my feet
Doth the same tale repeat :
Whither is fled the visionary gleam ?
Where is it now, the glory and the dream ?

v.

Our birth is but a sleep and a forgetting :

Figure 7. William Wordsworth, *Ode on Immortality and Lines on Tintern Abbey* (New York: Cassell and Co., 1885), 11 (detail).

of the mountain even has small pins depicted in the upper corners, as if it is at-tached to the book, in a scrapbooking style similar to the way the pansy is depicted on the earlier page. All of these pictures lie on a pair of "real" flowers that twine around the pile, while three birds and an insect flutter in some nowhere space, ap-parently confused about where exactly they belong. With such illustrations, this late nineteenth-century book represents the souveniring of Romantic poetry, echo-ing particular Wordsworthian themes: "the picture of the mind revives again" for the poet at the outset of "Tintern Abbey," and along with it a "sad perplexity" at his own changed view of the scene. Readers of this edition, almost a century later, en-counter pictures of pictures, remediated Wordsworthian scenes of memory pinned

Of the deep rivers, and
the lonely streams,
Wherever Nature led ; more like a man
Flying from something that he dreads, than one
Who sought the thing he loved. For Nature then
(The coarser pleasures of my boyish days,
And their glad animal movements all gone by)
To me was all in all. I cannot paint

38

Figure 8. William Wordsworth, *Ode on Immortality and Lines on Tintern Abbey* (New York: Cassell and Co., 1885), 38.

and augmented with virtual flowers that signify a permanent exile from those scenes. Rather like the birds hovering around the two-dimensional illustrations of nature, such readers are tacitly encouraged to peer into the poem, maybe with a perplexity of their own at the dark alienations of the bibliographic tableau. In its depiction of fresh flowers plucked and inserted around, beneath, and within printed material, the book both confirms the readerly practice I have been tracing and amplifies the Romantic themes of memorialization and loss that these Wordsworth poems typify. At the same time, its simulacra signify a conscription of

Ye that through your hearts to-day
Feel the gladness of the May!
What though the radiance which was once
    so bright
Be now for ever taken
    from my sight,

Though nothing can bring back the hour
Of splendour in the grass, of glory in the flower;
We will grieve not, rather find

22

Figure 9. William Wordsworth, *Ode on Immortality and Lines on Tintern Abbey* (New York: Cassell and Co., 1885), 22 (detail).

those themes into the book trade. Only once the books are collected and personalized can they be brought back into the orbit of the self. "[N]othing can bring back the hour / Of splendour in the grass, of glory in the flower" (Figure 9), except maybe, for a moment, poems as they exist in individuals' books, hybrid agents of a sentiment that returns those books to the horizon of personal memory.

Illustrations in this era not only reflected readers' habits of augmenting books with flowers, but also prompted further interactions. For example, an edition of Thomas Moore's *Irish Melodies*, illustrated by Daniel Maclise (1846), drips with flowers depicted on every page, most notably in the ornamental borders printed around the poems. In an edition from 1872, found on the shelf at Lied Library at the University of Nevada, Las Vegas, a reader (likely Annie Wheeler, whose name is inscribed on the flyleaf) has inserted a strikingly red, trumpetlike bloom between pages that are framed in an illustrated garland of very similar flowers that also serve as a kind of marginalia (Figure 10). We can see an interweaving of practices here: readers and publishers were finding reciprocal ways to get flowers into books of poetry, both reflecting and expanding an elaborate web of meaning making that surrounded poetic texts. The poem itself, entitled "I Saw from the Beach," laments the passing of youth's passionate fire—"the wild freshness of Morning"—and the "passing of the spring-like tide of joy" as we grow older, again in keeping with the complex figural nostalgia that this chapter has traced via botanicals culled and saved, discovered in library books whose fate is governed by a similar process.

Like the Grigg & Elliot editions of Hemans from Chapter 1, many editions of nineteenth-century poetry reveal more specific patterns when we are able to compare multiple marked copies of a frequently reprinted book: for instance, the popular Roberts Brothers illustrated editions of Jean Ingelow's *Songs of Seven* (1881 and 1884).[38] A sequence of seven first-person lyric poems devoted to progressive seven-year spans of a woman's life, *Songs of Seven* (originally published in 1866) tracks the speaker's progress from "Exultation," in which she is a child, toward her "Longing for Home," in which she is a bereaved widow at the age of forty-nine. The first four of these poems are joyous and keyed to flowers: "Seven Times One: Exultation" begins, "There's no dew left on the daisies and clover," and each of the stanzas of "Seven Times Four: Maternity" begins, "Heigh-ho! daisies and buttercups." The remaining three poems, "Widowhood," "Giving in Marriage," and "Longing for Home," are all about loss and are accordingly barren of flowers, the only exception proving the rule: a bitter reference to "a waste of reedy rills" in "Widowhood." The in-text engravings by Edmund H. Garrett are richly floral, done in the same trompe l'oeil style as the engravings in Cassell's edition of Wordsworth. Garrett's illustrations depict the specific flowers mentioned in the poems: images of columbine and cuckoopint curl around and shadow the virtual card upon which they are mentioned (Figure 11). In this particular copy, the stains of flowers once inserted are plainly visible—not only on this page, but on *every single page* of the book: some early reader placed a Woolfian "whole botanical collection" among the leaves. Each page appears as a palimpsest of floral evocation: the inserted flowers (now gone), the quasiphotographic stains they left behind, the illustrated flowers, and the flowers named in the poems. All of these elements commingle in the book, representing the agency of multiple actors, including the author Ingelow, the illustrator Garrett, the anonymous reader who placed the flowers, the person who removed them at

The minstrels have seized their harps of gold,
 And they sing such thrilling numbers,—
'T is like the voice of the Brave, of old,
 Breaking forth from their place of slumbers!
      Spear to buckler rang,
      As the minstrel sang,
And the Sun-burst⁺⁺ o'er them floated wide;
      While rememb'ring the yoke
      Which their fathers broke,
"On for liberty, for liberty!" the Finians cried.

Like clouds of the night the Northmen came,
 O'er the valley of Almhin lowering;
While onward moved, in the light of its fame,
 That banner of Erin, towering.
      With the mingling shock,
      Rung cliff and rock,
While, rank on rank, the invaders i·e·
      And the shout, that .ast
      O'er the dying pass'd,
Was "victory! victory!"—the Finian's cry.

226

I saw from the Beach.

I saw from the beach, when the morning was shining,
 A bark o'er the waters move gloriously on;
I came when the sun o'er that beach was declining,
 The bark was still there, but the waters were gone.

And such is the fate of our life's early promise,
 So passing the spring-tide of joy we have known;
Each wave, that we danc'd on at morning, ebbs from us,
 And leaves us, at eve, on the bleak shore alone.

Ne'er tell me of glories, serenely adorning
 The close of our day, the calm eve of our night;—
Give me back, give me back the wild freshness of Morning,
 Her clouds and her tears are worth Evening's best light.

Oh, who would not welcome that moment's returning,
 When passion first wak'd a new life thro' his frame,
And his soul, like the wood, that grows precious in burning,
 Gave out all its sweets to love's exquisite flame.

227

Figure 10. Flower pressed in *Literature, Art, and Song: Moore's Melodies and American Poems . . .* , ed. Sir John Stevenson, illus. Daniel Maclise and William Riches (New York: International Publishing, 1872), n.p. Annie Wheeler's copy. Lied Library, University of Nevada, Las Vegas.

some stage, and the flowers themselves, whose moisture and chemistry left their own traces.

Two other copies of *Songs of Seven* have similar stains on a few of their pages, indicating flowers that were once there; and they also both have an actual flower remaining in them. In one, a stem with a few broken blossoms sits next to the flyleaf, which bears an inscription to "Grace E. Terry from her Mother." In the other, inscribed to "Gracie," from "Mr. and Mrs. Walter Jones" on her birthday, a well-preserved single blossom on a stem appears at the close of "Seven Times Two: Romance" (Plate 5). The illustrator has done his part as well, placing an ornamental bouquet of foxgloves and asters after the poem, reflecting the language of its speaker, the fourteen-year-old maiden impatient for her own maturity (and for love, implied by Ingelow's poem foreshadowed in the facing-page illustration):

O columbine, open your folded wrapper,
  Where two twin turtle-doves dwell!
O cuckoopint, toll me the purple clapper
  That hangs in your clear green bell.

And show me your nest with the young
    ones in it;
  I will not steal them away;
I am old! you may trust me, linnet, linnet:
  I am seven times one to-day.

Figure 11. Jean Ingelow, *Songs of Seven* (Boston: Roberts Brothers, 1881), 14–15. Author's collection.

I wish, and I wish that the spring would go faster,
  Nor long summer bide so late;
And I could grow on like the foxglove and aster,
  For some things are ill to wait.

I wait for the day when dear hearts shall discover,
  While dear hands are laid on my head;
"The child is a woman, the book may close over,
  For all the lessons are said."

I wait for my story . . . (lines 21–29)

Wishing to "grow on like the foxglove and aster," the speaker finds in the flowers around her a model for her own self-development. Like the poem, which offers a stadial plan for the lives of its young female readers, the foxglove and aster (standing for youth and age, respectively) present themselves as models of growth for our heroine.[39]

These three copies of the Roberts Brothers edition of *Songs of Seven* were owned by three different female readers, all of whom inserted flowers in response to a poem that suggests simultaneously that each young woman must wait for her own story *and* that women's lives follow a scripted sequence of stages: that they all are, as Amy M. King writes, "waiting to 'bloom'" in a culture in which "conceptions of girlhood, maturation, and the social dispositions of marriage are buttressed by a botanical language strong and persuasive enough to uphold them" (3). Indeed, *Songs of Seven* reflects the heavy nineteenth-century investment in those scripts for women, visible in images like *The Life and Age of Woman* (1835; Figure 12), *The Life and Age of Woman: Stages of a Woman's Life from the Cradle to the Grave* (1848), and others like them. These images prompt these questions: Is there any meaningful variety in the life of a flower, or a Victorian girl, or a copy of the same book? Is there anything to wait for, or is the story always merely a version of the same tale? In the words of the title of a contemporary volume of floral poetry, is it always that the girl "Buds, Blossoms, and Leaves"?[40]

Ingelow's poem is certainly built on the framework of a traditional notion of a woman's "lot," which emerges most directly in the concluding stanza of "Seven Times Six: Giving in Marriage":

> To hear, to heed, to wed,
>   Fair lot that maidens choose,
> Thy mother's tenderest words are said,
>   Thy face no more she views;
> Thy mother's lot, my dear,
>   She doth in naught accuse;
> Her lot to bear, to nurse, to rear,
>   To love—and then to lose. (lines 25–32)

Maidens choose "[t]o hear, to heed, to wed" and thus take on the mother's lot, "to bear, to nurse, to rear, / To love—and then to lose." Those infinitive verbs reprise and reverse the well-known Victorian paean to masculine individualism that concludes Tennyson's "Ulysses" (published in 1842), whose hero rejects the domestic and administrative scripts laid out for him as an aging warrior-king. Leaving his spouse and desk job, he plans an odyssey that will allow him to incarnate again the name he has become: "To strive, to seek, to find, and not to

Figure 12. *The Life and Age of Woman* (Barre, MA: A. Alden, ca. 1835).

yield."[41] Ingelow's heroine, already wounded by the death of her husband and several of her children ("when God drew near / Among his own to choose" [lines 7–8]), can only lament and passive-aggressively address her daughter ("in naught accuse") who is fulfilling her "fair lot" by wedding a man and leaving her mother behind. By the time we get to "Seven Times Seven," that daughter has also died ("one after one they flew away / Far up to the heavenly blue") and all that is left is "Longing for Home" (the final poem of the sequence), in Heaven where the family might be reunited.

Strangely to our modern eyes, evidence suggests that these editions of Ingelow were a common gift to girls at an early age. In addition to the copy given to "Gracie" on her birthday (at Niagara Falls, on December 10, 1882), a shelf copy at Harvard University's Widener Library is inscribed to a seven-year-old girl named Florence McKeehan on "Xmas 1884" and then pre-annotated by the giver with the dates of Florence's birthday according to the poems that follow (Figure 13). "Seven Times One" is labeled for that year, July 12, 1884; "Seven Times Two" is labeled in advance, July 12, 1891; and "Seven Times Three" is labeled July 12, 1898, which will take her through her twenty-first birthday and includes the poem subtitled "Love."[42] Darker life events follow in Ingelow's poem, so our annotator wisely stopped there; but the assigning of those early stages to our young reader—the encouragement of her proleptic identification with a self the young girl should attain—becomes quite literal in this copy. The predictive date-stamping turns the book into a kind of fortune-teller, if an inaccurate one. In reality, Florence grew up to marry Louis John Magill (born in 1871), a Marine Corps officer, in May 1902, when she was twenty-four years old.[43] They had one son before Colonel Magill died at the age of fifty of a heart attack while shoveling snow at his home in Philadelphia on February 20, 1921.[44] And then, eight years later, when she was in her early fifties, Florence got married again, to a man thirteen years her junior (William Platt Pepper Jr., born in 1890), and managed to outlive him by six years. She died in 1941, at the age of sixty-three. All of these dates and events hover over Florence's copy of *Songs of Seven*, part of the networked and stadial chronology of a life, which is Ingelow's subject after all.

Perhaps most eloquent is a copy of *Songs of Seven* (1866) at Northeastern University, inscribed to "Miss Elsie Barlow," "presented on her fourteenth birthday / with the love and best wishes / of her friend / Cornelia W. Martin / Sept. 1867 / Willowbrook." Cornelia Williams Martin (1818–99) was a devout Christian heiress and, along with her successful husband, Enos Thompson Throop-Martin (1808–83), a member of fashionable society in New York City. She was forty-nine when she gave this book to Alice ("Elsie") Wadsworth Barlow (1853–82), and she included with it a letter about Ingelow's poem that is still tipped in to the book:

Dear Elsie,

It has given me great pleasure to make your acquaintance and particularly to have you spend your fourteenth birthday in our home. I always attach much importance to birthdays and those which mark the several distinct stages of life's journey are peculiarly interesting to one who sympathizes with the young as well as with the aged. Every seven years marks a decided change in appearance as well as in character. The first seven years of life are passed in comparative retirement, in the sports & pastimes of infancy and childhood, when all responsibility is borne by the parents and guardians. The second seven years are given to the elementary part of education fitting the child in some measure for the duties of life and

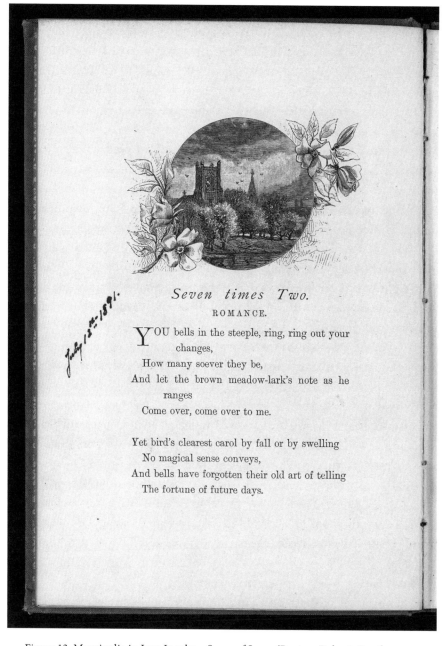

Seven times Two.

ROMANCE.

YOU bells in the steeple, ring, ring out your
    changes,
  How many soever they be,
And let the brown meadow-lark's note as he
    ranges
  Come over, come over to me.

Yet bird's clearest carol by fall or by swelling
  No magical sense conveys,
And bells have forgotten their old art of telling
  The fortune of future days.

Figure 13. Marginalia in Jean Ingelow, *Songs of Seven* (Boston: Roberts Brothers, 1884), 16. Florence McKeehan's copy, with the date of her seventh birthday added. Widener Library, Harvard University. Hollis Number 005386446.

giving her <u>some</u> responsibility—that period with you, dear Elsie, is just past and to-day you enter upon such responsibilities as you have never before known. The next seven years decide your character for life and perhaps will fix your destiny.

In this letter to the young Barlow, Martin uses Ingelow's time scheme to characterize the "distinct stages of life's journey," placing particular emphasis on the seven-year span Barlow has entered with the arrival of her fourteenth birthday (Ingelow's "Romance"), which Martin asserts will "decide your character for life and perhaps fix your destiny." Twelve years later, Barlow married one Stephen H. Olin. She died giving birth to her second daughter, Julia Lynch Olin, at the age of twenty-nine: seven times four—plus one. Grace, Gracie, Florence, Elsie: all of the girls and young women who received this book in the latter decades of the Victorian era grew up and took their own different paths, sometimes fulfilling and other times deviating from the narratives their early gift books offered them. These copies of *Songs of Seven* speak of a tension between social role and individual identity, between expectation and improvisation, between the duplicate and the unique. The flowers and inscriptions placed there, plangently or hopefully, recall the quotidian readers to whom these mass-produced books spoke: young women who grew on like the foxglove and aster and developed their own identities in dialogue with the popular poetry that they read and the books that they owned, marked, and saved.

The flower-wielding readers of nineteenth-century verse were not merely engaging in sentimental practices—although I hope that by now those practices look more complex than our scholarship has long assumed. Their alterations of their poetry books exist on a continuum with emerging modernist experiments in an era of industrial printing. Mrs. Dalloway said she would buy the flowers herself, but her Victorian precursors had already visited, if not cornered, that market. In modifying pages with botanicals and their impress, as well as with inscriptions, pastings, and cuttings, they prefigured the aesthetic movement that would champion the deformation of print, the defacing of the book, and the radical incisions made to objects of mass culture. As Bart Brinkman has argued, the personal Victorian scrapbook "models processes of accumulation, selection, and preservation" that "inform poetic modernism," just as its paper-collage format points to "a feminized origin for the découpage of the avant garde, celebrated in the works of such artists as Juan Gris."[45] The point is not that Victorian naïveté was wised up and therefore redeemed by modernism, but rather that so-called sentimental reading practices were experimental aesthetic engagements that had a formal sophistication all their own. We see in any one of these flower-strewn books the moment when a mass-produced object crosses over from replicable text to unique artifact (a one-off monotype, perhaps). And then, crossing back, in a book like Cassell's edition of Wordsworth, we observe that tromp l'oeil simulacrum as evidence of the recommodification of the personalized object and the readerly practices that produced it. Such books rehearse some of the central narratives of the Romantic century—the yielding of pastoral to industrial culture, the fall from individually expressive works to sleek copies (à la Ruskin)—and the modernist instantiations of and rebellions against that conflicted legacy.

Looking into this faraway garden now—leafing through the actual physical books once owned by nineteenth-century readers—offers a combination of delight and melancholy, a feeling captured perfectly in the concluding poem to that late-Victorian sequence beloved by so many across the century's divide, Stevenson's *A Child's Garden of Verses* (1885). Entitled "To Any Reader," the poem serves as an evocative envoi to the volume:

> As from the house your mother sees
> You playing round the garden trees,
> So you may see, if you will look
> Through the windows of this book,
> Another child, far, far away,
> And in another garden, play.
> But do not think you can at all,
> By knocking on the window, call
> That child to hear you. He intent
> Is all on his play-business bent.
> He does not hear; he will not look,
> Nor yet be lured out of this book.
> For, long ago, the truth to say,
> He has grown up and gone away,
> And it is but a child of air
> That lingers in the garden there. (lines 1–16)

Another garden there, visible "through the windows of this book" but forever closed (like those Wordsworthian scenes of nature virtually pinned to the pages of Cassell's edition). And in that *hortus conclusus*, that long-ago Eden, a child lingers as an unreachable phantom of lost youth: "far, far away."[46] Many of the poems in Stevenson's collection are written from the child's perspective, but this soft warning comes in an adult voice, and indeed begins by inviting the child-reader to share an adult's point of view: that of a mother looking out the window at her child "intent . . . on all his play-business bent" among the garden trees (bearing some resemblance to Wordsworth's play-busy "six-years' darling" of the Intimations Ode). And as an adult reads this poem aloud to a son or daughter, she may glimpse her own childhood in the pages, a version of an earlier self now "grown up and gone away" but still haunting the old book, the old garden, via a return to the "play-business" of reading. Now "it is but a child of air," which is to say, of *airs*—bound up with the verse and its gardenlike book, whose subtitle at this point might as well be "Paradise Lost."

The 1905 edition of *A Child's Garden of Verses*, illustrated by Jesse Wilcox Smith, is particularly evocative, providing an inset picture above "To Any Reader" that shows a flashback to an earlier *mise-en-page* in the same volume, the poem "Foreign Lands" and its arboreal illustration (Figure 14). "Foreign Lands" is another poem about surveying flowery gardens—call them "fresh woods, and pastures new"—that are also books: "I saw the next door garden lie / Adorned with flowers, before my eye / And many pleasant places more / That I had never seen before" (lines 5–8). Those adjacent gardens occupy shelf space, not acreage, recalling Keats's "On First Looking into Chapman's Homer," in which reading feels like gazing at the newly discovered Pacific Ocean with a "wild surmise." These are nested poems of longing after fields of gold, at once gardens and volumes that resolve uncannily into the object in the reader's hand; as Keats might say, this living book—see, here it is—I hold it toward you. One day, I may find a copy with a few old flowers pressed between these particular pages, but the magic is already there, encoded in poem, illustration, and bibliographic design, the braided result of the century's imagination of nature, its figurations of the self in time, and its practices of sentimental and epiphanic reading.

It will not have escaped my reader that this chapter is adorned with a virtual botanical collection in its own right, reproduced and inserted via photographic images meant not only as emblems of nineteenth-century reading but as souvenirs of discovery, of their own reemergence from the archive and that flash upon the inward page. In those apparitional moments, they evoke not only Wordsworth's remembered daffodils but also Walter Benjamin's model of history, of the past that "can only be seized as an image that flashes up at the moment of its recognizability."[47] As instances of such sudden flashing, the images are meant to evoke a certain immanence and fragility, borrowing from the emotional logic that prompted their original owners to augment their books with flowers and leaves. But now the ephemerality of the botanical insertions has been transferred to those books themselves, plucked from the shelves and bearing witness to the rich variety of individual bibliographic experience in an era of the downsizing of print collections. They have become unique, epiphanic moments amid a backdrop of

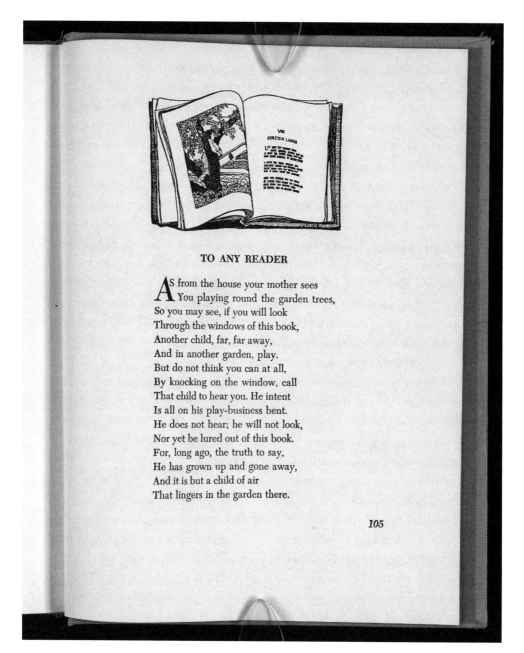

TO ANY READER

As from the house your mother sees
You playing round the garden trees,
So you may see, if you will look
Through the windows of this book,
Another child, far, far away,
And in another garden, play.
But do not think you can at all,
By knocking on the window, call
That child to hear you. He intent
Is all on his play-business bent.
He does not hear; he will not look,
Nor yet be lured out of this book.
For, long ago, the truth to say,
He has grown up and gone away,
And it is but a child of air
That lingers in the garden there.

105

Figure 14. R. L. Stevenson, "To Any Reader," in *A Child's Garden of Verses*, illus. Jesse Wilcox Smith (New York: Scribners, 1905), 105.

assumed similarity, redundancy, and text-as-data, pointing at once backward to the historical circumstances of their creation and forward to the nineteenth century as we will know it henceforth, after the great twenty-first-century winnowing of the libraries, already under way. We have inherited these books from past readers, but what choices will we make regarding their disposition in the digital age? "Take them, as I used to do / Thy flowers, and keep them where they shall not pine": Elizabeth Barrett's injunction to Robert Browning remains evergreen.

CHAPTER 3

Time Machines

Poetry, Memory, and the Date-Marked Book

I

If we look to nineteenth-century literature as a primer for its own reception, we find two broad mythic modes of Romantic reading: sublime discovery and nostalgic revisitation. Sublime discovery is typified by a poem like Keats's sonnet "On First Looking into Chapman's Homer," in which the experience of encountering a text involves a sudden shock of the new. For Keats, reading a fresh translation feels like gazing at a reconfigured world, "silent, upon a peak in Darien."[1] In many ways the birthright of modern lyric poetry, this mode of reading depends on imaginative energy flowing from the text to the self in surprising moments of identification. Keats's sonnet remarkably both describes and occasions this experience. For a moment, we are Keats reading Chapman's Homer and also Keats writing (and reading) his own sonnet as it emerges on the page while also remaining ourselves, viewed from a momentary, weird parallax. Readers in this mode are shaken and enlarged by novelty, whose signature in the long nineteenth century is mixed into the DNA of the genre that bears its name: be it gothic, sensation, detective, romantic, psychological, or even modern, the novel in its varying forms trades on unexpected turns, in the navigation of which the readers literally find themselves, uncovering or even making an identity as they consume the narrative (Frankenstein's creature may be said to enact a particularly literal version of the process, stumbling across books by Volney, Milton, and Goethe and using them as tools to sharpen a previously unformed idea of personhood). And novels often adopt such scenes of textual encounter as scenes of *Bildung*, in the lives of characters as diverse as Caleb Williams, Catherine Morland, and Emma Bovary, offering to their readers an image of the powerful communication circuit that the genre aimed to install at the heart of reading culture. Moreover, insofar as the novel aspired to the status of literature as opposed to mere enter-tainment, it endeavored to make its own novelty sustainable beyond a first read-ing and to excite similar feelings of surprise over multiple rereadings. In other words, the reader had to be put into the *mood* of discovery even when the *mode* was actually one of revisitation. Romantic poetry also had this technology of read-ing at its core, the motto for which is something close to the Wordsworthian oscil-lation between spontaneous overflows and emotions recollected in tranquility. In rendering a first reading as discovery, Keats's sonnet on Chapman's Homer con-veys that experience along its own frame; but its success depends upon rereadings that are simultaneously old and new, recollections and overflows. As a type of Romantic reading, then, discovery encodes its opposite: "On First Looking into Chapman's Homer" and "On Sitting Down to Read *King Lear* Once Again."[2]

This other mode, that of reading as nostalgic revisitation and recognition, has a curiously displaced power in Romantic poetry. We see the dynamic in founda-tional works like Wordsworth's "Tintern Abbey," where it is the natural world rather than a book that is being revisited and reread. Like Keats's sonnet, this poem presents reading as both revisitation and discovery, but with the emphasis reversed. In "Chapman's Homer," we slowly realize that our shock of discovery (like that of Keats with Homer, and Cortez with the Pacific) is also a shock of recognition; whereas in "Tintern Abbey," we come to see that Wordsworth's ini-tial nostalgic recognition of the Wye Valley is also a startling discovery about himself: a disabling "sad perplexity" that confirms his early days of "aching joys" and "dizzy raptures" as self-generated episodes.[3] That is, these two mythic modes of Romantic reading turn out to be opposite sides of the same coin. Yet in Words-worth's poem, the object of contemplation is a landscape, not a book. Similarly, in Coleridge's "Frost at Midnight," we more than half expect a book to appear as the focus of the poet's nocturnal reverie, but instead it is the fireplace, with its "film, which flutter'd on the grate," that provides the portal to memories of the past.[4] Frequently in Romantic poems, scenes of rereading often focus on nontex-tual features of the external world, leaving the book as a notional or apparitional phenomenon that can resolve itself only imaginatively into the volume held in the reader's hand.

Such resolution—from apparition to codex—is an image of the reception his-tory of Romanticism, beginning in the 1830s and 1840s, as the collected works of authors who wrote in the period then becoming known as "Romantic" emerged from the newly industrialized press and found their ways into the hands of in-heritors.[5] Romanticism became its printed record, and as a result, poetry and its scenes of reading in Victorian Britain and in nineteenth-century America were frequently marked by a mood of recognition and revisitation. As we saw in Chap-ter 2, flowers placed in books become both souvenirs and emblems of a reading moment; they virtually incarnate the experience of an encounter that is at least notionally traceable to a particular place and time. A spring morning in the garden or an autumn afternoon among the leaves becomes tethered to the book by means of the botanical material placed therein, occasioning a model of textual consumption based on the unique, punctuated moment. The little slip of paper we saw attached to the pasted floret in Annie Deering's copy of *The Changed Cross* makes explicit the silent date-stamping associated with many other floral insertions in books of poems in this era. Even when not accompanied by inscribed dates and locations, flower bookmarks focus bookish experience according to an epiphanic logic wherein reading is simultaneously arrested and memorialized, represented symbolically by the articulate, fading structure of the flower itself. Put another way, a flower in a book becomes an icon of a reading episode at once halted and sublimed, an incarnation of the singular branchings of the mind now transfixed and preserved but also lost, something like a wreath on a grave.

Yet flowers also fade, and degrade, and fall apart. Even as they figure a specific reading incident, they also evince their involvement with the slow time of the book.[6] In their physical attenuation, they remind us that bookmarks—flowers, inscriptions, and so forth—are placed there not just to pin down but also to link up multiple reading experiences. They make a specific locus of address repeatable, and, in so doing, they evoke plural occasions of reading across time. We know that reading is recursive and multitemporal, particularly when it comes to poetry as it was encountered in the nineteenth century. Poetry mattered because it continued to matter; and lyric poems ride upon energies harnessed by their own repeatability. Deering "often thought of" the poem "Coming" and turned to it on her deathbed precisely because of its familiarity. As Catherine Robson, Deidre Shauna Lynch, Meredith L. McGill, and others have shown, poetry was literature you lived with, not in a single moment of reading but over time, by means of the revisitings engendered by reading aloud, commonplacing, scrapbooking, memorization, and other readerly practices, as well as by anthologization, reprinting, and other modes of publishing that kept poems—often, the *same* poems— before the eyes of an increasingly literate public.[7] In short, poetry was for rereading. Much of its value was predicated upon and amplified by multiple investments over time, an economics that came more belatedly and always more partially to the genre named for its promise of the new, the novel. The increasing presence of books and periodicals in the middle-class home enabled such layered investments, as domestic libraries became sites for familiarization and personal associations through the years.

Testifying to this layered temporality, nineteenth-century readers frequently date-stamped the markings they made in their books. We saw in Chapter 1 how a grieving mother wrote not only "My darling William" next to Hemans's stanza (from "The Graves of a Household") about a dead child, but also the specific date on which she made that connection. In Chapter 2, we encountered birthdays inscribed in gift copies of Ingelow's *Songs of Seven*, as well as the dated slip affixed to a dried flower in Deering's copy of *The Changed Cross*. Now I turn to dated marginalia directly, and to books that were annotated and date-marked across time, ones that bear evidence of at least two occasions of nineteenth-century reading. Further, these examples all involve at least two hands: they were each inscribed by a different pair of lovers, with marks of flirtation, longing, affection, and loss, in explicit dialogue with the nineteenth-century poems that engaged their attention. Taken together, they reveal the Romantic practice of anchoring one's reading on a timeline and on the nostalgic re-revisitation that this installs at the heart of reading culture. Wordsworth's name for this phenomenon is familiar: "spots of time," certain experiences that retain "a distinct pre-eminence" along the topography of a life.[8]

One way to measure the legacy of Romanticism, then, is to use marks of date-stamping as an index of ideas about temporality and literary representation. Such marks highlight not only what books were as objects of practice for nineteenth-century readers but also the processive, layered nature of books as objects in time: date-marks momentarily bring to the surface and make traceable books' multiple horizons of temporality. The heterochronic book unevenly testifies to its times of composition, publication, purchase, gifting, reading, being damaged, and being conserved. The examples I present reveal the paradoxical power of revisited books to call forth the past while also emphasizing its pastness, to at once fulfill and continually defer readers' search for lost time. They become emblems not only for the Victorian reception of Romanticism but also for our own modern encounters with the nineteenth-century archive of which they are a part.

Like my earlier examples, the books that I present in this chapter were all found through guided browsing on open shelves of academic libraries. Their unexpected emergence from unspecial circulating collections is part of the story these books have to tell, part of their poignant, attenuated witness to the passions of a bygone world. The books are fading from our attention, moving out of libraries, being replaced by online surrogates, and turning brittle with age. But perhaps we can find ways to save them and make them matter again. Thanks to online databases, we can trace the lives these books call forth via their personalizing marks and connect the books to the emotional experiences of their owners. Personal annotations can become evidence of presumably widespread protocols, illuminated by tracking births, courtships, marriages, careers, and deaths. But even as it underwrites book history, this biographical detail competes for our attention, continually arcing the narrative toward sentimental tales of love and loss—which, in the end, perhaps resemble my story of the rediscovered nineteenth-century book in the twilight of the stacks, the late age of the print library. We are modern now; and it all happened so long ago. Implicitly this chapter asks, How do we care for these dated losses, these many old and fragile things?

II

Let me begin again, at the close of the nineteenth entury, with Thomas Hardy's short lyric "Her Initials," first published in 1898 in his *Wessex Poems and Other Verses*:

> Upon a poet's page I wrote
> Of old two letters of her name;
> Part seemed she of the effulgent thought
> Whence that high singer's rapture came.
> —When now I turn the leaf, the same
> Immortal light illumes the lay,
> But from the letters of her name
> The radiance has died away.
>   1869.[9]

Vintage Hardy, we might say of this melancholy, mordant narrative of fading enchantment. And indeed, it comes bearing a declaration of a vintage year: that closing date-stamp—1869—which signals its place in the poet's biography (when Hardy was twenty-nine), nearly thirty years prior to its date of publication. Before its medial em dash and the shift from past to present tense ("now I turn the leaf"), the poem itself evokes an even deeper past: that time "of old" when, in an assertion of recognition, the speaker inscribed the initials of his beloved "upon a poet's page." The poem reaches across half a century of interactive reading and inscriptive practice, looking backward from its fin de siècle publication through its moment of composition to its named episode of lovestruck annotation. Times and feelings have changed; that is the poem's burden—but the marginalium abides, a monument to a radiant moment of appropriative reading when the "high singer's rapture" evoked only thoughts of her, when the page with its inked letterforms fairly glowed with love borrowed from its reader's eye. The speaker's romantic love inspires the annotation, his reencounter with the annotation drives the poem, and the poem's publication many years later offers the linked but contrasting episodes as a post-Romantic parable of reading—and feeling—across time.

Hardy's subject in "Her Initials" is not only an evolving romantic relationship between two people but also a temporally layered encounter between a reader and a "poet's page," literally figured within the volume in the reader's hands. In *Wessex Poems*, the *mise-en-page* is deepened to *mise-en-abyme* by Hardy's inclusion of his own drawing at the top of the page, depicting an open book of poems with initials written in the left margin, a cryptic "Y. Z." (Figure 15). Hardy then signs the drawing with his own initials, a crossed "T. H." in the lower right-hand corner. One more pair of initials stands out in the drawing: the two ornamental capitals visible at the start of the two printed poems (an S and a W), themselves visual echoes of the majuscule U that starts the poem. Readers of this page of *Wessex Poems* are thus confronted with a kind of palimpsest: the material printed page itself depicting the imagined page with its printed (ornamental), inscribed

Figure 15. Thomas Hardy, "Her Initials," in *Wessex Poems and Other Verses* (New York: Harper and Brothers, 1898), 21.

(marginal), and notational (signatory) initials. The words of Hardy's poem may push sentiment aside in favor of disillusionment, but his drawing brings the erotically marked page before us like a revenant, a relic of a lost time whose deep resonance can be heard faintly, almost plaintively, in the poem's other bookend, that closing date-stamp: 1869. Moreover, the layout of the drawn page (ornamental capitals, running heads, top-corner pagination, poems running across page breaks) suggests that Hardy was working from a specific volume that he had read and marked. The illustration resembles pages from books in the Aldine Poets series, published by Bell and Daldy in the 1860s.[10] Hardy's page thus refers to the history of Victorian printing, recalling a specific format from an earlier era, the time of effulgent romance. The "immortal . . . lay" exists in distinct tension with the embodied, time-bound form in which it abides; such is the lesson of the marginalia. Although, for the poem's speaker, the radiance has died away from memories of his beloved, the image of a book from her high-Victorian moment remains enshrined on Hardy's fin de siècle page, a symbolic touchstone for the nineteenth-century book and the histories of longing that it so richly encodes. Not only is Hardy's poem about nostalgia, therefore, but it stages that longing precisely as a bookish affair.

A better-known example of such a dynamic is William Butler Yeats's "When You Are Old," his 1891 recasting of a lyric by Ronsard. Yeats imagines a time years hence, when his beloved is "old and grey and full of sleep / And nodding by the fire," when she will "take down this book, / And slowly read, and dream."[11] These lines adapt the famous Augustinian directive, the phrase that, as Augustine says in the *Confessions*, prompted his conversion: *tolle, lege*—take it (the book) and read. But for Yeats, the command becomes take it, read, and dream, in a nostalgic mode: "dream of the soft look / Your eyes had once, and of their shadows deep." Even at the moment of its first reading, then, the poem predicts (really, it demands) a second, slow reading that will make its addressee regret. That is, "When You Are Old" induces proleptic nostalgia for the current act of reading, for the "look" of the reader's eyes upon the very page in view. Originally printed in *The Countess Kathleen and Various Legends and Lyrics* (1892), the poem evokes its future reception as a scene of loss and reverie, when its Victorian reader, of the "changing face," will "[m]urmur, a little sadly" that "Love . . . hid his face amid a crowd of stars." Facing pages, the poem claims, she will be put out of face by them: confronted with the same physical document her eyes once knew, she will thereby measure her distance in time from the "one man" who had loved her then, before the book of poems was hidden amid a crowd of other books on the shelf.

As the 1892 book title suggests, "When You Are Old" is both a lyric and a legend, or rather a lyric that insists on becoming a legend in the reader's mind by establishing the present as a time to be mourned, one of deep shadows and pilgrim souls. *The Countess Kathleen* is dedicated to "Miss Maud Gonne" and contains various poems referring to her beauty and Yeats's love for her (e.g., "The Peace of the Rose," "The White Birds," and "The Pity of Love"). Thus "When You Are Old" is about a renewed encounter not only with itself as a poem but also with the entire book, one that she may "take down" and "slowly read" through. Indeed, the poem on the facing page, "The Sorrow of Love," picks up on the theme of sadness and weds it to "ever-singing . . . unquiet leaves" that evoke the leaves of the book. In this way, "When You Are Old" serves a dedicatory, inscriptive purpose in the volume: it approaches the condition of personal annotation insofar as it singles out "this book" as a souvenir, a gift that will be found in the beloved's library even when she is old and gray. But because it is printed, rather than handwritten, "When You Are Old" becomes portable: it has the potential, with reprintings, to transform *any* book that contains it into a remembrancer, as the poem—which has become one of Yeats's most popular lyrics—carries forward into later centuries its Victorian legend of reading as nostalgic reverie, and of books as domestic, fireside accessories.

Both "Her Initials" and "When You Are Old" emphasize the open book as a revisited scene to read and dream on, a future-perfect prompt to backward longing over the time-traveling codex. Emily Rohrbach and Jonathan Sachs have located this anticipation of the future backward glance (especially from a position of loss) as the definitive Romantic mode of imagining the self in time.[12] Hardy and Yeats, both Romantic inheritors, trade on this mode, providing figurations of nostalgic representation at the level of language, page, and individual volume, and their works have imaginative roots in the Romantic and Victorian practices of inscription, annotation, and marginalia writing that transformed copies into souvenirs of lost time. Andrew Piper has argued that nineteenth-century authors and readers dreamed in books, suggesting that their imagination of literature— its effects, its features, its ontologies, its possibilities—was based in the media in which it circulated.[13] To this I will add that the century's authors and readers dreamed *on* books in equally significant ways, ones that we have inherited. The reverie over the book implies that reading is an essentially epiphanic practice, shot through with nostalgia, by which the modern reading subject is made visible. Keats's "On First Looking into Chapman's Homer" evokes this process, in which the reader feels like "stout Cortes" gazing at the Pacific in silence, a still moment of both recognition and wonder as the old topographies pass away. Keats's metaphor suggests that poetic reading is available to representation only in the moment of its break or rupture: readers pause, gaze, muse, dream, "bend down beside the glowing bars" (in Yeats's words), and perhaps mark the page with pencil or forefinger. When we stop reading as processing, we start reading as longing and thereby find ourselves in books. The self and the physical book reappear simultaneously in the caesura, and the page becomes a mirror or dream tablet.[14] So even when readers do not write in their books, poetry makes them marginalians of the mind.

This phenomenology of reading could help explain our attachment to books as physical objects and their appearance in our hands in moments of personal reverie, when we are taken out of the flow of reading by affect and must pause for a moment to enfold it within a narrative of emotional experience. Reading the "immortal lay" in his particular volume in 1869, the speaker of Thomas Hardy's "Her Initials" is arrested by an affective recognition, which he assimilates to thoughts of his beloved "she" and then takes a moment to mark "two letters of her name" on the "poet's page." Thus consecrated as souvenir, the book bears a trace of the moment of shared "effulgent thought" in which reading yields to marking—a movement from trance to trace—and the material book returns as an object of sense. Marginalia make only a fraction of such countless moments visible, but they register a dynamic of investment in the codex that has formed the foundation of appropriative book love for the past two centuries. Recognition and nostalgia, epiphany and longing: these are the watchwords of Romantic reading practices that have shaped modern ideas of literature and its relation to the book; and marginalia are the traces of those practices.

Letitia Landon describes just such a reader's reverie in her 1834 poem "Emily" (or "The Wandering Thought"), written to accompany an image of a young woman holding a closed book and looking off into the middle distance.[15] The poem begins, "Her eye has wandered from the book / That rests upon her knee; / Gone from that page of love and war, / Where can her fancy be?" (lines 1–4). This "maiden with her wandering eye" (line 33) has been reading "A history of old romance," and the speaker asks rhetorically, "How can she read of others' love / And not recal her own?"(lines 17–20). Like the speaker of Hardy's "Her Initials" (and, for that matter, Dante's Paolo and Francesca), Emily recognizes her own erotic feelings in reading about similar feelings in others. Her attention moves naturally from the romance of her book to thoughts of her own "youthful knight" via an associative, identificatory mode of reading that yields to personal remembering. Emily does not write in her book, but the poem evokes the concept by suggesting marks left by and upon her. She thinks of the "scarf and glove / Which he is vow'd to wear," upon which "Her tears have left their stain" (lines 23–24, 26). Further, Emily herself seems to be turning into a book, as well she might, given Landon's focus on the engraved image printed on the facing page opposite the poem. The speaker notes of Emily, "there is color on her cheek" (line 13), a black-and-white blush signifying her "deeper, dearer thought" beyond the ostensible subject of her reading. And the poem concludes with an explicit comparison of her face to a book:

An innocent and happy love
  Is in that youthful face;
God grant that never coming years
  May leave a sadder trace!

Life's book has one or two fair leaves;
  Ah, such should be for thine!
That young face is too kind, too good
  To bear a harsher line. (lines 45–52)

Landon invokes at least three layers of figuration here: first, Emily as a real person represented through synecdoche by her "youthful face"; second, "that youthful face" as the engraved image in Finden's *Gallery*; and third, "Life's book" with the "fair leaves" of its facing pages. The poem wishes that no "sadder trace" or "harsher line" be left upon any of these surfaces, as scars, marginalia, or tragic content. So, the poem implies, stop reading now: close the book and remain suspended in "those gentle dreams" of romance (line 37). Fittingly, Landon's "Emily" is the final poem in the volume.

As Yeats's "When You Are Old" suggests, books could also become messengers, bearing inscriptions meant not just to record private feeling but also to communicate it to a beloved. An 1869 Boston copy (now at the University of Virginia) of the popular narrative poem *Lucile*, written in 1860 by Owen Meredith (the pseudonym of Bulwer-Lytton's son, Edward Robert) carries a gift inscription: "To Jennie Tayloe / From a friend / August 1869." The giver has used the language of a poem to convey a message, underscoring the lines on page 79, "our two paths are plain, / And those two paths divide us," and writing in the margin, "July '69" (Figure 16). The poem itself is about the rivalry between Lord Alfred and a French duke for the hand of the virtuous Lucile, and about the misunderstandings that separate lovers. Here, the unknown "friend" has date-stamped a portion and appropriated its language for his (or her) own lyric utterance, a timely comment on a relationship with Virginia Jennie Tayloe (1848–1929) of Roanoke, Virginia, presumably when it reached a kind of crisis, a month before the "friend" gave her the book as an appeal or a valediction (Tayloe would go on to marry Captain Mortimer M. Rogers in 1875). These markings help us see afresh the countless mute underscorings, check marks, and marginal brackets so common in nineteenth-century books: they must often have been autobiographical appropriations of this kind. A few pages earlier in this copy, the unknown friend has followed suit, marking such lines as "Thy place in my life is vacant forever / We have met; we have parted" (74); "Thou mightest have been to me much" (75); and, near the end, "How with love may be wreck'd a whole life!" (238). We can perceive

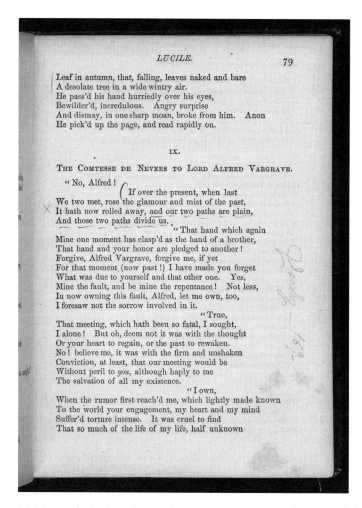

Figure 16. Marginalia in Owen Meredith, *Lucile* (Boston: Fields, Osgood and Co., 1869), 79. Jennie Tayloe's copy. Alderman Library, University of Virginia. PR 4954 . L7 1869.

the intention here because of the date-stamps and the inscription to Tayloe. This copy has been transformed into an interpersonal record of a relationship, predicated on repurposing and appropriation.

The habit of personalizing books grows in part out of widespread phenomena such as commonplacing, scrapbooking, and album verse, all of which involved the repurposing of poetic materials according to one's own associations and relationships.[16] Somewhere in the background also lies biblical reading in the Protestant tradition. The practice of applying poetic texts such as the Psalms or Jesus's parables to one's personal experience—especially in epiphanic moments of reading and recognition—was practically bred in the bone for the Anglo-American readership of this era. This mode of reading involves an intersection of the conventional and the personal that had much to do with poetry's popularity in the long nineteenth century. The moment of personal, private recognition is simultaneously an implicit gesture toward community, a moment of subjectivity that involves a reach for a common language, a common stock of emotions and beliefs.

That sense of community is evoked by Bayard Taylor's popular midcentury poem "The Song of the Camp," which depicts British soldiers before a battle in the Crimea singing together a ballad in praise of a beloved woman; at its center are the famous lines "Each heart recalled a different name, / But all sang 'Annie Laurie'" (lines 19–20).[17] Here the central poetic text—the old Scottish ballad "Annie Laurie"—becomes a rallying point for the singers, each of whom is brightened at once by the shared words of the song and the memory of his individual beloved. As Taylor writes,

> Voice after voice caught up the song,
>   Until its tender passion
> Rose like an anthem, rich and strong,—
>   Their battle-eve confession.
>
> Dear girl, her name he dare not speak,
>   But, as the song grew louder,
> Something upon the soldier's cheek
>   Washed off the stains of powder. (lines 21–28)

In this emblematic anecdote, we see dramatized the moment of recognition, love, and longing, as each soldier takes up the lyrics of the old ballad as an individual confession: "for bonnie Annie Laurie / I'd lay down my head and die."[18] The result is not marginalia exactly, but rather the tracks of tears, washing the gunpowder stains from "the soldier's cheek" in a baptism of sentiment as each one, singing of "Annie Laurie," thinks of his own "[d]ear girl" and his own death on this "battle-eve." The generic language and commonplace emotional register of the "Annie Laurie" ballad provide an opening for subjective experience, not a diffusion of it, in a moment of communal bonding that was repeated across the century in shared parlor songs and recited poems. For many Victorian readers of poetry, as for the soldiers, "each heart recalled a different name"—as Hardy does in "Her Initials"—and recorded their individual emotional epochs within the circumference of a book. How we read such records and the verse that prompted them touches on an unanswered challenge of the post-Enlightenment era: the question of the similitude of our inner lives, asserted by Wordsworth ("We have all of us one human heart") and Arnold ("The same heart beats in every human breast") in echo of what Robert Frost called that "hard mystery of Jefferson's," the idea that all humans are created equal.What would a literary criticism that believed that look like? My hope is that the actual books read and marked by nineteenth-century readers can help us toward an answer.

Before turning to some of those books, which were taken from university library shelves (at Virginia, Columbia, and Louisville), I want to linger in the nineteenth-century parlor or study for a moment—by the fireside, under the lamps, and among the shelves—in order to consider the book as medium, that is, as a technology of memory, a means of contacting the spirits of the past. In Robert Browning's "By the Fire-Side" (1853), the speaker's imagined reveries "by the fire . . . / O'er a great wise book" lead him back to Italy in the early days of love with the wife who will remain with him "[m]using by fire-light" over a book of her own.[19] For Browning, the old book offers "a vista opening far and wide" for him to "pass out where it ends" into the realm of memory, and back again to domestic bliss. This is Yeats's "When You Are Old" with a happy ending. Yet here the content of the book (ancient Greek prose) hardly matters. More apt, perhaps, is James Whitcomb Riley's sentimental chestnut, "An Old Sweetheart of Mine" (1889), a series of nostalgic memories of a childhood girlfriend, a reverie indulged in an upstairs study among "old bookshelves" while the speaker's wife and children are out of the way. Our narrator is smoking, not reading, but a book appears (in a simile) virtually right on schedule. In its first published version, the poem begins,

> As one who cons at evening o'er an album, all alone,
> And muses on the faces of the friends that he has known,
>
> So I turn the leaves of Fancy, till, in shadowy design,
> I find the smiling features of an old sweetheart of mine.

The experience of memory is figured as a search through a picture album, a book of souvenir images on "the leaves of Fancy." And the reverie is invoked by an allusion to Wordsworth, an evocation of the leech gatherer from "Resolution and Independence," who looks upon the pond, "which he conn'd, / As if he had been reading in a book."[20] In both cases, the simile relies on the idea that the act of reading produces recognizable postures of attention. Like Yeats's aging heroine "bending down beside the glowing bars" and dreaming over her book, or Browning's narrator musing over his in "By the Fire-Side," Riley's husband indulges in erotic reverie according to the logic of the open codex as a fixative of body and gaze, while the mind travels to other times and places. This one has a happy ending, too: it turns out that the wife downstairs *is* the "old sweetheart," who shows up at the end in her own "living presence," and domestic bliss trumps the "truant fancies" of nostalgia.

One more fireside tale: in July 1879, the aging Longfellow sat in the study of his historic home in Cambridge, Massachusetts, reading an illustrated book about the American West.[21] It told of the immense, never-melting snowy cross formed in the crevices on the face of the Sawatch mountain range in Colorado, on a peak known as the Mount of the Holy Cross. The book provided an illustration of the phenomenon by Thomas Moran (Figure 17). For Longfellow, who had never traveled anywhere west of New England, it was nevertheless a moment of recognition. Looking at the image, he was brought back to a night of horror exactly eighteen years earlier, when, in that same parlor, his wife, Fanny, had burned to death in his arms. She had been in the adjoining library, sealing a lock of their young daughter's hair in an envelope, when the hot wax dripped onto her dress and caught fire. Fanny rushed into the parlor, engulfed in flames that Longfellow attempted to extinguish with a small rug, and then with his body. He was burned and scarred severely, and she died the next morning.[22] Now, with this picture of the Mount of the Holy Cross before him, he was moved to write the famous sonnet "The Cross of Snow":

> In the long, sleepless watches of the night,
>> A gentle face—the face of one long dead—
>> Looks at me from the wall, where round its head
>> The night-lamp casts a halo of pale light.
> Here in this room she died; and soul more white
>> Never through martyrdom of fire was led
>> To its repose; nor can in books be read
>> The legend of a life more benedight.
> There is a mountain in the distant West
>> That, sun-defying, in its deep ravines
>> Displays a cross of snow upon its side.
> Such is the cross I wear upon my breast
>> These eighteen years, through all the changing scenes
>> And seasons, changeless since the day she died.

July 10, 1879[23]

Seeing the cross of snow, Longfellow feels it, in a Dimmesdale-like transfer, upon his own breast, where it becomes another scar of trauma and loss—a kind of

Figure 17. Thomas Moran's "Mountain of the Holy Cross," in *Picturesque America . . .* , ed. William Cullen Bryant and Oliver Bell Bunce (New York: D. Appleton, 1872).

typographical dagger indicating Fanny's mortality, symbolic on the page of Longfellow's book and adopted by him as a sign of changeless grief, the permafrost left after tragic bereavement. (Samuel Longfellow reprinted the image beneath the poem when he first published it in his 1886 edition of *Life of Henry Wadsworth Longfellow*.) Yet it is also a negative insignia, a white erasure on black ground that reverses the polarities of the typical *x* that marks the spot, or the black inscriptions on a white page of paper. It is the ghost of a mark, and it, in turn, leaves its mark. Through this image, Fanny's "legend," which Longfellow paradoxically claims outstrips those that can be "read in books," emerges. Even as the poet dismisses the reading of books, his open, marked codex becomes a portal to the past, to another life—and also a strange and enigmatic mirror. Like the closing date at the end of Hardy's "Her Initials," that "July 10, 1879" lingers after the poem as a reminder of its own mournful occasion, a testimony of the intransigence of his grief. One thinks, too, of Hardy's Virgilian epigraph to his poems for his dead wife, Emma: *veteris vestigia flammae*—the traces of an old flame, the scar left by an old wound.

Moran's image of the cross of snow is not marginalia, of course; but the flash of recognition it calls forth in Longfellow suggests the by-now familiar mode of epiphanic longing that I have called Romantic or lyric reading. The graying heroine of "When You Are Old," the disenchanted lover of "Her Initials," and the wistful-but-happy husbands of both "By the Fire-Side" and "An Old Sweetheart of Mine" all share in this attitude of bibliographic reverie, which involves an oscillation between reading and remembering, between turning leaves and leaving the present for the dreamtime of the past. It is a marginalian's posture, a moment for inscribing the self in relation to a beloved other, whose past existence is literally an open book. Thus the life and memory of the reader get bound up with that specific volume, in a series of nostalgic investments that sometimes leave their traces. The examples that follow, taken from the library stacks, are anecdotal cases of this kind, in which nineteenth-century books of poetry have become layered scenes of erotic memory. Their marginalia reveal interpersonal associations, nostalgic modes of reading, personal appropriations, and moments of encounter, in the manner of Hardy, Yeats, and others that we have explored thus far. As they do in "Her Initials," these annotations come bearing specific dates that refer to readers' lived experiences. Furthermore, the scene of reading is always at least doubled in time, as the books register mulitple encounters and interactions and the annotation of previous annotations. They are witnesses to the complex temporality of the book.

III

One evening in 1858, the Louisville native Mary Fontaine Cosby, then twenty-five, attended a party at the Green Street home of her recently married young friend, Catherine Caldwell, who was just twenty years old at the time.[24] Worth noting is the fact that the Caldwells lived about a block from Georgiana Keats, and it is possible that she or one of her daughters was at the party, too: Ella (born in 1833) and Alice Ann Keats (born in 1836) were exact contemporaries of Mary Cosby and the Caldwells.[25] A local historian of the era calls Cosby "a very beautiful woman, of most gentle and attractive manners," and says of Mrs. Caldwell, "She was one of the most accomplished women of her day in Louisville and a member of one of the leading families."[26] As an amusement, Cosby brought with her a book of poems: a copy of the collected works of a now-neglected British master of *verse de societé*, Winthrop Mackworth Praed. My guess is that she wanted to share Praed's "charades," sometimes called enigmas, with the guests: in pencil, she has inscribed the answers to these riddle poems (e.g., "Fireside," "Bridegroom," "Nightcap," "Moonshine"), and it seems likely that she read them aloud to the assembled company. (I wonder if a copy of Keats was also in the mix.)

The Praed book circulated that night, passing through the hands of other guests, most notably someone with the initials "C. A. P.," who took the opportunity to use it to flirt with Cosby and another woman named Emma. On two pages of Praed's longer poem "The Troubadour," the annotator has written in the margin, "Say 11 please, 10 is so early" and "dear Miss Emma stay all night" (132–33), apparently a message meant to be read semiprivately, like a note passed in class. One senses a casual hubris in these notes written in Cosby's book, even as we get a glimpse of the transactional, social role of books in a setting like this one. A few pages later, at a later moment in the evening, the annotator has added, "Goodnight. I am the victim of circumstances" (137), perhaps before being dragged away by friends or relations. But first, he (or she) had taken the opportunity that evening to write two notes meant especially for Cosby's eyes. Next to the title "The Belle of the Ball," we see written, "Miss Mary Cosby at Mrs. Caldwell's party / CAP"; and we find the same thing written again at the conclusion of the poem "Good Night," which ends, "The ball and my dream are all over—/ Good night to thee, lady! good night!" This annotation adds the date: "1858" (235). We can see the traces of the book's multiple roles in these annotations: not only as a source of entertainment, since the riddle poems were likely read aloud as a parlor game, but also as a venue for the text messaging occurring on the pages themselves. In the case of C. A. P.'s notes to "dear Miss Emma," the book provides a convenient substrate for communication, while flirtatious compliments to Cosby draw specifically on Praed's poems to engage her attention: good night to thee, lady, you're the belle of the ball.

Thus far, Mary Cosby's copy of Praed seems to have been read and used along the lines that the verse often encourages. Praed's style is lighthearted, flirtatious, and slightly rueful, very much a post-Byronic mode that manages youthful enthusiasms with half-jaded mockery. Some stanzas from "The Belle of the Ball" convey this:

> She smil'd on many just for fun—
>   I knew that there was nothing in it;
> I was the first, the only one
>   Her heart had thought of for a minute;
> I knew it, for she told me so,
>   In phrase which was divinely moulded;
> She wrote a charming hand, and oh!
>   How sweetly all her notes were folded!
>
> Our love was like most other loves—
>   A little glow, a little shiver;
> A rosebud and a pair of gloves,
>   And "Fly Not Yet," upon the river;
> Some jealousy of some one's heir,
>   Some hopes of dying broken-hearted,
> A miniature, a lock of hair,
>   The usual vows—and then we parted. (183)

Part of a series of poems called "Every-day Characters," "The Belle of the Ball" shows Praed gently mocking romantic love by emphasizing its conventionality. His list of the stock emotions, items (sweetly folded notes in a charming hand), and poems or songs (Thomas Moore's "Fly Not Yet," resonating nicely with C. A. P.'s plea to Miss Emma to "stay all night") that constitute a love affair culminates in "[t]he usual vows" never to part, followed by the just-as-usual parting. The poem ends as the couple meets again "[f]our summers after," by which time all has turned to "mirth and laughter": the speaker has moved on and "she was not the ball-room belle, / But only Mrs.—Something—Rogers." The belle has become a wife, and first love can be ironized into the folly of "young hearts romancing." This copy of Praed thus carries evidence of its use in very Praed-like scenes of flirtation and youthful romance, as these twentysomethings of the Kentucky elite take their places within the roles that the poems present. A year after Mrs. Caldwell's party, Mary Cosby married Lucius Loomis Rich (and not C. A. P.), becoming "Mrs.—Something—Rich," as foreshadowed in Praed's knowing poem.

Some years later, Cosby picked up her book again, at a very different stage of her life. Like the Byron of *Don Juan*, Praed seems to be predictably light and ironic but sometimes shifts into postures of sharp melancholy; and when Cosby returned to her book, she marked the following concluding lines from perhaps his darkest poem, a lament for lost love entitled merely "Stanzas":

> Thou may'st have comfort yet!
> Whate'er the source from which those waters glide,
> Thou hast found healing mercy in their tide;
>   Be happy and forget!
>
>   Forget me—and farewell!
> But say not that in me new hopes and fears,
> Or absence, or the lapse of gradual years,
>   Will break thy memory's spell!
>
>   Indelibly, within
> All I have lost is written; and the theme
> Which Silence whispers to my thoughts and dreams
>   Is sorrow still—and sin! (248–49)

Unlike the comedic "Belle of the Ball," this poems ends in a tragic, almost gothic key, emphasizing both loss and an abiding sense of guilt and sin. Enjoining the changed lover to "[b]e happy and forget," the poem asks, "Is not the damning line / Of guilt and grief engraven on me now?" For an uncanny moment or two, the book itself seems to be speaking of its own annotations: "Indelibly, within / All I have lost is written." And, in the margin underneath the poem, Cosby has written this plangent reflection (Figure 18): "I read this book years ago, a bright, joyous, happy girl—Life was all before me—& I wondered that there could be a heart sad enough to write these lines. Now long years have passed—I again take up this book. The best part of my life is passed. The bright, happy girl is changed into the lonely broken-hearted woman & of all that is written here the above is the truest expression of her feelings" (249). The note is undated; we know only that "long years have passed" since that party of 1858, when she was "a bright, joyous, happy girl." Cosby's husband, Lucius, was mortally wounded in 1862 at the Battle of Shiloh, fighting for the Confederate side as a colonel in the 1st Missouri infantry.[27] That was not the only loss: according to Johnson, "[t]heir two children, a son and a daughter, both died young" (485). Her mother had passed away long ago, when Cosby was fifteen. My best guess is that she returned to this book sometime in the late 1860s or early 1870s, a "lonely,

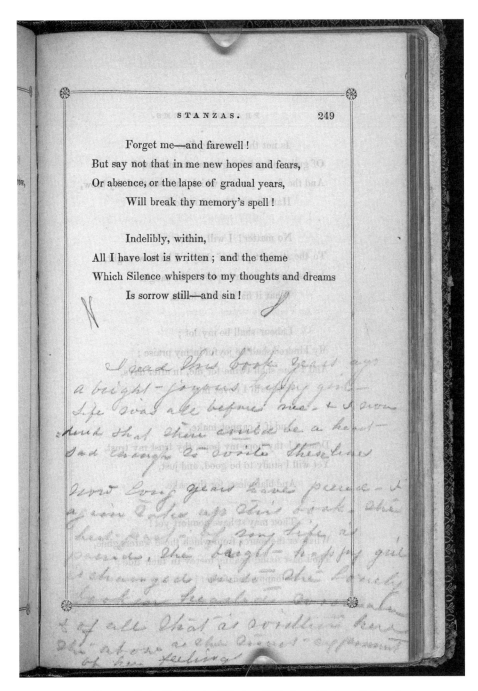

Forget me—and farewell !
But say not that in me new hopes and fears,
Or absence, or the lapse of gradual years,
Will break thy memory's spell !

Indelibly, within,
All I have lost is written ; and the theme
Which Silence whispers to my thoughts and dreams
Is sorrow still—and sin !

Figure 18. Marginalia in *The Poetical Works of Winthrop Mackworth Praed*, ed. R. W. Griswold (New York: Henry Langley, 1844), 249. Mary Cosby's copy. Ekstrom Library, University of Louisville. PR5189 .P7 1884.

broken-hearted woman" in her late thirties, looking back on happier times and a lover she could not forget.

Was it C. A. P.? Cosby makes one more intervention, adding a set of her characteristic four brackets to the penultimate stanza of "Good Night," the poem that C. A. P. had annotated with her name at Mrs. Caldwell's party in 1858. It reads in part, "There are tones that will haunt us, though lonely / Our path be o'er mountain or sea; / There are looks that will part from us only / When memory ceases to be." My guess is that her marks on the poem were made on the second occasion of reading. It seems likely that, in paging through a volume that she remembered from earlier days, Cosby reencountered the flirtatious notes by C. A. P. and allowed them to draw her back into a scene of youth and possibility. Haunted by the "tones" and "looks" of someone from her past, she uses this book to amplify that haunting; the presence of C. A. P.'s date-stamped handwriting would turn the book into a particularly powerful touchstone. Reencountering not only Praed's poems but also the traces of her romantic, hopeful reading of them that her book still preserves, she commits to the "indelibly" written sense of loss conveyed in "Stanzas," saying that they are "the truest expression of her feelings" now. Whether she was thinking of that night in 1858 specifically, let C. A. P. stand for the lost lovers of the past who "will part from us only / When memory ceases to be."

Cosby's story emerges incompletely from this book, yet enough details of genealogy and local history are available that we can move from speculation to probability. The location of the book itself—in the general library collection at the University of Louisville—is a crucial piece of evidence. It allowed me to place Cosby in the social network of nineteenth-century Louisville. Another name penciled into the book, Carpenter, has been covered by a pasted library charge slip, but it is enough to confirm Cosby's identity: her older sister Ellen Blake Cosby (born in 1828) married the Louisville resident John Slaughter Carpenter in 1850. They had eleven children, and the book seems to have passed into that branch of the family at some point. I feel fairly confident that "Mrs. Caldwell" is indeed Catherine Smith Caldwell, Cosby's contemporary and a leading Louisville hostess of the era. But who is C. A. P.? One tantalizing possibility is Charles A. Powell, the only young man fitting those initials in a Louisville address directory from 1860; Charles was working as a clerk for wholesale druggists R. A. Robinson at that time.[28] His story has a strange sequel: in 1868, he was arrested along with his brother George for larceny, having stolen and resold large amounts of opium from his employer. According to a local news report, "Charles A. Powell, a young man who had been employed [with the Robinson house] for twelve to fifteen years since he was a very small boy until last July, was implicated in the robbery, and he was arrested also." Charles confessed to moving at least two hundred pounds of opium over the previous few years.[29] His fate remains unknown to me, but his fall from grace corresponds to the period to which I date Cosby's melancholy re-reading of her Praed volume, and it may have contributed to her sense of having lost him for good. All of this is mostly reverie, of course. C. A. P. could have been someone else, male or female, associated with her younger years and the passionate evenings of 1858. In any case, books like this one prompt musings, like those of their original owners and readers. They are objects to read (and to investigate and analyze in terms of the evidence) but also to dream on. Their power lies in their ability not just to evoke the past but also to inspire in the reader the melancholy affect of pastness itself. The sense of history and the sense of loss, arriving together, bind us to these books just as they bound their nineteenth-century re-readers like Mary Cosby, the possessors and possesed.

*   *   *

My next example was also found in the University of Louisville library, but the book's history has nothing to do with that region of the country: it was acquired by the university as part of a large purchase (sixty thousand volumes) from a California dealer in the 1960s. On the inside flyleaf, the previous owner has written his name three times, along with a date, apparently experimenting with his own signature: first in pencil, "Geo. B. Griffin / 1854," then in ink, "Geo. Butler Griffin 1854," and again in pencil, larger and with a flourish underneath, "Geo. B. Griffin 1854." The book itself is a copy of James Wright Simmons's *The Greek Girl* (1852), a forgotten Byronic mash-up, two cantos of ottava rima that blend certain moods and postures from *Childe Harold's Pilgrimage* into an approximate ventriloquizing of *Don Juan*. Simmons's romance plot provides occasion for playful *sententiae* delivered with mordant cleverness, making it into a kind of anthology of Byronisms, a mixtape of tribute and cover tunes created by a true fan.[30] That Griffin found it congenial says something about how far Byron had seeped into the groundwater of antebellum American culture, particularly for young men trying on models of sentimental masculinity. Yet in this volume, we also see another annotator—I believe a female one—gently modifying those early identifications and urging Griffin to a new reading of the poem and himself.

George Butler Griffin was born in 1840 in New York; he acquired his copy of *The Greek Girl* when he was fourteen.[31] He was a student at Columbia College at the time, graduating at seventeen and heading off on a surveying schooner to Panama that fall, and thence to Mexico to survey for a railway. By 1859, George was back in New York, and he attended Albany Law School until 1861. My best guess is that the second layer of annotations—made by "Fred"—date from this Albany period. George underlined and bracketed a number of passages at some point during his time at Columbia, and "Fred" has picked up the book later and added more commentary. Some of these offer confirmation of George's emphases: in a note to bracketed lines reading, "He had renounc'd his birth-right sooner than / Conform to other men's opinions," Fred has written, "yourself perfectly. Fred" (33, canto 1, stanza 43). And to a pair of bracketed stanzas lamenting sorrows that make us abandon our "dear illusions. . . . Till life becomes a cold and cheerless mart; / The past has perish'd! and we feel no more / The beacon burns to light us to that shore," Fred has added, "I never read anything that surmised more <u>your own thoughts</u> than this—Fred" (47, stanza 73). An obvious paradox emerges: the nonconformist who is "perfectly" reflected in a mass-produced cultural object. Like Mary Cosby, who wrote that certain lines in her Praed book were "the truest expression of her feeling," Fred here draws an equivalence between poetic language and interior subjectivity, a primary mode of poetic appreciation in the nineteenth century, as we have seen exemplified in other cases. Elswhere in this copy, as a comment on lines reading in part, "In years a boy . . . he grew in loneliness. . . . Of his own mind he fashion'd his own world," Fred has written, "these were your thoughts in 1854. Fred" (11, stanza 18).

But whose thoughts, and whose mind, given the imaginative modeling going on in this scene? After all, reading to find a language for the self is risky: someone else's thoughts become your own, just as they have for many others. Adela Pinch has explored the ways in which nineteenth-century readers located their emotions via the quotation of others' words; as she says, "Romanticism's expressions of emotions are situated in a culture of quotation."[32] In recognizing and affirming a poem's formulation, a reader finds a language for, and gives up a piece of, a unique identity. Byronism mitigates the accompanying anxiety of interior similitude by doubling down on this paradox, offering a rhetoric of singular alienation that any middle-class reader may imaginatively inhabit, at least temporarily. The popularity of the Byronic mode depends on its rhetoric of elite estrangement being relatable. The teenage George Griffin found it so. He even composed his own stanza to add to *The Greek Girl*, writing it in pencil on the last page of the poem; and, although he later crossed it out heavily, fragments here and there are visible: "But still . . . / . . . has resigned / All hope of happiness / . . . ne'er could he find . . . / . . . ne'er took pains" (117). The Byronic rhetoric emerges despite Griffin's overstrike, although the secrecy communicated by the cancelation has itself a quasi-Byronic air. Fred writes after this crossed-out section, "Why did you mark this so it could not be read—what was it?" (117).

In fact, many of Fred's later notes offer corrections to George's earlier sympathetic underlining of this Byronic poem: for example, to the bracketed line "One lesson still remains, 'tis—to *conceal*," Fred has underlined "conceal" and written, "you would not express yourself in this way now? Fred" (5, stanza 15). Further, as a comment on the line "I know it is decided, and—we part!" Fred has written, "quite appropos [*sic*] at the time. Not so. Fred" (25, stanza 25). And so a love story begins to emerge out of the marginalia. In a note next to the bracketed lines "And what remains? Can either love again? / Ah no! regret, remorse, pride— all forbid!" Fred has written, "yes, I know of one instance to prove they can—not so? Fred" (42, stanza 62). And to the bracketed lines "But with lost love, we feel that all is lost—/ We are alone upon a desert coast," Fred has added, "do you still think so? Fred" (97, stanza 60). Fred's flirtatious, corrective notes culminate in a comment on a stanza in which the narrator reflects on the death of Oscar's beloved Inez (Figure 19). The stanza ends, "No star shall rise upon his path again!"

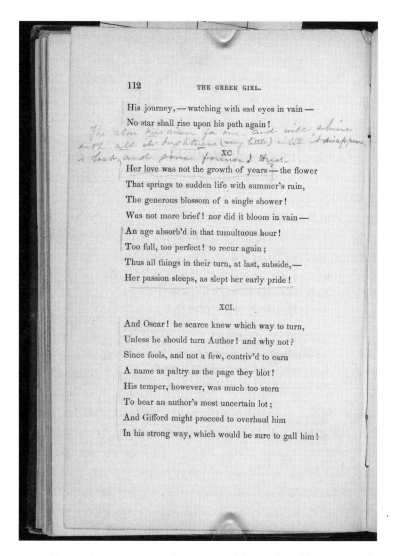

Figure 19. Marginalia in James Wright Simmons, *The Greek Girl* (Boston, 1852), 112. George Butler Griffin's copy. Ekstrom Library, University of Louisville. PR 2839 .S4 c. 1.

Fred has written the following self-deprecating declaration below it: "The star <u>has</u> risen for one—and will shine with <u>all its brightness</u> (very little) until it disappears, is lost, and gone forever! Fred" (112, stanza 89).[33]

Fred's notes (not all of which I am able to present here) evoke a personality, as the notes tease and woo George by means of Simmons's poem and this book. For example, in a note to a stanza about the hero Oscar, who, "[w]on by the solemn stillness of the hour . . . sought the terrace," Fred writes, "you have sought the terrace with cara Cora often—not so? Fred" (108, stanza 82)—apparently a reference to a previous female love interest. As I was with "C. A. P.," I am left wondering about the identity of "Fred." It could have been an intimate male friend, or a female love interest, as "Fred" is a plausible nickname for a woman of that period. My only guess is Sara Edwards, whom George Griffin would marry in Albany in November 1861; the dates fit, as do the substance and context of the notes, including the proprietary nature of Fred's commentary in this book. She may well have made her additions after their marriage, finding the book as the couple established their household. In the end, George and Sara Griffin did not get much time together: they had two sons, both of whom died before the age of two, and Sara herself died a few weeks before her second son, in 1866, at the age of twenty-five. George moved to South America the following year, leaving this book behind; through various episodes and agents, it eventually ended up in the stacks at Louisville.[34] Like my other examples, the book partially illuminates the readers who read and marked it and who measured their own identities and romantic lives by means of its pages, its language, and its date-stamped layers of reception.

*   *   *

An edition of *The Poetical Works of Thomas Moore*, published in Buffalo, New York, in 1852, was found on the shelves of Butler Library at Columbia University.[35] In the later years of the nineteenth century, it belonged to Juliana Catherine Shields (1875–1949) of Norwich, Connecticut. The book has the following gift inscription on the front free endpaper: "To Miss Juliana / It gives me great pleasure to inscribe myself / Your sincere friend, / R. E. L. Barnum / Savannah, GA / M[ar]ch 25, 1893." Like my other examples, this copy has been marked by a romantically entangled couple, who conducted a part of their relationship using the language of Moore's poetry and the spaces of the book. Juliana was seventeen when she met the twenty-nine-year-old physician Robert E. Lee Barnum (1863–1908) in Georgia in the spring of 1893, and they embarked on a short-lived romance. Marked with various dates in 1892 and 1893, Juliana's copy offers a record of experiences and evolving feelings by repurposing lines and phrases from Moore.

Throughout the book, and particularly in the long stretches of *Lalla Rookh*, Juliana's use of Moore often seems adventitious. For example, remembering a shared trip to Bonaventure Cemetery in Savannah, she underlines the phrase "jasmine bowers" and writes next to it, "Bonaventure with R. E. L. B." (169). In instances like this one, her copy of Moore becomes a kind of sourcebook: not for poems as such, but for passages of verse that resonate with her own life and feelings. More extreme than commonplacing, this practice is closer to falling into quotation à la Anne Eliot in *Persuasion*. As Pinch writes, "Falling into quotation . . . was something that romantic writers did impulsively, when the matter at hand was feelings" (165). Rather than commenting on poems as such, Shields is adorning her annotating voice with samples from Moore. As an extreme example of such appropriation, someone—likely Shields—has neatly cut out a stanza from a page containing a lyric song by a chorus of maidens in *Lalla Rookh* (57–58). The resulting fragment would have presented one complete stanza on either side:

A Spirit there is, whose fragrant sigh
    Is burning now through earth and air;
Where cheeks are blushing, the Spirit is nigh,
    Where lips are meeting, the Spirit is there! (57)

By the first love-beat
    Of the youthful heart,
By the bliss to meet,
    And the pain to part; (58)

Whether she took it for the meeting of lips or the pain of parting, Juliana may have pasted this fragment into an album or even a letter to R. E. L. B.; but in any case, the resulting page, with its little cutout window, becomes an emblem of appropriative reading. It offers a different type of trace: an absence as evidence of a particularly invested episode in the consumption of the book.

Sometimes, Juliana takes the opportunity to send a message to R. E. L. B., as when she brackets this snippet of dialogue: "'Like me?'—weak wretch, I wrong him—not like me; / No—he's all truth and strength and purity!" (37). To this, she adds in pencil, "Sav.[annah] 3/25/93" and "R.E.L.B." Furthermore, R. E. L. B. has added his own response in the lower margin: "The sentiment with which you here associate me, I know is but the emanation of a gentle nature, & a pure life, and like the sweet perfume of a delicate flower is . . ." The remainder of the note was cut off when the book was trimmed for rebinding (Figure 20). Abstracted entirely from the plot and flow of Moore's poem, these lines about "truth and strength and purity" become a fragment of rhetoric in an interpersonal

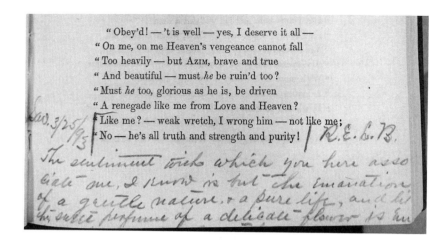

" Obey'd! — 't is well — yes, I deserve it all —
" On me, on me Heaven's vengeance cannot fall
" Too heavily — but Azim, brave and true
" And beautiful — must *he* be ruin'd too?
"Must *he* too, glorious as he is, be driven
" A renegade like me from Love and Heaven?
"Like me? — weak wretch, I wrong him — not like me;
"No — he's all truth and strength and purity!

Figure 20. Marginalia in *The Poetical Works of Thomas Moore* (Buffalo: George H. Derby and Co., 1852), 37. Juliana Shields Haskell's copy. Butler Library, Columbia University. PR 5054 .P6 1852g.

communication field. Shields's labels—place, date, person—claim a segment of the printed page for her own use, a mode of reading (and writing) at once familiar and in various ways outside the protocols of critical practice. On the one hand, Shields seems hardly to be "reading" at all. On the other, her annotations are evidence of her extensive and detailed engagement with the book, carried out via language-specific attention that might fairly be called close reading—but without any beholdenness to attending to the poem as a whole.

At other places in the volume, Shields and R. E. L. B. use Moore's language as a prompt for their own flirtatious exchanges, apparently conducted while the two were in close physical proximity and writing alternately in the book, like texting at close range. They tease one another back and forth in the margin next to the lines, "And with some maid, who breathes but love / To walk at noontide, through the grove, / Or sit in some cool, green recess—/ Oh, is not this true happiness?":

JS: No!
RELB: Yes!!
JS: Yes!!
RELB: No
JS: Yes (?)
RELB: (No) [underlined six times]
JS: No. (333)

Similarly, on a different page, next to the bracketed phrase "I am not thine," they write the following: "JS: Thank———/ RELB: Gott fur Danke ["Thank God"]"

(69). And finally, next to a passage Juliana has bracketed regarding the "lingering press / Of hands, that for the last time sever," R. E. L. B. was written another note in German: "Vielleicht! / und wenn deine / kleine Hand ich drucke [Perhaps! / and if your little hand I press]" (222).[36] In all of these examples, we can see this pair of readers adopting Moore's phrases for private riffs and exchanges, using the book itself as a platform for a mutual flirtation.

As a result, the book itself became a souvenir. Juliana adds R. E. L. B.'s initials in pencil to a stanza of Moore's poem "Take Back the Virgin Page," about turning books into forget-me-nots via the inscriptive practice of album verse: "Yet let me keep the book: / Oft shall my heart renew, / When on its leaves I look, / Dear thoughts of you" (295).[37] The book stayed with her all her life, even if R. E. L. B. did not. Their shared annotations seem to have been made in the weeks leading up to March 25, 1893, when he inscribed himself her "sincere friend" on the flyleaf. It was apparently a moment of parting: the following day, she wrote "R.E.L.B." and "Mar. 26, 1893," next to these lines, which she bracketed: "Oh! had we never, never met, / Or could this heart ev'n now forget" (161). That seems to mark the end of their relationship. A month later, R. E. L. Barnum gave a toast, "To Woman," at the dinner of the Medical Association of Georgia at the Windsor Hotel in Americus, "the dining room being taxed to its utmost capacity"— amid other toasts such as "The Triumphs of Modern Surgery" and "Our Country"; I wonder if he had Juliana Shields on his mind.[38] And whether or not it can be attributed to the aftereffects of this parting, Shields expresses in her Moore volume a sense of pain months later, in December 1893: to the bracketed line "Earth has no sorrow that Heaven cannot heal," she had at one point written, "Healed May, 1892," but revisits and adds to that annotation, "Oh that it were now true / Dec 93" (418). That is the latest date-mark in the volume.

We know R. E. L. Barnum married in 1896 and that Juliana went on to marry Henry S. Haskell in 1899, earn her PhD at Columbia in 1908 (Barnum died that year of meningitis, at the age of forty-four), and teach German at Barnard soon thereafter; she lived until 1949. On the same day we discovered her copy of Moore in the stacks at Columbia, we also found her Italian travel guide from 1932, annotated heavily regarding a trip with her husband: prices paid for wine and coffee and sites visited on certain dates, including a moonlight visit to the Colosseum on May 17, 1932, just about forty years after her visit to Bonaventure with R. E. L. B.[39] Distributed by call number in the Columbia library circulating collection, Juliana's date-marked books still speak to one another across the shelves and can be provisionally reunited because they are part of the same institutional history, the set of objects, spaces, and lives to which they have belonged. Juliana donated her books to Columbia in 1948, the year before she died, and they are duly stamped with dates of acquisition, having acquired one more layer of date-marking before coming to rest on the library shelves.

*   *   *

My last example is a brittle, poorly printed copy of Longfellow's *Poems and Ballads* published in New York in 1891 and now in the circulating collection at the University of Virginia. It bears the following note written in pencil by its former owner, Jane Chapman Slaughter, on the front free endpaper:

> Our readings together were in this book, ere you went to your life of work and sacrifice, and I remained to my life of infinite yearning for your presence, the sound of your voice; a yearning never to be satisfied in this world or the next.
>
> Now never I see thee,
> Never more hear, the voice of my
> Comrade, ever more dear.
> "And he never came back!"[40]

This retrospective lament attaches the Longfellow book to a particular moment in Slaughter's romantic life. She has annotated a number of the poems in this copy, with reference to her detailed memories of reading them, apparently with John H. Adamson, whose name is also inscribed in the book as its first owner as of Christmas 1892 (her ownership inscription is dated 1900). Some of these notes were made immediately following the moment of shared reading, and some have been added years later, when she reencountered the book as an older woman. For Slaughter, this copy of Longfellow has become a Yeatsian book to dream on, a window to the past by means of her own earlier annotations, which seem to have been meant for him to see. Her Longfellow book has been repurposed, its poetic content integrated into the erotic and nostalgic epochs of its readers' lives, its pages transformed into private souvenirs, Dear John letters (of a kind), pages of a diary, and ultimately touchstones of loss.

For example, in the bottom margin after "The Skeleton in Armor"—Longfellow's ballad in which a ghostly Viking tells a story of winning the love of "the blue-eyed maid"—Slaughter has written in a note, "Then you looked at your watch & said—'Now shall *we* go & make that visit, for at 5 o'clock I have to go to Washington,' & *we* meant you & I, & *we* had a happy walk." Then, in a later hand, after a gap of some years, she has added the following on the facing page: "Our last walk together in this world. Never to see each other more—Never, oh, never! It was after this I called you—'Norseman,' the name we always used to the end, in our letters. Do you remember?—You added to it 'your Norseman,' and 'your devoted Norseman'" (186–87; Plate 6). In the Longfellow poem, the Viking warrior inspires the maiden's love through storytelling: "'Once as I told in glee / Tales of the stormy sea, / Soft eyes did gaze on me, / Burning yet tender" (lines 57–60). We can imagine the lines formed an echo to what was happening with these Victorian lovers as Adamson read the lines aloud (Slaughter's marginalia tells us precisely) at 10:00 p.m. on Sunday, July 1, 1900, in the parlor of the Alexandria Infirmary in Virginia.[41] Slaughter also notes in the margin to this poem, "You read this and I said—'It just suits your voice—'" (177).

We can see a similar annotation-plus-revision above Longfellow's poem "Footsteps of Angels," where Slaughter wrote in 1900, "You read this, July 1st, Sunday, the day you said—'goodbye,' sitting in the great armchair in the Infirmary parlor—O friend of <u>mine</u>!"; then, in the later hand, she has commented on her previous note: "Once, mine! Now, <u>mine</u> no more!" (29). It is a haunted moment, particularly since the poem "Footsteps of Angels" (first published in 1839) is itself a meditation on nostalgic longing so intense that it seems to summon the spirits of the departed, in particular that of Longfellow's young wife, Mary, who had died after a miscarriage several years earlier. The poem begins,

> When the hours of Day are numbered,
>   And the voices of the Night
> Wake the better soul, that slumbered,
>   To a holy, calm delight;
>
> Ere the evening lamps are lighted,
>   And, like phantoms grim and tall,
> Shadows from the fitful fire-light
>   Dance upon the parlor wall;
>
> Then the forms of the departed
>   Enter at the open door;
> The beloved, the true-hearted,
>   Come to visit me once more; (lines 1–12)

Around these final two lines, the presumably older Slaughter has added a set of brackets, registering their applicability to her situation in encountering this book with its encoded memories of her lost companion. The scene that Longfellow's poem evokes is precisely that of "The Cross of Snow," but much earlier in his lifetime. It is another fireside poem, mourning a different wife below the same lamplight, in the same room that would eventually witness Fanny's death and its later, bookish scene of mourning. One thinks of Moore's popular lines that evoke this quintessentially nineteenth-century mood: "Oft, in the stilly night, / Ere slumber's chain has bound me, / Fond memory brings the light / Of other days around me."[42] In addition, Poe's "The Raven" may draw upon the haunted amosphere of "Footsteps of Angels" in presenting night thoughts about a dead woman and the "angel footfalls" that visit a reader of "a quaint and curious volume" in his study.[43] For Slaughter, the page becomes a similar palimpsest of bereavement, as she reannotates the earlier "goodbye" with a Poe-like coda: "no more."

We find more annotations of this kind made upon Longfellow's translation of "Coplas de Manrique" in this copy. Above the poem, Slaughter has written, "Sunday May 6, 1900, The Infirmary Parlor, Time 10 p.m. You took the book from me & you said 'Now shall I read the Coplas de Manrique & pronounce it wrong.' I corrected you & you only smiled. You said, 'If I don't do it well you will remember it is the first time & excuse'" (71). Like the other dated notes in Jane's copy, this marginal comment places the reading of Longfellow's poem into a private narrative of courtship. At the conclusion of the poem, she writes the date again, "Sunday, May 6th," and follows it with "N'oubliez pas," another message for John (100). Yet below this, at a later period, Slaughter has written in an altered, older hand, "Read to me by 'My Norseman' O, so long ago, before he went on his 'crusade' in Liberia at Capetown, on the West Coast" (100). Of course, Capetown is not in Liberia; but there was an Episcopal mission at Cape Mount, Liberia, and Slaughter may have been thinking of that as the destination of her beloved.[44] As she writes on the flyleaf, "And he never came back!" Jane Slaughter never married; she was one of the first women to receive a PhD from the University of Virginia, and her books were given to the university's library when she passed away.[45] As with "Footsteps of Angels," the poem within the book has become a layered, revisited scene—a memorial site tied to those early summer evenings in the Infirmary parlor, a kind of beacon in Slaughter's memory, and now for us a partial way back into those reading moments as well. At the same time, our affective response to the historical marginalia leads us to reencounter these sentimental poems with our defenses at least partly disabled, our own reading strategies newly scrambled and emotionally charged by the models in front of us.

*   *   *

Four examples of owners and their books: Mary Cosby's Praed, George Griffin's *Greek Girl*, Juliana Shields's Moore, and Jane Slaughter's Longfellow. Scenes of encounter and reencounter, they reveal ways that books and poems served their nineteenth-century readers as touchstones for their personal histories containing those *veteris vestigia flammae*: the traces of an old flame. In these examples, the doubled sets of annotation emphasize the sociality of books along the timeline of readers' lives, the ways they became entwined with love and its sequels. Poems keep time with metrical allegiances that conduce to memory; poetry books keep time as capsules, filled at the intersection of reading and marking, charged with the familiarity of the revisited trace. Particularly when they are given specific dates, such marks help us more clearly to see nineteenth-century books as objects in process, as layered sites of production, use, and archiving that bear the signs of ongoing change. As Christina Lupton writes, "Book history has been seen . . . as an understanding of the ways lives and texts unfolded in the past. But the boundedness of books has never been just a sign that they are over: it has always been a sign of that time for reading that is still to come."[46]

In other words, all these stories bear on the future of books, of every book. We might think of them as ongoing travelers or relay communiqués from the nineteenth century to this era and others, offering these deeply personal histories as part of what poetry was: both a public and a private art, illumined by Moore's "light of other days." In an 1838 lyric epigraph to a sequence of poems written about pictures, Letitia Landon writes, "What seek I here to gather into words? / The scenes that rise before me as I turn / The pages of old times. A word—a name—/ Conjures the past before me."[47] Landon's dizzying, Möbius-strip metaphor—pictures gathered into words and words conjuring scenes that are also turned as pages—serves as an apt emblem for encounters with books transfigured by sentimental annotation. Neither close nor distant reading of poems, nor the descriptive protocols of bibliography, can give us fully apt instruments to attend to those personalized books, whose voices are "[h]eard only in the trances of the blast," as Coleridge puts it—in those moments of silence in which we hang listening, eavesdropping on the pages of old times.[48]

CHAPTER 4

Velveteen Rabbits

Sentiment and the Transfiguration of Books

I

Maurice Halbwachs begins his classic 1925 study *On Collective Memory* with an anecdote about the phenomenology of reading old books: "When one of the books which were the joy of our childhood, which we have not opened since, falls into our hands, it is not without a certain curiosity, an anticipation of a recurrence of memories and a kind of interior rejuvenation that we begin to read it. . . . But what happens most frequently is that we actually seem to be reading a new book, or at least an altered version. The book seems to lack pages, developments, that were there when we first read it."[1] For Halbwachs, the cause of this bewilderment when reading a favorite book from childhood lies in the way memory is always a socially and temporally embedded phenomenon, a product of repetitions that necessarily evolve with time.[2] When we come back to the books of our youth, we bring to the experience a remembered copy that, upon collation with the original, reveals Wordsworthian discontinuities and sad perplexities.[3] Born in 1877, Halbwachs is testifying here to a reading experience that spans the century's divide. His encounter with those early volumes—"the books which were the joy of our childhood"—involves a step back to the nineteenth century, to the belle époque, a time of splendor in the leaves. The revisited book, like a Wordsworthian landscape, offers a way of measuring internal changes following youthful experience, an intimation of mortality. As David Simpson writes, "When we read the stories favored in our youth and find them empty, we are brought up against our own passing away as still to come but not to be avoided," adding, "These are more than merely bookish thoughts."[4] In turning to a nineteenth-century book (that is, one that was "the joy of [his] childhood") as an anchor for meditations on the dynamics of memory, Halbwachs suggests the deep connections between consciousness and codices—overlaid with a species of bittersweet longing—in that historical period. It is no coincidence that Walter Benjamin speaks wistfully of his collection of nineteenth-century children's books in his 1931 essay "Unpacking My Library."[5] Modernist literary precepts famously pushed the nineteenth century aside in order to "make it new," but Victorian book encounters had already profoundly shaped the sensibilities of that generation of writers and cultural critics.

Halbwachs's anecdote also evokes the ways that ideas of affection and loss are bound up with nineteenth-century books, especially from the vantage of twentieth- and twenty-first-century readers. Products of a bygone era of technology and social relations, old books incarnate myriad forms of life that have moved out of reach—like A. E. Housman's "land of lost content" (or is it "*con*tent") that "cannot come again"—and yet the books remain, now facing an indefinite future in libraries.[6] Deidre Lynch has recently reminded us that "literature is never more loveable than when at death's door," that, "since the Romantic period, declarations of love for literature" have frequently "been framed in elegiac terms."[7] Our attachment to books of literature is, as with most things, dependent on our sense of their continually but never completely slipping away. Maybe it has to do with our childhood memories of books, a recollection of reading in the laps of our mothers and fathers, a phenomenon that the act of rereading as an adult amplifies. As Lynch demonstrates, this elegiac attachment is also predicated on the rise of mass print and the installation of books in the bourgeois household as objects of domestic affection, which began during the same period when children's books were assuming their modern form.[8]

We might say (following Nicholson Baker's allegory for the old card catalogues) that nineteenth-century books were the Velveteen Rabbits of the modern era, loved into shabbiness and becoming Real—and lost—through the nursery magic of early reading.[9] We all know the 1922 story by Margery Williams: a plush toy bunny becomes a boy's beloved plaything and bedfellow, getting worn and dirty and thereby becoming a Real rabbit. The venerable Skin Horse delivers the moral early on: "When you are Real, you don't mind being hurt. . . . It doesn't happen all at once. . . . You become. It takes a long time. . . . Generally, by the time you are Real, most of your hair has been loved off, and your eyes drop out, and you get loose in the joints and very shabby. But these things don't matter at all, because once you are Real, you can't be ugly, except to those who don't understand."[10]

After the boy suffers an episode of scarlet fever, his doctor orders his toys to be burned: "the little Rabbit was put into a sack with the old picture-books and a lot of rubbish, and carried out to the end of the garden behind the fowl-house. That was a fine place to make a bonfire" (26–27). Thanks to a magic fairy, the once-velveteen rabbit—now *really* real—bounds off into the bracken with the other real bunnies, but the books, now rubbish, presumably meet the flames. And in any case, the boy never gets to hold his toy rabbit again. Becoming *really* real, it leaves the world of objects just as surely as if it had been burned, sublimed into a life beyond human hands. And it is this parable that haunts our reception of the nineteenth-century print record: its tenderness and loss, its leaping free of material and its lonely burning, its intimacies and our consequent betrayals. Above all, its wave of sentiment that so subsumes our thinking about old books as to become the only real we know. Derrida suggests that all archival urges to preserve are twin-born with appetites to erase—the leaping bunny and the picture books in ashes. Maybe the problem was not scarlet fever after all: maybe it was a case of what Derrida calls archive fever.[11]

This chapter moves beyond poetry to think more broadly about investment and damage in the realm of books, and about the implications of Romantic modes of object attachment that have shaped our bibliographic inheritance from the nineteenth century—both the physical contours of that archive and our attitudes toward it. As we have seen, books accrue layers of meaning and significance over time via chains of attachment and investment made by their possessors. Some of these are the result of reading moments, visible most clearly in dated marginal notes.[12] Others are oriented to the book itself, either as an object of value (ownership and gift inscriptions suggest this) or as a physical resource providing blank paper for writing or a stable structure for storing things like pressed flowers and other ephemera. Along with these practices, books also inspire a type of sentimental investiture that transforms them into personal and familial relics—and, for us, into touchstones to which we give a collective honorific: the archive or library.

In Chapter 2, I discussed how flowers were turned into fading souvenirs by Victorian readers, who loaded them with associations that were braided with the poems printed on pages, often decorated with floral engravings, between which flowers were pressed and stored: flower, poem, and book, all fused in a nexus of sentiment. Such overloading and its consequences are in fact common to all my examples: as books were transformed by interactions and use into gardens of verse, images in lava, and time machines, they accumulated content, some of it legible to us now. At the same time, those interactions were wearing down the books, marking and damaging them according to a logic wherein defacement becomes transfiguration. Call it Velveteen logic: damage resulting from investments and interactions across time becomes enhancement, a process of real-ization and transfiguration whereby a book is actualized and also threatened with disintegration—something like what happens to the mother and child in, and by means of, Hemans's "The Image in Lava." The process is one of preservation and destruction, in which care is expressed not only as protection but also as damaging marks made both consciously and unconsciously: the side effects of cherishing.

Depending on your perspective, marginalia and other marks made by readers are never far from defacement, graffiti, and dirt. As William Sherman reports, "soiled by use" was bookseller Quaritch's verdict on a heavily annotated 1586 Psalter, the same copy that the Huntington Library describes as "well and piously used," containing "marginal notations in an Eizabethan hand" that "bring to life an early and earnest owner."[13] The disagreement here turns on the imagined virtues of old books. Collectors have long prized pristine copies in fine condition, and most readers have similarly wanted no distractions from the printed text. However, researchers, in particular scholars of the history of reception, value marginal notations in older materials. Moreover, many book lovers have felt the emotional pull of annotated or otherwise battered volumes from earlier eras. In his 1822 essay "Detached Thoughts on Books and Reading" (discussed in Chapter 1), Charles Lamb professes a preference for "sullied leaves," which lead him to reveries of former readers with their "thousand thumbs":

> How beautiful to a genuine lover of reading are the sullied leaves, and worn out appearance, nay, the very odour . . . of an old "Circulating Library" Tom Jones, or Vicar of Wakefield! How they speak of the thousand thumbs, that have turned over their pages with delight!—of the lone sempstress, whom they may have cheered . . . after her long day's needle-toil, running far into midnight, when she has snatched an hour, ill spared from sleep, to steep her cares, as in some Lethean cup, in spelling out their enchanting contents! Who would have them a whit less soiled? What better condition could we desire to see them in?[14]

Like that annotated Psalter that the Huntington claims "bring[s] to life" an earlier owner, Lamb's "sullied leaves" of old books "speak" of a previous reader: he imagines a "lone sempstress" reading at night, enchanted by her book in an erotic posture of absorption. Part reconnection and part projection, that imagined reanimation connects to the nineteenth-century discourse of antiquarianism and bibliophilia, born out of Romanticism's melancholy desire to summon the past, what Longfellow calls the "voices of the night" and "forms of the departed" that old books can help generate as objects to dream upon.[15]

Instead of primarily delivering their printed contents, then, old books seen as such "speak" of their own reception, even when the traces of that reception are only the nonsemantic, unintended marks of use: soiled leaves, thumb-marked pages, battered bindings. Sherlock Holmes might be able to interpret them, as he does scuffs on a pocket watch, but in reality such nonverbal marks resolve only into phantasmal projections of past readers, ones that sit uncomfortably close to the actual past readers that marginalia and annotations encourage the literary historian to "bring to life" or reanimate. Consider "On the Fly-Leaf of a Book of Old Plays," published in 1889 and written by the obscure American poet Walter Learned (1847–1915), in which the narrator envisions a bookbinder in eighteenth-century London:

> At Cato's Head in Russell Street
>   These leaves she sat a-stitching;
> I fancy she was trim and neat,
>   Blue-eyed and quite bewitching.
> . . . .
> For beau nor wit had she a look;
>   Nor lord nor lady minding,
> She bent her head above this book,
>   Attentive to her binding.
>
> And one stray thread of golden hair,
>   Caught on her nimble fingers,
> Was stitched within this volume, where
>   Until to-day it lingers.
> . . . .
> Yet as I turn these odd, old plays,
>   This single stray lock finding,
> I'm back in those forgotten days
>   And watch her at her binding.[16]

Like Lamb's "lone sempstress," Learned's heroine both sews and uses books, a figure that evokes the crossover between text and textile, the tactility of the bibliographic encounter. The narrator's chance discovery of a "thread of golden hair" sewn into the binding of an eighteenth-century book (we might posit a volume of Colley Cibber's plays, printed for William Chetwood at Cato's Head in Russell Street in 1721) triggers a fantasy of a "trim" and "bewitching" blue-eyed maid (perhaps channeling Cibber's faithful heroines from *Love's Last Shift* and *The Careless Husband*, both contained in the first volume of Chetwood's edition). Like Lamb, Learned uses the old volume to "fancy" a beautiful female counterpart who handled this particular book before him: "these leaves she sat a-stitching." The bookbinder's unnoticed strand of hair signifies the peculiar combination of distraction and absorption that books demand, suggesting a private moment that the later reader can voyeuristically, if tenderly, invade: watching "her at her binding" while she bends her head obliviously over her work.[17] The "single stray lock" becomes a key, opening the book in which it is found as a portal onto an imagined past. It also inspires appropriation: Learned frames his poem as if it were written on the flyleaf of the same volume, an inscription of his own trace next to the one the bookbinder at Cato's Head inadvertently left behind.

Offering a kind of mute commentary on this scene—on Lamb's sempstress and Learned's bookbinder—a sewing needle (Figure 21) was found stuck in an 1860 copy of *Letters of Hannah More to Zachary Macaulay* in Alderman Library at the University of Virginia. It was formerly owned by one Lucy Nelson, who wrote in the book that it was "brought me by Sister from Baltimore, Sept. 1860":

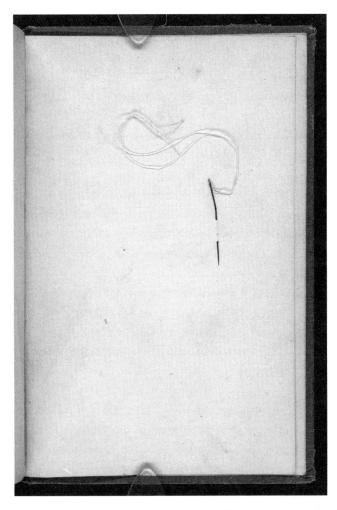

Figure 21. Nineteenth-century sewing needle inserted into a rear endpaper of *Letters of Hannah More to Zachary Macaulay* (New York, 1860). Ivy Stacks, Alderman Library, University of Virginia. PR3605 .M6 A8 1860.

another souvenir, another loose thread.[18] It becomes almost an incarnation of the poignancy of these book artifacts: their traces sharp-pointed, affectively piercing, like a needle. We know that these books called forth many, many kinds of interactions, between texts and their readers, between books and other objects, between human bodies and other human bodies. We tend to think of the history of reading as centered on the consumption of verbal texts; but some examples encourage us to go beyond linguistic forms and to think about texts as something closer to textiles, woven creations of material and semantic content—always incarnate, each body bearing traces of its many experiences through its long journey into our hands.

Another minor American writer, Frank L. Stanton (1857–1927), presents a similar bibliographic encounter with a previous female reader in his 1892 poem, "Annetta Jones—Her Book," a reverie over an old copy of Shakespeare's works "in boards of brown": "here and there the yellow leaves turned down / Where sweet, love-breathing Juliet speaks, and as I lean and look, / Traced in pale, faded ink, these words: 'Annetta Jones: Her Book.'"[19] Annetta Jones's ownership inscription prompts further examination. The "yellow leaves turned down" and the underlining of Juliet's speeches in turn speak volumes to the narrator. He determines, "She was no saint . . . for I discover / By these sublime marked sentences, Annetta had a lover!" Then the reverie takes off:

> And I believe her eyes were blue—her lips as cherries red,
> And many a shy, sweet kiss they knew, and tender words they said;
> And from her powdered brows gold hair fell cloud-like—soft and sweet,
> Down-streaming, gleaming, dreaming in her silver-slippered feet!
>
> She lived—she loved—was wedded; the romance of her life
> Perchance was toned a trifle when her lover called her "wife;"
> But what a glorious fate is hers! for as I lean and look
> Her name still shines with Shakespeare's: "Annetta Jones: Her Book."
>   (lines 13–20)

Golden-haired, red-lipped, and dreaming, Annetta Jones (as imagined by Stanton) read purposefully and personally, transforming her copy of Shakespeare into a private confessional of desire: her dog-earing of pages from *Romeo and Juliet* is enough for him to improvise upon. In a similar vein, the narrator of Stanton's poem "A Little Book" laments over a "little book, with here and there a leaf / Turned at some tender passage; how it seems / To speak to me—to fill my soul with dreams."[20] For both Learned and Stanton, old books are objects of erotic reverie, artifacts out of which emerge blonde, blue-eyed women of past eras. Male readers imagine bewitching lovers whose lives remain bound up with the volumes they hold. Parables of the power of books as fetish objects, these late-Victorian verses reveal the layers of projection involved in the history of reading. Annetta appropriates Juliet for her own ends, Frank appropriates Annetta, and so it goes on, all made visible in this case by marks made on the pages.

These forgotten late nineteenth-century poems are examples of the potent cocktail of nostalgia and desire that leads us to imaginatively engage with old books, and the winding together of speculation and empiricism that often characterizes histories of reading. As Patricia Crain reminds us, "Marks in books . . . often remain ineluctably mysterious, . . . inviting readerly projection" that "writes its own chapter in the afterlife of these books" (110–11). The extended, mostly occluded backstories of the volumes are crucial to their allure and magic. For Learned and Stanton, a female reader posited as the object of desire is both a muse (of history, of memory) and a transmuted incarnation of the sensual aspects of the old book itself: the smoothed binding, the soft paper, the opening cleft. One thinks of the question that concludes Robert Browning's "A Toccata of Galuppi's" (from *Men and Women* [1855]), another erotic, elegiac fantasy prompted by old media (in this case, music) and featuring eighteenth-century blondes: "Dear dead women, with such hair too—what's become of all the gold / Used to hang and brush their bosoms?"[21] In Learned's poem, a volume of old plays contains one such golden strand, providing a partial, bookish answer to Browning's *ubi sunt* rhetoric. But in all of these poems, loss serves as the pretext for an atmosphere of sentimental luxury and incipient eroticism surrounding the encounter with the past: the romance of the trace.

In the Alderman stacks at the University of Virginia, there is an 1847 copy of Shakespeare's plays that belonged to a young woman named Sallie Anne Meredith (1829–89).[22] On the front free endpaper, she has written "Miss Sallie A. Meredith's book" and added some lines on love: "Love is a spark, a glance; it can kindle but not then again quench." On the following blank page, under the heading "Multum in Parvo" she has written playfully, "Oh! When shall I reach that 'ultimum maximum' of human desires, that 'ne plus ultra' of human imagination, that 'magnum bonum' of all of earth's most transcendently sublime joys—the married state—" (Figure 22). Recalling Annetta Jones and her dog-eared Shakespeare in Stanton's poem, Meredith has penciled in numerous marginal brackets and enthusiastic underlinings of the balcony scene of *Romeo and Juliet* (956–57). The appeal of the book lies in its snapshot capture of a scene in the emotional life of a nineteenth-century reader. But rather than merely imagine her, I turn to the historical archive for a brief evocation. In 1858, when she was twenty-nine, Sallie Meredith married John Barrett Pendleton; they had a daughter, Elizabeth, and he went off to fight for the Confederacy in the Virginia Volunteers. In his penultimate letter home,

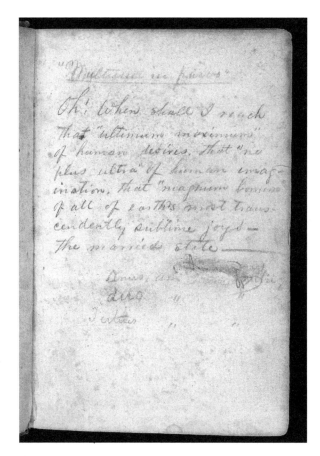

Figure 22. Inscription on front free endpaper of *The Dramatic Works of William Shakespeare* (Philadelphia: J. B. Lippincott, 1847). Sallie Anne Meredith's copy, Alderman Library, University of Virginia. PR2752 .J7 1847.

written in 1861, John writes, "Kiss my sweet little Bettie for me. Oh! Sallie you do not know how my heart longs to see you all. I must now bid you an affectionate Goodbye my dear wife, and may God bless and protect you all is my fervent prayer."[23] He was killed in action a few weeks later at Laurel Hill.

II

Love and damage, investments and transfiguration: the histories of individual copies of nineteenth-century books emerge from our processing of the marks they bear, itself conditioned by historiographical and sentimental regimes of the post-Romantic century. Leah Price has suggested we might "trace different models of textuality back to their *generic* origins—to determine in what contexts, both for-

mal and material, competing understandings of . . . the book take shape."[24] She
has shown how the Victorian "it-narrative" genre allowed for the anthropomor-
phization of the book, whose many adventures could be related as the story of a
"Veteran, Invalid, Prostitute," or other long-suffering, chronically ambulatory
creature. This personification has in part provided a model for book history insofar as it focuses on circulation (120). The story of the Velveteen Rabbit points
to another role for books, one that reflects a nineteenth-century mode of imaginatively framing objects of affectionate use. In previous chapters, we have seen
books of poetry turned into souvenirs by their readers via additions and alterations linked to specific episodes of those readers' lives. In Sara Ahmed's terms,
such books become "sticky objects" to which emotional associations cling; and
some are literally adorned and augmented with items stuck to or between their
pages.[25] For example, Chapter 2 explored how pressed flowers within books become emblems of such a process, marking a place and alluding to a moment even
as they damage and are damaged by the pages that preserve them. As we look
into those faraway gardens or handle those cloth-bound creatures, our reactions
as book historians are inevitably shaped and colored by the same forces that produced them and ourselves. And as we decide what to do with the books from the
nineteenth century, we have to think about what they are and where they came
from—not only material products but also imaginary objects, sites of feeling
shaped by cultural discourses that we also have partly inherited.

Two similar poems of the era (both written circa 1840) may be taken to represent post-Romantic expressions of this imaginative construction of sentimental objects: Felicia Hemans's sonnet "To a Family Bible" and Eliza Cook's "The
Old Arm-Chair."[26] Both center on memories of a mother's interactions with object and narrator, a triangle of mutual investments across time that transform
the object into what Cook calls "a sacred thing" (line 8); and both present a scene
of reading. In the case of Hemans's "Family Bible," that sacralization occurs primarily not according to the Good Book's holy content, but rather as a result of
its domestic associations. The sonnet begins,

> What household thoughts around thee, as their shrine,
> Cling reverently!—of anxious looks beguiled,
> My mother's eyes, upon thy page divine,
> Each day were bent;—her accents, gravely mild,
> Breathed out thy lore. (380, lines 1–5)

This Bible has become a "shrine" for "household thoughts," which "cling rever-
ently" to it, a barely concealed figure for the ubiquitous practices of enshrinement
that turned family Bibles into miniature archives in this era: for example, Bibles

with inscriptions of marriages, births, and deaths (as we saw in Chapter 1) and the insertion of ephemera of various kinds within them. Here the "mother's eyes" and "accents" have proved ephemeral (she is among the "holy dead" [line 14]) but are still present as memories attached to this "book of Heaven" (line 13); as Hemans puts it, "I pour, with grateful tears, / Heart blessings on the holy dead and thee!" (lines 13–14). Similarly, Cook's popular lyric "The Old Arm-Chair" offers memories of "Childhood's hour" spent "near / The hallowed seat" when a mother taught the narrator "to lisp my earliest prayer" (lines 9–10, 15), and when the mother "turned from her Bible, to bless her child" (line 20). Here the memories attach not to the Bible itself but to the "mother's old Arm-chair" (line 32), the abiding household nexus of associations: "'Twas there she nursed me: 'twas there she died" (line 27). As a result, the narrator says, "I've treasured it long as a sainted prize; / I've bedewed it with tears, and embalmed it with sighs. / 'Tis bound by a thousand bands to my heart" (lines 3–5). Because "a mother sat there . . . a sacred thing is that old Arm-chair" (lines 7–8). Embalmed, bedewed, treasured, bound, and made sacred by love and loss, the armchair has become a domestic relic, part surrogate and part transitional object: in other words, something like a book. It is a family heirloom whose invested value pays a dividend of tears, told in the "quivering breath and throbbing brow" it evokes in its long-term housemate and inheritor (line 26).[27]

Marked and personalized copies of nineteenth-century books, especially of poetry, may be thought of as syntheses of Hemans's family Bible and Cook's old armchair: books and furniture, at once sacred and homely, common and unique, worn and brought to life by use. Bibles had long accreted such memories and records within them. It was the nineteenth century that witnessed the great expansion of bibliographic range within the domestic interior and the widespread emergence of the secular book as a familiar souvenir.[28] Richard Henry Dana's popular midcentury anthology *The Household Book of Poetry* (published in various editions between 1857 and 1872) is a representative of the phenomenon. Another example is the dedicatory poem to Longfellow's 1850 volume, *The Seaside and the Fireside*: "The pleasant books, that silently among / Our household treasures take familiar places, / And are to us as if a living tongue / Spake from the printed leaves or pictured faces!"[29] The "living tongue" suggests Keats's "living hand" (not published until 1898), and the uncanny effect of both poems is similar, as the "printed leaves" of "pleasant books" evoke what Longfellow calls elsewhere "the voices of the night": the silent but internally audible ghosts of readings past.[30] Products of the age of industrial reproduction, books as "household treasures" in middle-class homes have become "familiar" both as physical objects and verbal content, taking their places by the fireside like old friends and in the minds of their owners as household words. The "printed leaves" attest to the layered memorial power of a physical book to evoke not just memories of its theme or subject or of its specific verbal phrases, but also the history of one's personal interactions with the volume and its pages: the visual and tactile engagements of readers with the book itself. As John Plotz writes, "Phenomenologies of reading too often imagine that books can be assimilated as pure mental phenomena, straight from the page to the far-off landscape inside. But book collecting ought to remind us that the material facts of the book—its year, its binding, its place in the series, even where it sits on the shelf—influence the world the text creates."[31]

Plotz registers the fact that in the mid–twentieth century, as the field of reader-response criticism took shape, the physical book moved to an uncertain position. Formalists and phenomenologists of reading often proceeded as if the book itself existed only as a groundwork interface, the first duty of which was to disappear. As George Poulet puts it, once reading proper starts, "the book is no longer a material reality. It has become a series of words, of images, of ideas." And "in order to exist as mental objects, [books] must relinquish their existence as real objects."[32] The goal, as Roman Ingarden writes, is for readers to be possessed by the writer's prose, to get "immersed in the flow of *satzdenken* (sentence-thought)" and forget about the object in their hands, a process that Kevin McLaughlin describes similarly as "the withdrawal of the material support in the act of reading."[33] In this view, physical books are all mute potential, and their material features and structures are attendants meant to enable (and withdraw silently before) the main event of reading the text. Moreover, in part because of the prominence such critics gave to narrative and expository writing, that event was consistently imagined as decoding and imaginative completion, the concretization (Ingarden) of language and the grasp of a work's gestalt (Iser) or an author's cogito (Poulet): reading as a meeting of the minds.

Yet Poulet also describes books as objects almost alive, almost real, like the Velveteen Rabbit: he begins his "Phenomenology of Reading" with a consideration of the book as a particular kind of object in need of redemption, like an animal in a cage:

> Books are objects. On a table, on bookshelves, in store windows, they wait for someone to come and deliver them from their materiality, from their immobility. When I see them on display, I look at them as I would at animals for sale, kept in little cages, and so obviously hoping for a buyer. For—there is no doubting it—animals do know that their fate depends on a human intervention, thanks to which they will be delivered from the shame of being treated as objects. Isn't the same true of books? Made of paper and ink, they lie where they are put, until the moment someone shows an interest in them. They wait. Are they aware that an act of man

might suddenly transform their existence? They appear to be lit up with that hope. Read me, they seem to say. I find it hard to resist their appeal. No, books are not just objects among others. (53)

Characterizing books as a particularly vital sort of object, Poulet says they "appear to be lit up with . . . hope" that someone will "deliver them from their materiality"; they are vessels to be transformed and filled with life by "an act of man." In his imagining, books wait, hope, and make appeals for human intervention, much like animals in a pet-store window. But in attributing consciousness to books, Poulet is actually closer to Williams's fable, in which the Velveteen Rabbit can hope for its own transubstantiation into the order of the Real—its own deliverance from the shame of mere materiality—before it happens. For Poulet, books have this power because they are repositories of human thought, awaiting reconstitution in reading. But his metaphors also suggest a latent awareness that their embodiment, their abiding materiality, is crucial to the ways books exist, for us, in the world.

More recently, book historians have reminded us that bodies are always part of the scene—both the material books and their embodied human users, as well as the histories of production and reception that have been brought to bear on networks of reading. Global book history, cultural criticism, and race and gender theory have emphasized the importance of material and bodily contexts for understanding the readerly encounter. Moving away from idealized phenomenologies of reading, critics such as Christina Lupton, Gillian Silverman, and Abigail Williams have emphasized the social lives of books and readers, their mutual embeddedness in material networks that both constrain and enable textual encounters and book use.[34] Along these same lines, Joshua Calhoun and Jonathan Senchyne have recently written on the material turn in book history, emphasizing the histories and interactions encoded in rag paper.[35] And Lisa Gitelman and Ben Kafka have demonstrated the role paper documents have played in the construction and maintenance of the modern self in relation to the techno-capitalist state.[36] Ordinary reading, or what Eric Livingstone calls "reading *simpliciter*," is more various, active, site-specific, socially inflected, and materially determined than theorists like Iser, Ingarden, and Poulet have typically allowed for, insofar as they have bracketed the evidence of the archive—that is, the evidence of how reading interfaces evolved and were altered, and how reading communities emerged and engaged, in specific historical and cultural contexts.[37] Rather than asking what reading *is*, book historians are asking what it *was*, taking the historical specifics of book production and reading publics as their base of evidence. The reader's body and the body of the book are always part of the scene.

I briefly rehearse this genealogy out of a desire to connect our current critical practice back to nineteenth-century ideas of the book, drawing a line from my annotators and marginalians through to our own conceptions of what books are. I intend my examples throughout this study not only to reveal the lives and bookish engagements of people from that earlier era but also to illuminate the deep roots of current practice and belief regarding nineteenth-century books and their value in relation to reading. As we have seen, poetic volumes contain a particularly concentrated distillate of the sentiment, personalization, and affective braiding of textual content and physical format that characterized nineteenth-century reading. Books of poetry impel rather different modes of engagement or entanglement from those of prose fiction, which has been the groundwork genre for most theories of reading. Herbert Tucker writes of the "multisensory appeal that imagery and prosody make to the inward eye and ear and tongue," adding, "The physical properties of the verse medium will never let us forget—as all told it is the prose fictionist's or essayist's business to make us forget—the brokerage of the signifier."[38] Extend that logic outward to the material page and the precincts of physical books, particularly in the bibliographically diverse nineteenth century, and you realize that volumes of verse were particularly bent toward that unforgettable brokerage or multisensory realization, toward appearing suddenly like a rabbit in a magician's hand.

Such objects remind us forcefully and clearly that books have bodies and interact with bodies, that the mental operation of reading is predicated on the hardware of the bibliographic object and the wetware of its human user. Traces and marks left behind make visible those transactions and symbolically encode them. If a flower pressed in a book can be seen as an emblem of the preserved moment of reading, a lock of hair placed between pages can be a synecdoche for the many bodily interactions that have determined the book's trajectory across time and space. One such lock, tied neatly with silken thread, was found in a copy of *The Whittier Year Book* (1895) in Alderman Library (Plate 7). Its location next to quotations for February 28 and 29 embeds it visibly within the cycle of the year, even as the calendrically minded verse selections make reference to "[t]he fruits and flowers of time" (February 28) and a "winter noon" that "[s]eems warm as a summer's day" (February 29). One reacts first to the intimacy of the hair as a thing, its insistently human, particular, and sensual qualities that are almost embarrassing in their details: those wispy strands, that reddish shade, its silken feel. Yet its anonymity preserves distance also, allowing it to become in some way emblematic of biblio-human relations, of our embodied loves and losses of books—and of one another. Even as locks of hair bring us close to the bodies of historical readers, they assert the finality of our separation from those readers. They hover between material and figural orders of being. As Deborah Lutz has written of such objects, "To pore over the relic is to fall into the reverie of memory, to call to mind the absent being. The object disappears and becomes pure symbol, pointing only outside of itself. Yet the texture, its somewhat shocking substantiality as a thing, as an actual piece of that person can call back from reverie to feel its bluntness, its weighty, obstinate 'thingness,' its non-symbolic quality which refers to nothing but its own presence . . . made strange as tactile, silent material."[39] That oscillation between reverie and materiality mimics the process of reading—the immersion in *satzdenken* and its opposite, the awareness of the book as an object. It also follows a familiar path in Romantic poems, one that leads from the sensual world of Grecian urns, birdsongs, and inspiring breezes to states of reverie and back again. Encountering a tress of Milton's hair, Keats is drawn into a sudden and startling sense of embodiment: "I feel my forehead hot and flush'd, / Even at the simplest vassal of thy Power,—/ A Lock of thy bright hair! / Sudden it came, / And I was startled when I heard thy name / Coupled so unaware."[40] In a Romantic horizon, the book, poem, and lock of hair all become sites for the sublation of reverie and its material origins.

Again, Elizabeth Barrett Browning's *Sonnets from the Portuguese* provides a poetic analogue here in its figuration of the lock of hair as at once a remembrancer, herald, and bearer of an embodied legacy.[41] Sonnet 18 begins,

> I never gave a lock of hair away
> To a man, Dearest, except this to thee,
> Which now upon my fingers thoughtfully
> I ring out to the full brown length and say
> "Take it." (lines 1–5)

"I ring out": in Barrett Browning's ambiguous formulation, her thoughtful fingers transform the wrung lock from ringlet to "full brown length," which thereafter becomes something like a wedding band in its signifying power, re-coiled, given, and rung out—like the "Wild bells" of Tennyson's *In Memoriam* 40—as a messenger of a new order of things.[42] Further, like the moment in sonnet 44 in which flowers and poems morph into one another (discussed in Chapter 2), the lock of hair merges with the poem that describes it, both love gifts meant to signify a length of days now committed to their receiver's care: the ringlet and the book. The growth of flowers, hair, and poems takes time, and those things almost incarnate the hours, the "warm and cold days" (sonnet 44, line 7) that saw their lengthening. In the remainder of sonnet 18, Barrett Browning speaks directly of the clipped tress as a bearer of the past, not only of the speaker's lost "day of youth" or of the past sorrows that have caused her hair to droop, but more specifically "pure, from all those years, / The kiss my mother left here when she died" (lines 5, 13–14). Like Hemans's "Family Bible" and Cook's "Old Arm-Chair," Barrett Browning's sonnet presents an object that has been sanctified by maternal contact, by associations gathered from a mother's touch—and from her death. Moreover, Barrett Browning's lock of hair strangely carries that kiss within it, a trace upon the tress, something that the receiver can find like a relic or legacy in its own right, "pure, from all those years." The hair itself is the incarnation of lost time; the phantom kiss remains as a trace of memory entangled with that object.

The next sonnet in Barrett Browning's sequence is about her reception of a lock of her beloved's hair in return: "The soul's Rialto hath its merchandise; / I barter curl for curl upon that mart" (sonnet 19, lines 1–2). And in a manner similar to the way she imagines her mother's kiss left upon her own hair, she surmises that the "bay-crown's shade . . . / Still lingers" on Robert's curl, "it is so black!" (lines 8–9). Like Wendy to Peter Pan, Barrett Browning says she will "tie the shadow safe from gliding back," not with thread but "with a fillet of smooth-kissing breath" so that she may "lay the gift where nothing hindereth / Here on my heart" (lines 10–13). Like sonnet 18, the poem does its work between trace and transfiguration: each curl has been visited by an intervention, one real (the mother's kiss) and one symbolic (the bay crown's shadow). Yet the shadow can be "seen" in the real blackness of Robert's hair, whereas the kiss of the mother can only be imagined as a blessing on Elizabeth's. That is, both poems present a lock of hair as a crossing point, a nexus of the real and the imagined, material and reverie, wherein a part of the beloved's body has been marked, clipped, coiled, and given as a material container of immaterial things. Like the marked book, the curl shimmers between artifactual and symbolic orders—trembling like a Velveteen Rabbit (another transitional object) on the edge of the Real.

III

Thinking of books as objects of tender affect and attachment, like stuffed animals, brings forward the child as an emblem of the reader. In *Reading Children*, Crain examines "children's marks of engagement with their books," finding in their "inscriptions, notes, blots," and other traces the evidence of books "as surrogate selves, and as memorial artifacts" (109). Like me, Crain is interested in "the ways in which . . . books became repositories, registers, and mediums for social and emotional attachments" (109), and she shows how the personalized book "opens and closes upon surrogate selves, embodied . . . in things like paper dolls and locks of hair" (113), suggesting D. W. Winnicott's concept of the transitional object. Further, that childhood self survives in the adult reader—like the child playing in the garden book at the end of Stevenson's *Garden of Verses* (discussed in

Chapter 2)—as an introjection of a "protected" imaginary realm.[43] Winnicott makes explicit the connection between the child's "realm of illusion," mediated by objects like books and stuffed animals, and the imaginative life of adults. He writes, "Transitional objects . . . belong to the realm of illusion which is at the basis of initiation of experience"; and further, "This intermediate area of experience," which belongs simultaneously "to inner and external (shared) reality, constitutes the greater part of the infant's experience, and throughout life is retained in the intense experiencing that belongs to the arts and to religion and to imaginative living."[44] Wordsworth made a similar point, that the childhood experience of a permeable internal and external reality forms the basis of the adult's "intense experiencing" via the imagination: those "first affections" become "a master light of all our seeing."[45] In Winnicott's view, that would include reading as well. Like the child, a "Seer blest," the Romantic observer insists on free commerce between the subjective and objective, on the enveloping of objects of the external world with what Coleridge calls "a light, a glory, a fair luminous cloud" issuing "from the soul itself," so that "we receive but what we give, / And in our life alone does nature live."[46] And so the stuffed rabbit comes alive before our eyes, like the "fair luminous cloud" of Coleridge's that follows the hare as a glittering mist in Wordsworth's "Resolution and Independence": "The Hare is running races in her mirth; / And with her feet she from the plashy earth / Raises a mist, which, glittering in the sun, / Runs with her all the way, wherever she doth run."[47] As it does in Poulet's account of reading, the material world truly lives via the gift of the observer's attention and imagination, in a state of Winnicott's childlike "intense experiencing."

Crain's most striking conclusion is that the nineteenth century saw the rise of a "chiastic relationship between children and books," in which childhood and reading became deeply and mutually associated with Romantic ideas of reverie, absorption, self-forgetting, and, ultimately, redemption (8). Thus the haunting, ensorcelling nature of the child's old book, which seems to offer a way back, through some combination of its verbal and material content, to an earlier self: it becomes an emblem for Stevenson's "child of air," sequestered in those faraway gardens of verse (see Chapter 2). As an emblem for that lost child, consider the hand-decorated paper-doll clothes found in an 1833 copy of the works of Walter Scott in the University of Virginia stacks: fittingly, the human figure itself is missing (Plate 8).[48] Or perhaps even more to the point is a battered, well-loved copy of an illustrated gift book of poems by Edith Thomas called *Babes of the Year*, also from the Virginia stacks, in which poems are keyed to the seasons of the year and decorated with smiling, cherubic children. It was owned by Emily Tapscott Clark (1891–1953), who has carefully written her full name, two dates (February 8 and 10, 1898), and her Richmond address (110 N. 5th St.) twice. She also drew

Figure 23. Childhood drawings in Edith M. Thomas, *Babes of the Year*, illus. Maud Humphrey (New York: Frederick A. Stokes, 1898). Emily Tapscott Clark's copy, Alderman Library, University of Virginia. PS 3027.B3 1888.

pictures of people, teacups, and a three-chimney house on the free endpaper, cre-ating a representation not unlike the composite illustration on the book's well-worn cover (Figure 23). Emily Douglas Tapscott Clark was seven years old at the time. Her mother had died when she was three, and her father, William Meade Clark, had recently (in 1896) moved them to Richmond; he would remarry the following year.[49] The figures in her drawing are unidentified, but they seem to portray visitors coming to the house, welcomed by a flower-bearing gentleman; then again, the circular headgear on a number of them just might be halos.

These examples of childhood book use take my subject farther into the realm of the pure sentimental emblem than I had perhaps intended to go. Yet they do serve to bring our own responses to such found objects into the foreground, reminding us that we are adult scholars working to manage affectionate reactions alongside the business of literary historiography and the pressing issues of library collection management. Seth Lerer writes that children's marginalia is best thought of as an index of "how the adult reads the child"; it provokes "scholarly inquiry into an understanding of the annotator as an imaginative subject."[50] It also leads us back to our own childhoods as well, our own origins as readers. I began with Halbwachs's reflection on "the books which were the joy of our childhood" and with his sense that our later encounters with them will always reveal discontinuities with our earlier selves. Moreover, he suggests that such discontinuities are themselves the only assurances that we were ever children—that we ever had a childhood—in the first place. We saw in Chapter 3 how books are time machines, calibrating and confirming a remembered self via rereadings and remarkings over the years. Attesting to the transitions of readers' lives and the involvement of poetry with them, such books can be thought of as transitional objects in another sense, stadial markers of readers' evolving understandings of themselves as they pass through developmental stages and particular social contexts. As the Skin Horse puts it, "It doesn't happen all at once. . . . You become."

The books evolve, too, as we have seen—not only via the marks and scars that they accumulate but also in their transition from domestic objects to institutional ones: once personal relics, now academic resources. Their survival, like that of the poems they contain, is predicated on what Anne-Lise François has called "those delicate practices of transmission inseparable from the work of release and abandonment."[51] Recall, too, that we are dealing with nonrare library books, donated by former owners or their heirs and placed in the circulating collections, catalogued as copies rather than as artifacts. Because of this trajectory, their markings have been treated as damage under library policies that typically do not distinguish between patrons' graffiti and owners' markings. When I first introduced this project to the librarians at my university, one told me that when preservation librarians see marginalia in the circulating books, they typically erase it. Along the same lines, a copy of a preservation review sheet from our library tells part of the story of the present status and likely future of these battered, out-of-copyright volumes in the stacks. It amounts to a checklist of diagnostic categories that lead to a handful of actions, including "repair," "purchase another copy," and "withdraw." Among the considerations that go into

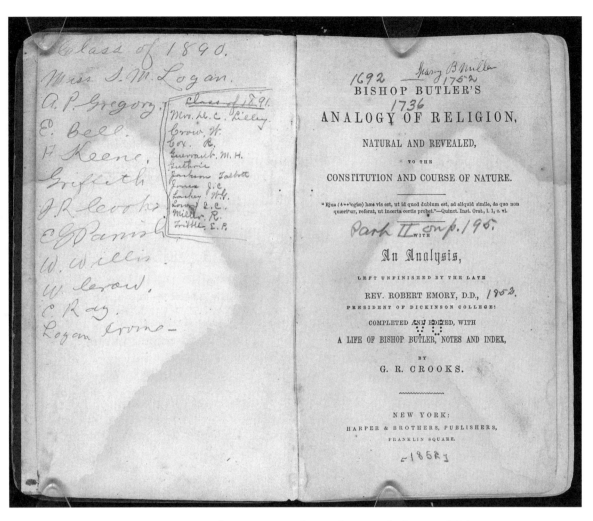

Figure 24. Inscription and annotations on front endpaper and title page of *Bishop Butler's Analogy of Religion*, ed. G. R. Crooks (New York: Harper and Brothers, 1852). Mary Belle Miller's copy. Formerly held by the University of Virginia. BT1100. B9 1852. Author's collection.

those categories are (1) the number of times the book has been checked out, (2) whether other editions are available at the library, (3) whether there are digital copies on Google Books, (4) how many copies are available nationwide, and (5) what type of damage is visible in the book. A librarian friend once passed a withdrawn book to me, with its accompanying form filled out. The book—*Bishop Butler's Analogy of Religion* (1852)—contains copious marginalia from 1867, including the name of one of its former owners (Mary Belle Miller, from Lexington, Kentucky), a penciled list of young women from the "Class of 1890" and "Class of 1891," a weekly class schedule, and a good deal of substantive annotation on the free endpapers and throughout the volume (Figure 24). In fact, the book could provide a fascinating window onto theological and philosophical education for Southern women in the latter part of the century, probably at one of the women's institutes of that era. But according to its preservation review form, the book had been checked out only once, the library had "many, many, many" other editions, ninety other copies of this particular edition were available nationwide, "several editions" were noted as appearing "in full text in Google," and the book was marked as being "brittle" and full of "graffiti." For these intersecting reasons, it was withdrawn from the library collection.

Yet each reason is problematic. First, a book that has not circulated recently might well be a very important one for humanities research, given the discipline's grounding in history and its need to reach backward to rethink, reintroduce, and redescribe things that have been neglected. And the book is worn with use: it clearly had an active role in the lives of several readers, which we might well take as an index of its influence beyond postacquisition circulation statistics. Second, we know that editions differ in significant ways relevant to scholarship, so those "many, many, many" editions at Virginia and on Google cannot serve as surrogates for this particular one—much less for this unique artifact. Further, the insufficiency of Google scans as research surrogates has been established in a number of quarters, so that the book's availability "in full text in Google" matters only in part.[52] The ninety copies of this book in other libraries are significant, but they, too, will differ from one another in more or less signficant ways, as this heavily annotated example demonstrates. Finally, I hope I have shown that historical annotation of one's own books is something different from patrons' marks in the books belonging to an institution (although that also might be profitably collected and studied) and often adds to the research value of a book rather than amounting to mere damage that disqualifies it from use.

"The little Rabbit was put into a sack with the old picture-books and a lot of rubbish, and carried out to the end of the garden behind the fowl-house." The fate of nineteenth-century books in libraries depends on the policies and prescriptions of those libraries, even as we admit that this national collection is, in some ways, an accidental archive, predicated on the local inflections of what was donated. Accident and surprise are actually part of the reason for valuing and retaining library materials; a collection's unruliness makes it possible to elude the managerial and categorical ideologies of the library system. To be sure, all libraries and archives have an element of randomness, just as they also inevitably reflect the structures of power—economic, cultural, linguistic, racial, sexual—that determined what would not be preserved, what was excluded, what was passed over, and what was not passed on: the silences of the archive, the inheritance of loss. As I have said, the pre-owned nineteenth-century books of poetry now in

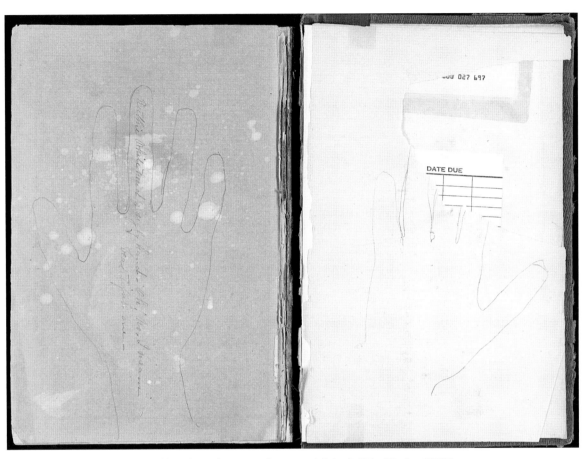

Plate 1. Traced hands on the rear endpaper and flyleaf of *The Works of William Shakespeare* (New York: Redfield, 1853). Miriam Trowbridge's copy. Alderman Library, University of Virginia. PR 2753 .C75 1853.

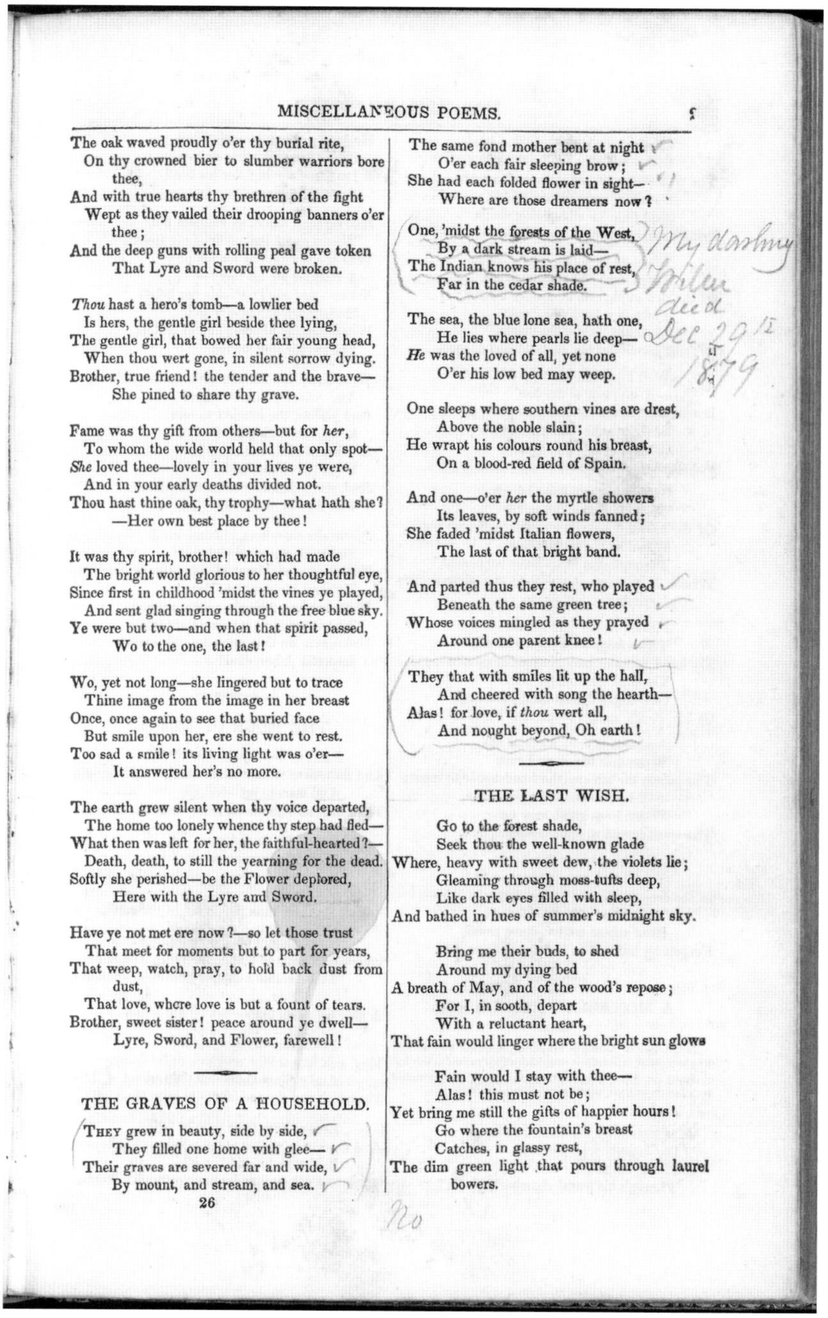

The oak waved proudly o'er thy burial rite,
  On thy crowned bier to slumber warriors bore
    thee,
And with true hearts thy brethren of the fight
  Wept as they vailed their drooping banners o'er
    thee ;
And the deep guns with rolling peal gave token
    That Lyre and Sword were broken.

Thou hast a hero's tomb—a lowlier bed
  Is hers, the gentle girl beside thee lying,
The gentle girl, that bowed her fair young head,
  When thou wert gone, in silent sorrow dying.
Brother, true friend ! the tender and the brave—
    She pined to share thy grave.

Fame was thy gift from others—but for *her*,
  To whom the wide world held that only spot—
She loved thee—lovely in your lives ye were,
  And in your early deaths divided not.
Thou hast thine oak, thy trophy—what hath she?
    —Her own best place by thee !

It was thy spirit, brother ! which had made
  The bright world glorious to her thoughtful eye,
Since first in childhood 'midst the vines ye played,
  And sent glad singing through the free blue sky.
Ye were but two—and when that spirit passed,
    Wo to the one, the last !

Wo, yet not long—she lingered but to trace
  Thine image from the image in her breast
Once, once again to see that buried face
  But smile upon her, ere she went to rest.
Too sad a smile ! its living light was o'er—
    It answered her's no more.

The earth grew silent when thy voice departed,
  The home too lonely whence thy step had fled—
What then was left for her, the faithful-hearted?—
  Death, death, to still the yearning for the dead.
Softly she perished—be the Flower deplored,
    Here with the Lyre and Sword.

Have ye not met ere now ?—so let those trust
  That meet for moments but to part for years,
That weep, watch, pray, to hold back dust from
    dust,
  That love, where love is but a fount of tears.
Brother, sweet sister ! peace around ye dwell—
    Lyre, Sword, and Flower, farewell !

THE GRAVES OF A HOUSEHOLD.

THEY grew in beauty, side by side,
  They filled one home with glee—
Their graves are severed far and wide,
  By mount, and stream, and sea.
26

The same fond mother bent at night
  O'er each fair sleeping brow ;
She had each folded flower in sight—
  Where are those dreamers now ?

One, 'midst the forests of the West,
  By a dark stream is laid—
The Indian knows his place of rest,
  Far in the cedar shade.

The sea, the blue lone sea, hath one,
  He lies where pearls lie deep—
He was the loved of all, yet none
  O'er his low bed may weep.

One sleeps where southern vines are drest,
  Above the noble slain ;
He wrapt his colours round his breast,
  On a blood-red field of Spain.

And one—o'er *her* the myrtle showers
  Its leaves, by soft winds fanned ;
She faded 'midst Italian flowers,
  The last of that bright band.

And parted thus they rest, who played
  Beneath the same green tree ;
Whose voices mingled as they prayed
  Around one parent knee !

They that with smiles lit up the hall,
  And cheered with song the hearth—
Alas ! for love, if *thou* wert all,
  And nought beyond, Oh earth !

THE LAST WISH.

Go to the forest shade,
  Seek thou the well-known glade
Where, heavy with sweet dew, the violets lie ;
  Gleaming through moss-tufts deep,
  Like dark eyes filled with sleep,
And bathed in hues of summer's midnight sky.

  Bring me their buds, to shed
  Around my dying bed
A breath of May, and of the wood's repose ;
  For I, in sooth, depart
  With a reluctant heart,
That fain would linger where the bright sun glows

  Fain would I stay with thee—
  Alas ! this must not be ;
Yet bring me still the gifts of happier hours !
  Go where the fountain's breast
  Catches, in glassy rest,
The dim green light that pours through laurel
    bowers.

Plate 2. Marginalia in *The Poetical Works of Mrs. Felicia Hemans* (Philadelphia: Grigg & Elliot, 1839), 277. Charlotte Cocke Gordon's copy. Albert and Shirley Small Special Collections Library, University of Virginia. PR4780 .A1 1839.

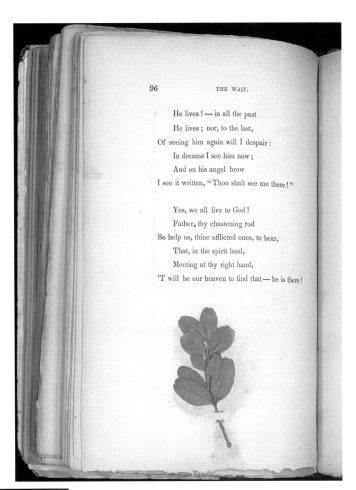

Plate 3. Green sprig inserted in *The Waif: A Collection of Poems*, ed. Henry Wadsworth Longfellow (Cambridge, MA: J. Owen, 1845), 96. Adams family copy. Richter Library, University of Miami.

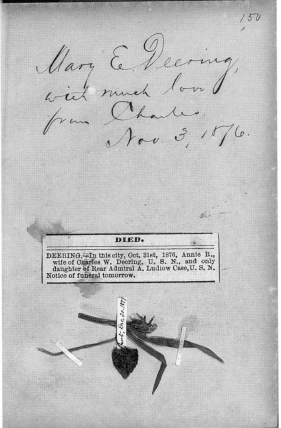

Plate 4. Inscription and augmentations on front endpaper of *The Changed Cross and Other Religious Poems*, 2nd ed. (New York: Anson Randolph, 1872). Deering family copy. Richter Library, University of Miami.

I wish, and I wish that the spring would go faster,
   Nor long summer bide so late;
And I could grow on like the foxglove and aster,
   For some things are ill to wait.

I wait for the day when dear hearts shall discover,
   While dear hands are laid on my head;
"The child is a woman, the book may close over,
   For all the lessons are said."

I wait for my story — the birds cannot sing it,
   Not one, as he sits on the tree;
The bells cannot ring it, but long years, O bring it!
   Such as I wish it to be.

LOVE.
"*Dark, dark was the garden, I saw not the gate.*"

Plate 5. Flower pressed in Jean Ingelow, *Songs of Seven* (Boston: Roberts Brothers, 1881), 20–21. Copy given to "Gracie," December 10, 1882. Author's collection.

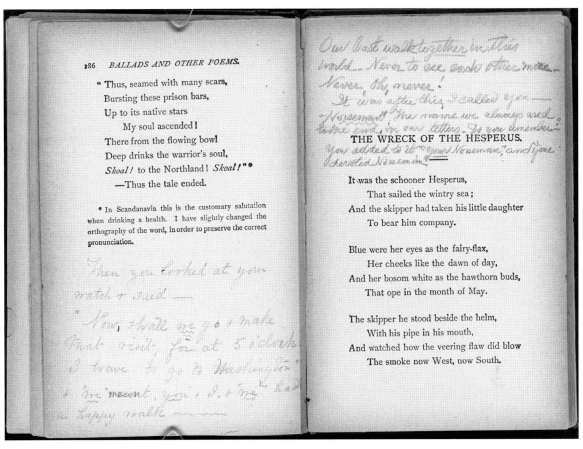

Plate 6. Marginalia in Henry Wadsworth Longfellow, *Poems and Ballads* (New York: Worthington Company, 1891), 186–87. Jane Slaughter's copy. Alderman Library, University of Virginia. PS 2252 .W6 1891.

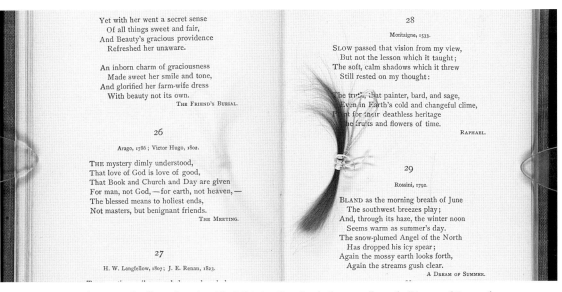

Plate 7. Lock of hair found in *The Whittier Year Book: Passages from the Verse and Prose of John Greenleaf Whittier* (Boston: Houghton Mifflin, 1895). Ivy Stacks, Alderman Library, University of Virginia. PS3253 .H62 1895.

Plate 8. Doll clothes found in *The Complete Works of Sir Walter Scott*, vol. 7 (New York, 1833). Ivy Stacks, Alderman Library, University of Virginia. PR5300 1833.

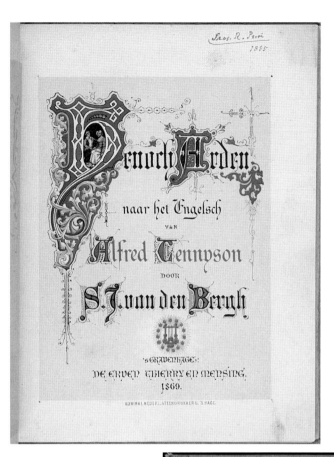

Plate 9a and b. Gift inscription and marginalia in *Henoch Arden naar het Engelsch*, trans. S. J. van den Bergh (The Hague, 1869). Thomas Randolph Price's copy. Alderman library, University of Virginia. PR 5556 .A63 1869.

Plate 10. Bookmark found in *The Holy Bible* (New York: Daniel D. Smith, 1820).
Papers of the Pierrepont and Minor families, 7286-c, Albert and Shirley Small
Special Collections Library, University of Virginia.

academic libraries were overwhelmingly the property of white, upper-middle-class families, with enough money to accumulate collections worth donating and enough cultural capital to get those collections into academic institutions. Indeed, at my university, below the Mason-Dixon Line, some of those same families owned people at the same time as they owned these books; at least one volume we found in Alderman Library, from the Esmont plantation in Virginia, has a list of what seem to be slave names written on an endpaper.[53] In a kind of despair, and objecting to the whole edifice, one might think these books the detritus of a world well lost, the dominant world of white culture, of white supremacy. "That was a fine place to make a bonfire. . . ."

Yet we are just beginning to take stock of this archive, spread as it is across hundreds of academic libraries with various constituencies and histories of collection building. But what is on academic library shelves in Missouri, in Alabama, in Ohio? What provenance have the nineteenth-century books now held by historically black colleges and universities?[54] We cannot know what we will find until we *open every book*. That is the task urgently in front of us, before the print collections are stored away and managed down for good. The results, so far, are promising, complicated—even bewildering. I have more to say about all this in the next chapter, but, for now, I want to conclude with a book that takes us right to the heart of the issue: a Dutch translation of Tennyson's "Enoch Arden"— *Henoch Arden*, published in the Hague in 1869 and now in the stacks at Virginia (Plates 9a and 9b).[55] It once belonged to Thomas Randoloph Price (1839–1903), a literature professor and former Confederate officer whose books were given to the university by his widow and daughter in a formal presentation ceremony in the Rotunda in November 1904.[56] A native Virginian and a graduate of the University of Virginia, Price was studying classics in Berlin when the news of the Confederate secession came to him, and he instantly made his way home to enlist (which involved running the Union blockade of Charleston, with the help of Captain John Wilkinson, on Christmas Eve in 1862).[57] After the war, he taught Greek at Randolph-Macon College and at Virginia, finally ending his career as a professor of English at Columbia University. One memorialist said of Price, "What we used to call Southern chivalry was in him fully expressed." Another, William Gordon McCabe (a Virginia colleague and fellow Confederate officer), elaborated further at Price's death: "[Price] himself represented all that was finest and best in the civilization of what is so often called to-day 'The Old South.' . . . Where Virginia flew her 'sic semper' on its azure field, there lay his paramount and complete allegiance. . . . Beyond all honors in scholarship and letters that came to him in after years, he counted the honor of having served the Confederate cause, which in his maturer manhood became to him, as it were, a religion."[58] Following these eulogists, one could say that Price was a representative man of this era in the history of the University of Virginia, one who, like McCabe and others (and certainly like most of the white Southern students of the Civil War years), embraced the Confederate cause and who left his mark on the university—for better and worse. Price was also a formidable scholar of languages and someone who frequently wrote in his books—an aspect of the collection that was (at the time of its acquisition) deemed part of its value to the university. At the 1904 library presentation, McCabe noted with enthusiasm that "in many a volume of this noble collection, . . . eager students . . . shall find page after page of these books filled with annotations of amazing apposite learning and acute suggestion, written in that fine, microscopic hand" (15–16).

A number of Price's books that have emerged from the stacks bear out McCabe's claim: Price was a learned marginalian. But his copy of *Henoch Arden* is different: it is not annotated by Price himself but inscribed by a friend, on the verso of the title page:

Rotterdam Aug. 28, '84

Dear Tom

While looking in a booksellers window just now, & smiling at "Dombey En Zoon," and other English works in Dutch, I got caught in a shower. So I got this book & retreated to a "café," and got a bottle of Rhine wine, & have taken the two together. I know the English poem almost by heart, & so I can read this Dutch without the dictionary; and it comes back to me, as I read, that we read it together in dear Richmond nineteen years ago. Some of the lines that you read aloud then seem vivid & fresh in my memory—things not to die until I do. And so it seemed to me that it might be a pleasure to you to see clearly—as I do through the mists of another tongue—Enoch Arden from another point of view; and therefore through the golden light of this "flask" of Rhine wine, I give you this book to show you how dear to me our past has been, and how much I think of you.

James R.

Growing expansive over a bottle of wine and a Dutch translation of "Enoch Arden" at a Rotterdam café in 1884, James R. fondly recalls Tennyson's poem, which the two friends read in the midst of war.[59] When James and Tom were reading aloud the newly published "Enoch Arden" together "nineteen years ago" (that is, in 1865), "dear Richmond" was making its last, weak stand against Union forces. Price's native city would soon be burning as the Confederate army withdrew; in early April, Lee surrendered. In the book, next to certain passages that he knows "by heart," James has written "Do you remember?" and "I remember when you read this," emphasizing the complex layers of memory at work on these pages of the Dutch "Enoch Arden," a poem whose sentimental mainspring is the idea of coming home to a place where one has been forgotten.[60]

James R.'s inscription is a vignette of poetry reading in nineteenth-century America and provides a window onto various aspects of that culture: memorization ("almost by heart") of long poems was a common practice; men read poems aloud to one another; poetry (including a newly published best seller like "Enoch Arden") was part of the Civil War experience for soldiers; the memory of poetry was often involved with a particular reader's voice ("I remember when you read this"); and shared sentiment over poems became part of lifelong friendships and memories, here shading into an almost erotic tenderness ("not to die until I do").[61] Dear Tom, dear Richmond, and the dear past emerge out of *Henoch Arden* for James, conveyed on its endpaper in neat pencil script and sent, through various paths, to the library shelves. Like Enoch himself, the book seems a traveler: from the Hague where it was published in 1869 to Rotterdam in 1884 to Price at his New York home soon thereafter and to Charlottesville in 1904 when it was donated to the university library—carrying within it an imagined return to Richmond in 1865 (not to mention Tennyson's England and the poem's setting in an English seaport town "a hundred years ago"). Like all the books we have inherited from the past, it encodes a partial history of its production, use, and circulation. The inscriptions and annotations in this copy of *Henoch Arden* make legible more details than is typical for a nineteenth-century book, in ways that can reveal larger pathways and networks of print culture and the history of reading. Like a chemical tracer, inscriptions can make those pathways and networks visible: another kind of book trace.

Henoch Arden is an uncommon book, one that Virginia is fortunate to have, particularly because of the inscription and marginalia that it contains and the sentimental investiture that those things index. Yet such special features have been obscured in the wake of Google Books, in that our online library catalogue (as is now common) offers access to digital page images of such books directly from the catalogue entry. Users most frequently choose that access option rather than hunting down print volumes in the library stacks. But the Google page images of *Henoch Arden* are taken from a clean copy in the National Library of the Netherlands (Koninklijke Bibliotek). A single-copy surrogate thus threatens to supplant the whole range of variously marked and inscribed copies in libraries (like Price's copy at Virginia), as is the case with virtually all the out-of-copyright material on library shelves that Google and HathiTrust provide access to. We have seen how nineteenth-century books were transfigured by their readers' sentimental investments, expressed at the intersection of damage and care, of love and use. Such books reveal in part how they became something more than material supports for verbal content, something else than the physical packaging of texts. Like the locks of hair they sometimes contain, they became sensual objects and souvenirs, simultaneously embodied and ideal, loaded with sentiment, fragile, and liable to loss. How will they fare in the new informational structures of the library and the twenty-first-century university?

When Tennyson's Enoch Arden leaves on the fateful sea voyage that will separate him from home and family, his wife, Annie, "from her baby's forehead clipt / A tiny curl and gave it" as a remembrancer (lines 234–35). That child dies soon after Enoch's departure, and on his own deathbed years later, having been replaced as Annie's husband by Philip (his friend and rival), Enoch recalls his youngest son via that lock of hair:

> And now there is but one of all my blood,
> Who will embrace me in the world-to-be:
> This hair is his: she cut it off and gave it,
> And I have borne it with me all these years,
> And thought to bear it with me to my grave;
> But now my mind is changed, for I shall see him,
> My babe in bliss: wherefore when I am gone,
> Take, give her this, for it may comfort her:
> It will moreover be a token to her,
> That I am he. (lines 888–97)

Souvenir and synecdoche, surrogate and token: for Enoch, the child's curl has done material and symbolic service "all these years" in connecting him to memories of home and to the absent body of his youngest child. Only upon his return has Enoch learned of that child's death, and so, as he says, he no longer needs to retain it: "my mind is changed, for I shall see him, / My babe in bliss." Like the Velveteen Rabbit at the end of its story, Enoch's boy has become real—lost to the arms of his parents in this world but translated to another order of existence, "the world-to-be," in which he alone of Enoch's children will greet Enoch as a father (because of Philip's gentle usurpation). In the end, the curl of hair yields to its sublime referent: the soul of Enoch and Annie's nameless child.

I recall now Mary Montague Minor, introduced in Chapter 1, whose death in 1862 at the age of seven prompted her mother, Ellen, to write in her book of Hemans's poetry: the book that inspired this project when my students discovered it on the Alderman Library shelves. In the Minor family papers at the University of Virginia, in one of their nineteenth-century Bibles in which births and deaths were so carefully recorded—itself now water-damaged and torn—I found a bookmark with the cross-stitched motto "May we meet in Heaven" (Plate 10): a plangent hope for a future state in which the family circle will be unbroken. For now, the library is the closest thing we have, our storehouse of mortal remains that can still evoke the networks of the past, momentarily real in our handling, attending, and reading of them. Nineteenth-century books come to us as relics of lost practices of reading and interacting with books, offering variously legible traces of the individual and social uses to which the volumes and their contents were put. Much of this material now resides in the circulating collections of academic libraries, and in this book I offer a plea on its collective behalf: for the preservation of as many copies and as much bibliodiversity as we can maintain.

Yet I want to return to my anecdotes involving the nineteenth-century book as a scene of loss and to a central paradox of this study—namely, its basis in the book trace, which is another way of saying its predication on damage and absences. Insofar as I aim to preserve endangered archival materials, I am defending plenitude; and yet the books that matter most to my project are the battered, haunted ones, with their vestigial markings and their tenuous voices, with their scars and gaps to dream on. In those books, we can see most clearly the movement of human memory into the realm of the perishable: the melancholy, post-Enlightenment bargain with the archive that it will take the place of any divine recordkeeping or ritual folk memory. For our part, we will become people of the document. As Pierre Nora writes, "Even as traditional memory disappears, we feel obliged assiduously to collect remains, testimonies, documents, images, speeches, any visible signs of what has been, as if this burgeoning dossier were to be called upon to furnish some proof to who knows what tribunal of history."[62] Collection, yes—but also a kind of uncertain, faith-based dispersal. All this annotation was wedded to particular volumes, which became memorials vulnerable to time and damage but also sent obliquely forth, via their envoys of marginalia, that the world might find them after many days. The inscriptions may have been written for the contemporaries of the book owners, but they were also for us: they were all written under a horizon of legacy.[63] And so we have these books, what Byron calls "dear objects of defeated care," that, as I have attempted to show here, may help us rethink the relations among media, poetry, affect, and memory in the nineteenth century and today.[64]

CHAPTER 5

Postcard from the Volcano

On the Future of Library Print Collections

Children picking up our bones
Will never know that these were once
As quick as foxes on the hill
—*Wallace Stevens, "A Postcard from the Volcano"*

From its beginnings, *Book Traces* has relied heavily on time spent in the stacks, among the printed volumes. Yet through the past decade, while visiting academic library buildings and relying on their built structures of knowledge, I have wondered to what extent my interactions with them and their contents are becoming anomalous, a twilit posture of library use. Many institutions have moved or are on the verge of moving significant portions of their collections off-site. Some are embarking on large-scale deaccessioning projects. Across the country, academic library buildings are being reconfigured as information hubs and learning spaces, and the books are on the move. What does the future hold for nonrare (or medium-rare) legacy collections? Going forward, what will be the claim of printed materials on our resources, our scholarship, and our imaginations? How much bibliodiversity does humanities scholarship and teaching require, and how much can our academic libraries afford to maintain? In terms of the future of print collections, these are the central questions of our time.

Digital technology and electronic media are the primary drivers of the profound changes that libraries are experiencing. Searching, retrieving, reading, and analyzing textual content frequently happen now from a patron's laptop connected to myriad digital resources, and the physical books themselves are consigned mostly to the background. During this same period, the digital humanities has emerged as an evolving set of practical and theoretical moves for reengaging the cultural record by means of new technologies. From 2008 to 2018, I directed the digital humanities organization NINES (Networked Infrastructure for Nineteenth-century Electronic Scholarship) at the University of Virginia, working with scholarly projects involved in digitizing the historical record of the long Romantic and Victorian eras in Britain and America.[1] Our collective goal was to open up these materials to various kinds of search, discovery, visualization, commentary, contextualization, and collaborative research. At the same time, we always stressed that digital archives are not replacements for the material texts they represent; rather, they are simulations or models. The books on the shelves carry plenty of information lost in the process of digitization, no matter how lovingly a particular copy is rendered for the screen. Electronic texts (so tied to immediate functionalities and the logic of the update) become amnesiac without ongoing reference to those multidimensional objects they appear to simulate. The Book Traces project evolved from NINES as a demonstration of the limits of electronic surrogates and of the abiding historical force of the nineteenth-century print record.

Marginalia, annotations, and insertions (e.g., flowers, locks of hair) make parts of a book's history particularly visible. In previous chapters, we saw a mother mourn her daughter on the flyleaf of her copy of Hemans; a husband attach a memorial flower to the book of poems that his wife read on her deathbed; a group of women add evaluative comments in the margins of a narrative romance; a former soldier inscribe a copy of Tennyson to a friend based on his memories of reading together during the Civil War; a woman annotate her beloved's copy of Longfellow and revisit those annotations many years later to lament his loss; and many more examples of the personal alteration of nineteenth-century books. These instances clarify the fact that the meanings of all books are tied inextricably to their specific material forms and the reception of those forms across time. Books are an advanced technology of memory, each one a complex record of its own making and use. Copies with marginalia and other legible interventions throw this general truth into sharp relief, as they give us rich scenes of history in the making. And they likewise illuminate the threat to cultural memory represented by the downsizing of library print collections.

Beyond this monograph, Book Traces exists as a collaborative initiative among librarians, humanities faculty members, and students across a growing number of institutions. In both its origins and aims, the project involves many hands and eyes on individual physical volumes in the circulating collections of academic libraries. Over the past decade, Book Traces has proceeded through exploration and discovery in the stacks. It has involved a series of practical and experimental investigations that have raised awareness about the artifactual value of nineteenth-century books. Throughout, the intellectual labor of librarians, the enthusiastic curiosity of undergraduate students, and the critical engagement of graduate students and faculty colleagues have been crucial to the joint project. Book Traces has always been an educational experiment that aims to change the conversation about books as theaters of cultural memory and also about the future of the library.

Our primary goal has been to discover and catalogue inscriptions, annotations, and insertions in pre-1923 imprints in the circulating collections, and to bring to view the uniquely marked and modified copies of books that help us understand the history of reading and book use in the long nineteenth century. The project aims to demonstrate how specific copies of books carry individual and collective historical meanings. Digitization projects, shared print initiatives, and preservation guidelines all tend to favor clean, unmarked copies of books, ones most suitable for delivering their printed contents. If two libraries are deciding which copy of a book to share between them, they tend to choose the clean, bright copy over the one marked by signs of heavy use. But what if the calculus should be more complex? Between 10 and 12 percent of pre-1923 imprints in circulating collections of academic libraries have recognizable interventions made by their original readers.[2] This finding, confirmed by Book Traces searches at various colleges and universities, might alter our formulae when it comes to retention and preservation decisions, productively blurring the lines between general and special collections.

Since 2014, Book Traces events and searches have been organized at over two dozen academic libraries in the United States and Canada, and more are planned.[3] In addition, the website Booktraces.org has invited anyone who finds contemporary owner markings in a pre-1923 book held in a library circulating collection to submit a photo along with some tracking information. Graduate and undergraduate classes at various institutions have adopted this procedure, which brings students into the stacks to make original discoveries and contribute to our knowledge about the collections and about the history of reading and book use. Focusing on specific call number ranges allows instructors to tailor such assignments to their discipline, be it literature, history, philosophy, or religious studies—all subject areas with high rates of marking. Most fruitful have been library stacks filled with nineteenth-century books that have been little used since their acquisition. Books by popular or commonly taught authors tend to have more modern student and patron marks, which stand outside the scope of the project. We look for older handwriting and dates, and other interventions that can be convincingly tied to the owners and handlers of the books before they came into the library. To be sure, someone might want to track patron annotation of academic library books through the present day, but that is not this project.

Following certain protocols for searching, data gathering, and book handling, Book Traces has depended on a tactic of guided serendipity. The books have been catalogued, arranged, and made available, but their unique markings can be found only by opening and examining every volume. Librarians rightly object to fantasy narratives of serendipity and discovery, in which researchers elide the work done by library professionals in acquiring, cataloguing, preserving, and making accessible the materials that a patron claims to have magically discovered. But often it does take a content specialist to recognize the particular significance of a given book, even after it has been catalogued and shelved. Perhaps "recognition" is a better term than "discovery." Likewise, "serendipity" describes the timely meetings of engaged researchers with relevant materials: happy convergences that can only be prepared for, guided but not scripted, because humanities research is fundamentally associative in its methods. Those convergences tend to happen in research libraries—something like laboratories, something like archaeological sites—that provide ready access to rich collections of print and digital materials with histories of their own.

On the shelves of a great library, researchers can see the history of a discipline, or the publication and reception history of an author, or the evolution of history itself, as they move from older to more recent books. Those histories are often our primary subjects, embedded within the contexts of the culture, the academy, the library, and even the individual institution. And for the bibliographer and book historian, each of those volumes also carries data regarding its own production and use, further ramifying the evidentiary scene of the library shelf. All this is to say that humanists value print collections not out of mere nostalgia but from a keen awareness of the intricate, enfolded orders of historical information those collections contain and embody.

Part of supporting the library means using its collections avidly and not simply paying lip service to their importance. If we lament the loss of library books but rarely find ourselves using the print collections, our lament will not register. A 2001 Council on Library and Information Resources (CLIR) report by Stephen G. Nichols and Abby Smith warns, "Scholars may not see preservation of research collections as their responsibility, but until they do, there is a risk that many valuable research sources will not be preserved."[4] To bring the legacy print collections back into circulation and demonstrate their variety and importance, humanities departments would do well to reintegrate bibliography, textual criticism, scholarly editing, and book history into undergraduate and graduate curricula, as well as into more of their scholarly work. Particularly at this moment of media change, of digital textuality, and of the transformation of the library, that work, what Jerome McGann has called "philology in a new key," is more urgent than ever.[5] As the print collections recede from everyday view, the coming generations of students (and faculty members) will have to be taught what books were: they will need new ways to develop familiarity with book technologies and to be able to recognize and defend their scholarly significance as meaningful cultural objects. Originating in the classroom and employing and engaging many undergraduate and graduate students, Book Traces is one example of how just such an educational initiative can become a social action.

I. Print Collections Management

When I first heard about the managing down of print and the rightsizing of circulating collections, and for a long time afterward, I felt it with the force of scandal. First, I had assumed that libraries had an inalienable attachment to their legacy print collections, because I had learned and become a scholar among them and had imbibed a great reverence for the stacks. Bibliography and librarianship were closely intertwined disciplines in my understanding, which was shaped by the University of Virginia's legendary culture of book studies and its commitment to its collections. Like many of my colleagues in English and other humanities departments, I had assumed that the books, so long the primary feature of our research library, were not going anywhere. I thought that ideas of deduplication and arguments for the large-scale withdrawal of support from print were coming from the fringes, or from efficiency-minded corporate thought leaders, and that these ideas would surely be resisted by librarians and humanities faculty members acting together. Finally, I was driven by a belief that, because disagreements about the value of the print collections depended on a relatively simple misunderstanding about the evidence that books contain and the research operations they enable, the issues could easily be resolved through a few influential conversations among the stakeholders. It turns out that almost none of that is true.

As this book was being written, print-sharing and deduplication programs moved steadily to the center of academic library policy circles. Indeed, such programs emerged from and have been nurtured within those circles all along. As the global library cooperative OCLC states on its "Shared Print Management" web page, "Academic and research libraries increasingly are planning and implementing programs to share the responsibility and costs of maintaining print collections. These shared print projects also help library groups reclaim library space."[6] Its website goes on to affirm that "many libraries are already managing down their local print collections with OCLC's help."[7] It is now a commonplace in the library literature that, as Alex D. McAllister and Allan Scherlen write, "many libraries are undertaking massive book deselection projects."[8] The digital vendor ProQuest recently announced "that out of more than 400 librarians surveyed, 78% of the respondents reported that they are deselecting print book collections" to reclaim library space for other purposes.[9] The motivations for these reductions are obvious: the usage rate of nonrare physical library collections is down everywhere, and tight budgets are increasingly being directed to digital resources.[10] Students and faculty members want more spaces to work and collaborate, but they do not use as many physical books as in the past. The availability of digital texts and digitally gathered data about collections has made printed books newly manageable, more reorganizable at scale. And since it has been calculated that every book retained by a library costs between one and four dollars per year to store and circulate, management has tended toward reductions.[11]

Objections to the downsizing of print collections have been raised in local contexts, most visibly by faculty members and students who fear the loss of research capacity at their institutions. But these have generally been rearguard operations, sometimes successful in slowing the movement of books from the shelves (as in cases at Syracuse, the University of Texas, Yale, and elsewhere) but only glancingly impactful on the larger shared print movement and the tenets that underlie it.[12] Further, such protests often seem to deepen lines of division. Productive policy conversations among librarians, archivists, and humanities faculty members and students have been difficult to engineer, in part because of the lack of a common language that could do equal justice to bibliographic, historical, administrative, organizational, technological, and economic concerns. Any conversation about book removal tends to be polarizing, and libraries tend to be pushed into defensive postures from which they react by labeling attempts to save books "sentimental," "exaggerated," and "nostalgic." For example, Nicholson Baker offered a trenchant but at times overly polemical critique of libraries' deaccessioning of print in the name of progress.[13] Baker's analysis was taken seriously if warily by library and archivist communities at the time, but they were also put on the defensive by his rhetoric. As years passed, *Double Fold* was remembered by the library community as an eccentric and ultimately nostalgic call to save everything.[14]

Certainly, "save everything" is not a responsible directive. Librarians have always weeded the stacks. But the core of Baker's arguments cannot be so easily dismissed. Nor can sentiment and nostalgia, given the involvement of those attitudes with the culture of the book and their salutary resistance to the presentism and techno-futurism of the American Now. Baker correctly and presciently described the technologically driven discarding of print in favor of more efficient but inadequate surrogates like microfilm and digital scans. His objections are to an ideology of substitution that can drive the wholesale removal of historical material in the name of convenience. Starting around 2001, massive digitization programs have pushed many libraries toward just such a systemic transformation, whereby entire classes of materials are either being moved off-site or being discarded. The title of a 2015 report from the University of Texas at Tyler gives a snapshot of this process: "Books Be Gone! Reducing an Academic Library's Print

Collection by Half to Meet Strategic Planning Initiatives and Participate in a Joint Library Resource-Sharing Facility."[15] Professional deselection has always been part of the process of maintaining a healthy library system. But we are now confronting a new vision of the library as such. In 2014, David Woolwine stated plainly, "Academic libraries are in a transitional period to what will, most likely, become almost entirely electronic collections," even as he called for attention to the specific needs of humanistic research.[16] As Robert H. Kieft and Lizanne Payne envision it, the "ideal state for academic library print collections" in this decade is one in which "all except a few campuses are repurposing the majority of their libraries' square footage to create . . . work spaces," devoting "much less of their on-campus space to housing general collection print materials in open stacks" and working in partnerships with other libraries "to maintain a relatively small number of print copies for use by everyone."[17] Along the same lines, a 2010 OCLC report by Constance Malpas concludes that "it is in the interest of all academic libraries that mass-digitized collections . . . improve to the degree that low-use print inventory can be retired in favor of increased reliance on digital surrogate[s]."[18] That is more than weeding: it sounds like a clear-cutting of the old-growth collections to make room for new developments.[19]

Other library policy organizations have produced similar or related visions of the academic research library's digital future. In September 2009, an ITHAKA Strategy and Research report appeared, written by Roger C. Schonfeld and Ross Housewright, with the ominous title "What to Withdraw: Print Collections Management in the Wake of Digitization." Having recently merged with JSTOR to provide access to scholarly journals online, ITHAKA made the case that university libraries should start deaccessioning collections of print journals and rely solely on digital versions: "The large-scale digitization of print journal collections has led to most access needs being met via digital surrogates. Numerous libraries would therefore like to reassign the space occupied by print collections towards higher-value uses."[20] Although the recommendations are ostensibly confined to journals, the language of the report encourages a slide away from print collections generally: "we do not assume that there is any intrinsic value to the maintenance of collections of print artifacts but rather take a critical perspective to analyze why the community might want to keep any print at all" (3). Furthermore, the ITHAKA report displays a troubling attitude toward faculty resistance to deaccessioning, lamenting that "the risk that faculty will protest the removal of even the most rarely used print collections inhibits decision-making about print collections. . . . [However,] due to a decline in faculty interest in print preservation both locally and remotely in recent years, the political necessity of maintaining even remote access to print collections will probably remain a requirement only in the medium term" (12–13). Perhaps most worrisome here are the ideas that the faculty serves as only a temporary, inhibiting presence on library policy making and that maintaining print collections is a political requirement, not an essential component of the mission of academic research libraries.

Rebecca Lossin has recently written of her graduate education in library science, circa 2004, as the digitization of library materials was beginning in earnest (Google Books debuted that same year):

> Instead of talking about this threat honestly, my colleagues dreamt up euphemisms like "digital migration"—as if books were flying north to the Internet rather than being destroyed and replaced by digital copies. They adopted an advertiser's devotion to satisfying the desires of adolescents for new media. . . . [F]antasies of saving space, cutting costs and keeping everything online tended toward the evacuation of the idea of the library as a place to hold physical objects. Librarians, in other words, were beginning to conceive of the library as something other than a library. They were anticipating its disappearance.[21]

Lossin's experience attests to a movement away from investments in local print collections and toward technologically driven models of access. She writes, "The new professional ethos demands a set of skills and interests that have nothing to do with historical holdings or research. . . . In self-reinforcing fashion, the demands of technological change attract techno-enthusiasts; and with techno-enthusiasts in charge, technological change becomes the agenda" (110). According to Lossin, digitization and the management of print collections are part of the corporatization of the university and the embrace of technocratic, managerial economies by libraries, amid a concomitant downsizing of humanities budgets.[22] Information science rather than bibliography governs the training of librarians, a shift over the past century that makes practical sense alongside the rise of digital information, but that has had implications that now need our collective attention. Library culture is changing; books are moving away from the center, both figuratively and literally. We are on the event horizon of the surrogate, the shared copy, and the downsizing of the historical printed record.

II. Duplicate Copies

Many individual librarians fiercely defend the legacy print volumes, devoting their careers to the preservation of the books on the shelves; and some institutions attempt to make strong commitments to keeping their legacy physical collections intact and accessible. But at the highest levels of policy and administration, deduplication is the new normal, which portends a significant reduction in printed books in academic libraries nationwide. At first, the management of the print record at regional or national levels sounds like a good idea: libraries will be better able to ensure preservation and ongoing access by coordinating their efforts. But such high-level organization relies on formalized, abstract, bird's-eye views of the collections, so local nuances are then lost. Ultimately, such coordination seems predicated on a radical downsizing of print. In their CLIR report "The Evidence in Hand," Nichols and Smith conclude that "it is not too early to plan for the eventual disposition of the scores, or even hundreds, of duplicate copies of individual items that scholars, voting with mouse clicks, prefer to use online" (27). As Malpas opines in the OCLC report on managing print, "Popular titles like Defoe's *Robinson Crusoe* or Swift's *Gulliver's Travels* . . . are each represented by hundreds of digitized editions in the HathiTrust Digital Library; the long-term preservation of the intellectual work embodied in these manifestations is, to coin a phrase, virtually guaranteed" (24). Offered as a reassurance that we can safely cull the physical books, this statement actually reads as a guarantee of loss, predicated on a vision of books as utterly interchangeable manifestations of their verbal content. Scholars see the matter differently, of course. But the idea of the redundant, duplicate book is driving a substantial portion of the conversation about the future of print collections.

The shared print movement depends on the savings generated by reducing volume counts, a shrinking of the footprint of print.[23] Given the scope and current pace of the work, librarians have to rely on general principles and digital metadata to ascribe redundancy to a certain portion of the collections. But what counts as a duplicate copy depends in large part on the granularity of your vision, and it is not all about marginalia. I recently demonstrated that ten copies of the same edition of the same 1902 book, acquired at random through interlibrary loan from the same catalogue record, all differed from one another in significant ways, including the text, illustrations, binding, page count, and marks of use.[24] Some librarians have drawn similar conclusions. Michael Garabedian determined, via surveys of the conditions of books at various libraries, that "random deselection of books would result in deaccessioning 'duplicates' with artifactual value."[25] And Ian Bogus and Zach Maiorana have recently shown that "inaccurate and incomplete bibliographic data themselves present a significant challenge to effective cross-institutional analysis of collections, and this challenge is compounded by a lack of certainty over the overall rate of accuracy for the collective metadata corpus."[26] Put simply, we do not know enough about our collections to deduplicate with confidence. And we cannot predict how many copies will be enough to save: the Risk Working Group of the Partnership for Shared Book Collections acknowledged in 2019 that "it is all but impossible to calculate the likelihood of a single copy's surviving without knowing intended use, loss rates, current conditions, and storage environments."[27] The data that *can* be easily gathered on existing volumes—number of checkouts, number of copies, whether a copy is available online—tell us almost nothing about the artifactual condition, the printing variants, and ultimately the research value of the books on the shelves. This is particularly true for humanities disciplines, in which reaching backward to analyze neglected materials is fundamental.

For well over a century, the scholarly community has warned against discarding so-called duplicate copies of books. In 1911, Falconer Madan was already claiming that "there is little opportunity to be original on the subject of Duplicates," so well developed were the basic outlines of the conversation. Madan argued "that our present methods for detecting duplicates are inadequate" and that "it is dangerous to part with any book as a duplicate, if printed before 1800, without close inspection."[28] In 1937, Randolph G. Adams warned even more stringently that "the problem of determining what books are duplicates is . . . not one upon which a librarian is entitled to trust his own judgment unless he is also an expert bibliographer, which many librarians are not. . . . [I]f the head of a library of deposit and reference arrogates to himself the right to make decisions about books which are seldom, or never, used during his own brief life span, he cannot complain if he is classed as an enemy of books" (329).

Madan and Adams present two related strictures: first, that bibliographic expertise is necessary to make decisions about whether books are duplicates, and second, that deaccessioning books due to infrequent use within one or two generations contravenes the mission of the library. Both Madan and Adams focused primarily on books from the handpress era, printed before 1800. But books printed in the nineteenth and early twentieth centuries reveal similar kinds and levels of significant variability. The governing directive of these remarks by Madan and Adams—never assume you know—still has the force of a counterweight to data-driven deselection.

As the twentieth century advanced, Madan's and Adams's positions continued to be elaborated and solidified by bibliographers, especially G. Thomas Tanselle, who in 1994 led a Modern Language Association committee on the future of the print record. That committee's report states, "The loss of any copy of any edition—from the earliest incunables to the latest paperback reprints (regardless of whether its text is considered interesting or consequential at the present time)—diminishes the body of evidence on which historical understanding depends."[29] This general point forms the basis of the entire Book Traces project: copies of books contain information that we do not know is there, and we cannot know what is there until we examine them. Of course, copies will be lost. But collaborative thinking among librarians, humanities content experts, and bibliographers should precede, if not preclude, any programmatic removal of books. As Susan Staves writes, "No one, after all, can really tell what a good copy is without collating it with others. . . . Not only do we now not know what we do not know, we cannot predict what scholars or what society will want to know a hundred years from now."[30] Madan, Adams, Tanselle, and Staves all make the point that developing criteria now for what counts as significant in a particular book risks winnowing the historical record to what we already recognize, to what is popular, and to current trends and ways of seeing.

In terms of nineteenth-century and early twentieth-century textual studies, the work of Jerome McGann has been most influential in establishing the scholarly importance of books' significant details. For McGann, a braided helix of publication and reception events constitutes literary works as evolving social acts, and those events are traceable only within specific documents. As he writes, "Every document, every copy of every edition, is unique; and this uniqueness grows more clear, more articulate, more significant as the document undergoes its historical passage."[31] It is easy to class books as duplicates based on the simple catalogue data that we capture from a title page, such as the author, title, edition, and place and year of publication. But much variation is hidden behind that data, variation that becomes visible only under evolving protocols of examination. New modes of analyzing cultural artifacts are always emerging, both technological (e.g., advanced imaging capabilities and DNA analysis) and intellectual (e.g., attention to once-neglected content like marginalia). We will not be able to use new methods on old digital scans, or on old metadata, or on collections that have been rightsized according to the views of the early twenty-first century. Discarding little-used books will limit possibilities. You cannot do MRI spectroscopy on black-and-white photographs of mummies taken in the 1880s, and you will not be able to do book history on single-copy digital surrogates produced quickly by Google Books circa 2010.

Because we typically do not know what evidence the books on the shelves contain, any distant or algorithmic attempt to collapse them into singular representative copies will inevitably produce losses. This is true not only for individual titles but also for the entire bibliographic system in its historical complexity. Books speak to one another as networked objects within cultural systems. Many meaningful features of books can be understood only as part of larger contexts of making and use. The books themselves are not merely reports on the nineteenth century; they are individual nineteenth-century scenes of evidence that were produced, conveyed, sold, handled, read, and marked by the culture of study. This archive of the history of the making and consumption of books cannot be replaced by representative copies or digital scans, and new scholars of the historical record cannot be trained on simulations.

Those of us who work on nineteenth-century materials have a particular stake in these matters, given that many of our primary bibliographic materials are still in library circulating collections. As I have said elsewhere, most libraries have moved books issued before 1800 to rare-book rooms; and books published after 1924 remain in copyright and thus are more likely to stay on the shelves for circulation (although twentieth-century books may also be winnowed heavily as books move into the public domain and as digital licensing develops). But the middle layer—the products of the great age of industrial printing, representing the zenith of book culture in the West—could form the leading edge of obsolescence. Books printed in the nineteenth century were often printed on cheap, acidic paper, making them turn fragile over time (although they are not doomed to turn to dust, a baleful diagnosis that was used to justify destructive reformatting in the twentieth century).[32] Also, they no longer get much use by patrons: their typeface and layout can make them hard to read, and many of the important titles can be obtained in more convenient modern editions. Unless they had no other option, most people today—except specialist scholars or bibliomaniacs—would not read a book printed in the nineteenth century. And since Google, HathiTrust, and other sites offer scanned versions of many nineteenth-century books, people interested in historical copies often need not visit the library at all.

As usage drops, libraries have trouble justifying storing these materials on valuable shelf space in central locations. Many books are being moved to off-site warehouses, where they will remain accessible to researchers who request them while benefitting from better storage conditions. However, such storage is also predicated on the assumption that those volumes will be requested only rarely, since it is costly to retrieve them. Off-site storage confirms and abets the paucity of use that has drawn resources away from nineteenth-century books, even as it preserves and protects them. Once they are stored in temperature-controlled warehouses, organized by size rather than by subject, such books are less likely to be used. They can be found only via the digital library catalogue, and catalogues often lead users first to online content rather than print materials, since (motivated by convenience and not necessarily by preference) most patrons will "click here for full-text access."[33] The books themselves—the individual copies held by each library—get less attention in this model, and less attention means greater justification for moving and keeping them off-site. Moreover, those volumes become inaccessible to certain kinds of search and discovery, including the research underlying this book.

In my own university library, one that has an extraordinary commitment to its physical collections, roughly half—about one hundred thousand—of our circulating books published between 1800 and 1923 have already been moved to our remote storage facility, which in 2019 had a total capacity to redeliver about ten thousand books per year. Obviously, this is much preferable to deaccessioning those books, and it is conducive to their long-term preservation, but it does limit certain kinds of research. For Book Traces, we could not browse the off-site materials, and we would have overwhelmed the system if we had tried to recall every book in our range of interest. As a result, we can only sample the holdings in the remote storage facility. Achingly and also predictably, our sampling revealed that books in remote storage were up to *twice* as likely to contain marks and interventions made by their original nineteenth-century readers.[34] Mostly left unused on the shelves, these donated volumes were some of the first to go off-site, making room for more modern acquisitions. When that happened, the unique aspects of these historical books, having never been catalogued as such in the first place, were submerged. Off-site storage takes underused materials whose primary interest (given the putative availability of their verbal content online or elsewhere) often resides in their unique bibliographic and physical features, and places those features out of view. As I have said, such relocation does protect the books: they are safely stored in boxes on tall shelves in cool, dark warehouses, away from the fluctuations of open-shelf temperatures and the scuffs of use. But my worry is that these books are more vulnerable to large-scale, administrative redefinition than they are to the comparatively dull tooth of time. Moving books off-site makes them less likely to catch the attention of a student or researcher and enhances their apparent uselessness in the eyes of data gatherers.[35] At some institutions, such moves will be preparatory to rounds of deaccessioning, which will happen after an appropriate period of distant monitoring that will almost inevitably confirm that no one needs these volumes.

So even as nineteenth-century materials seem to be becoming more visible and searchable thanks to digital scans, our access to robust and varied print collections for large-scale browsing and surveying is at risk. Scholars and librarians bear a shared responsibility here: the protocols of our institutions have conformed to the priorities of our discipline, which has not, in the main, required the presence of large numbers of nineteenth-century printed books, especially nonrare ones. We teach mostly from modern anthologies, cite recent editions, and consult digital scans of early books and periodicals when we need them. Furthermore, in the past generation or two, bibliography, textual criticism, and scholarly editing have in large part disappeared from English department curricula. Less time is spent among the books in the library, by all of us. And the library goes forward according to the priorities we express with every mouse click, every deferred trip to the stacks. As a result, librarians are making deselection decisions based on efficiency, relying on quantitative criteria such as age and circulation rates that can be applied administratively across the collection.[36] McAllister and Scherlen warn that the needs of humanities disciplines "for older, lesser-used books may be overlooked" because "libraries are moving swiftly to deselect with brittle criteria based on quantitative rubrics alone" (85). Print collections management is a driving force in librarianship now, and its main goal is the efficient rightsizing of physical library holdings at the regional and national level.[37] We need fewer copies of little-used books: follow that logic to its end and almost every nineteenth-century book will become a rare book after all.

III. What Remains

A library stack collection is not a random assortment of old books. It has been shaped by professionals—librarians and faculty members working together over generations—as well as by collectors and donors, by students and researchers, by coincidence and accident, by happy acquisitions and unintended losses. Not just its titles but its *particular volumes* contain layers of overlapping coherence, determined by various priorities, policies, and bequests over time. In every library that has accepted donations, there are recurring names, patterns of reading, and interwoven family histories that can be observed in the strata of the collections. Not all library books survive, of course: David F. Kohl estimates an annual loss of about 0.3 percent from circulating collections, although the newer and most heavily used titles are most vulnerable.[38] Nevertheless, the books are one primary index of the history of the institution and its local reading communities. The provenance of the volumes, particularly the older ones, is part of their significance for scholarly research.[39] The complex origins and orders of a legacy collection cannot be replicated via interlibrary loans of alternate copies. Nor can that collection be replaced by Google Book scans (of items from different collections) or other forms of electronic access to a single scanned copy.

One glaring problem with libraries' increasing reliance on digital texts is the relatively large number of errors in the Google Books corpus and thus in HathiTrust surrogates. As Paul Conway has shown, "the imperfection of digital surrogates is an obvious and nearly ubiquitous feature of Google Books. . . . [S]uch imperfection has become and will remain firmly ensconced in collaborative preservation repositories."[40] This is particularly troubling because we know that among libraries there is "significant reliance on the HathiTrust Digital Library in making withdrawal decisions" (Bogus and Maiorana). Regardless of the outright errors in the scanned pages, my point is that content—what books contain—goes far beyond words in a particular order, and beyond page images of a single representative copy. As we detach texts from books, we enable a certain range of procedures while disabling others. Online editions can open texts to investigation and discovery, but they are not replacements for the material they represent. This is obvious for rare books and manuscripts, which would never be discarded just because someone put scanned images of them online. But in the realm of the medium-rare nineteenth-century book, digitization is being used as a justification for declaring "redundant copies" obsolete—in direct contravention of the Modern Language Association's "Statement on the Significance of Primary Records."

The Google Books cover sheet, prefixed to all downloaded books, is revealing in that it recognizes the value of historical annotations and the unique, artifactual nature of individual copies: "This is a digital copy of a book that was preserved for generations on library shelves before it was carefully scanned by Google. . . . It has survived long enough for the copyright to expire and the book to enter the public domain. . . . Marks, notations and other marginalia present in the original volume will appear in this file—a reminder of this book's long journey from the publisher to a library and finally to you." Leaving aside the suggestion that the book "*was* preserved" by libraries until it was scanned (and is now disposable), the similarly problematic phrase "It has survived long enough," and the concluding "*finally* to you" (which suggests that the Google-user dyad is the teleological endpoint of a book's journey), I stress only Google's reminder that "marks, notations, and other marginalia" were frequently captured in its multimillion-volume-scanning project of academic library books (yet those notations are often illegible as such because of the low quality of the images; we can only speculate as to what happened to the flowers and other insertions during the scanning process). Google seems to be apologizing for this fact, excusing these marks by redescribing them as interesting noise. But these scans tell their own stories. And they remind us of the idiosyncratic nature of old books and of their unique features, which are not reflected by the single-copy digital surrogates with which Google aims to replace our varied library collections. If we and our students always turn to the digital versions, we will neglect all the unscanned copies and the scenes of evidence they have become. And then, according to a library resource economy in which unused books are useless, those copies will go away.

Academic and research libraries have long taken the preservation of the historically layered material record as their premier duty, but priorities are changing. To keep the books, librarians along with humanities faculty members and students will need to find common ground from which to articulate the ongoing value of the print collections and to demand more resources for their preservation. The struggle of the humanities in the modern university is completely bound up with the future of the library collections; you will not save one without inspiring strong support for the other, given that both are predicated on the value of the specific details of the historical cultural record. Careful curatorial attention to the individual historical books in university libraries can be taken up only by a combined force of content specialists, bibliographers, library professionals, and students. The status of many older books as merely circulating materials leaves them generally unsponsored, physically deteriorating, and vulnerable to replacement by digital modes of access to their verbal contents. To enhance their stewardship of these materials, libraries will need more financial support from their universities and their donors, and I hope that the teaching faculty and students will want to help make that case.

To do our work as literary critics and cultural historians, we need nineteenth-century books to remain available in academic libraries, repeatedly addressable by scholars through the years, and visible in all of their individual historical details. We need both a virtual and a material purchase on that grand archive of bibliographic production and consumption that defined the status of the book and of reading for so long. Libraries have to focus in part on present needs and on innovation: how to keep the lights on, satisfy user demands, and adapt to new technologies. But academic libraries are also our guardians of the past, which is to say of the textual humanities. Museum-labs of the printed cultural record, they have a fiduciary responsibility to their historical collections, which cannot be reconstituted elsewhere. Given this responsibility, libraries have to do some things as institutions of memory (not just service), in full cognizance of their transhistorical role in culture. The embedded coherence of their collections, which emerges from patterns of donation and amounts to a shadow archive of the institution itself, cannot be duplicated by alternate copies. There is an ethics of this archive: created by layers of management, its multiple embedded orderings resist later managerial deletions (particularly at scale and at a distance) so that the archive may remain an authentic witness to the past. In both its aggregate and singular qualities, our national library collections contain not only the history of the republic but also the record of our collective archiving of that history.

It is important to remember that the constitution of library print collections in America reflects the inequalities of the nation. As Kevin Seeber has written,

> Legacy print collections in academic libraries . . . represent racist and patriarchal systems that have dominated the U.S., including its higher education system, for way too long. To browse the stacks of an academic library is to look at books that are overwhelmingly—*overwhelmingly*—written by white men, about white men, for white men. Maybe approaching any old shelf in a library and finding something that's interesting and relevant to you really is serendipitous, but it's serendipity operating within a closed system that was informed by privileged structures that kept a lot of books

out of our collections, and a lot of views out of our academies. That same level of serendipity is not experienced by those researchers who are investigating the countless communities whose stories have been erased, as their books were never on the shelf in the first place.[41]

Seeber's reflection on the history of library collections is salutary. We need to be much more aware of the forces that have shaped those aggregations of materials, which have privileged certain kinds of research and disabled others. Yet Seeber and I draw opposite conclusions from this state of affairs. He recommends "deselecting print volumes in the name of creating a more equitable collection"; I see that as an erasure of the very history he calls to our attention. Library print collections are the ever-evolving result of decisions and chance events, and certainly more books by and about marginalized populations need to be written, published, and made available by libraries. But the national print collections have a historical integrity as an archive of what we gathered and what we knew. Discarding books until the library more closely mirrors our current perspectives undermines the historiographic basis of the humanistic enterprise. McGann warns against "a presentist view of scholarship that is alien to the humanities. . . . Humanities scholarship is rooted in the past, in our theaters of memory, even as it is executed in the present with a view toward creating a usable future."[42] Both directly and inadvertently, for better and worse, the old shelves tell stories that we still need to hear. Moreover, future generations will need to know that we heard them, in all of their specific details.

In "Church Going"—Philip Larkin's 1955 poem on the fade-out of religious faith in the modern world—the narrator wonders why, despite his own apathy and ignorance, he keeps visiting churches. Bicycling on Sunday afternoons, he finds himself "tending to this cross of ground"—that is, both unaccountably inclining toward and gently caring for these "accoutered frowsty barn[s]," even as he recognizes that they no longer have the power to hold "unspilt . . . what since is found / Only in separation."[43] Looking forward, he wonders, "When churches will fall completely out of use / What we shall turn them into," imagining most of them slowly crumbling to ruin amid rain and sheep, with only "A few cathedrals" kept "chronically on show" (lines 22–24). The poem ends as he tries to foresee "who / Will be the last, the very last," to seek a church "for what it was," the final representative of beliefs wedded to practices within "the special shell" created to house them (lines 38–40, 52). Are book-filled libraries, like Larkin's churches, falling out of use? At Alderman Library at Virginia, the shelves of books were once literally holding up the structure of the building, which is now being demolished and rebuilt along more modern lines. What the individual places of those books will be after the rebuilding is uncertain, that uncertainty a part of the troubled future of the print record: *habent sua fata libelli*. Now is the time to speak for those books. Looking backward, I think of the many nineteenth-century volumes on the shelves, with their momently audible voices and their rich layers of evidentiary data, and I imagine future scholars who might one day find themselves, like Larkin with his churches, tending and attending to them as patrons and scholars. And with that, with the books before them, in what Wallace Stevens might have called the holy hush of ancient sacrifice, they may pursue the work of the humanities. In the modern university, the book-filled library can never be obsolete, "since," as Larkin concludes,

> someone will forever be surprising
> A hunger in himself to be more serious,
> And gravitating with it to this ground,
> Which, he once heard, was proper to grow wise in,
> If only that so many dead lie round. (lines 59–63)

Envoi

A final word: when my daughter turned six, I gave her a copy of A. A. Milne's *Now We Are Six*, in which she had zero interest, like any reasonable twenty-first-century child of that age. I had inscribed it with a fatherly message and the date, telling her how proud I was of her, how much she had grown, things like that. Before she went to sleep on the night of her birthday, I read Milne's poem to her—*I think I'll be six now, for ever and ever*—along with what I had written. She was only half-awake and had drifted off before I finished. But someday when she is older, she may find the book again and see the message-in-a-bottle I sent to her. And maybe it will, in its own way, testify "before who knows what tribunal of history"[1] to the fact that, as I wrote on the flyleaf, she was always on my mind. Go, little book.

Notes

Introduction

1. Michel Foucault, "Lives of Infamous Men," in *Power*, ed. James D. Faubion, trans. Robert Hurley (New York: New Press, 2001), 157.

2. Catherine Gallagher and Stephen Greenblatt, *Practicing New Historicism* (Chicago: University of Chicago Press, 2001), 70–71.

3. Alan Liu, "The Power of Formalism: The New Historicism," *ELH* 56, no. 4 (Winter 1989): 721.

4. Percy Bysshe Shelley, "Ozymandias," in *Shelley's Poetry and Prose*, ed. Donald Reiman and Neil Fraistat (New York: W. W. Norton), 109–10; Walter Benjamin, "Theses on the Philosophy of History," in *Illuminations: Essays and Reflections,* ed. Hannah Arendt, trans. Harry Zohn (New York. Schocken, 1969), 257.

5. Most of the primary-source evidence gathered for this project emerged from the Book Traces project (http://booktraces.org and http://booktraces.library.virginia.edu), a NINES (Networked Infrastructure for Nineteenth-century Electronic Scholarship) initiative funded by the University of Virginia, and was discovered in books on library shelves at many institutions, thanks to the efforts of students, librarians, faculty, and volunteers, many of whom are named in the acknowledgments section of this book.

6. This book took its origins from the Book Traces project and was strengthened by a 2015–17 Hidden Collections grant from the Council on Library and Information Resources. A white paper on that aspect of the project, focused on the University of Virginia collections, can be found here: https://booktraces.library.virginia.edu/white-paper/. Mary J. Morrogh's MA thesis on the Book Traces project, "Poetry and the Evidence of Nineteenth-Century Reading" (University of Virginia, 2017), is also an informative predicate to my work.

7. Alphonso Alva Hopkins, *Geraldine: A Souvenir of the St. Lawrence* (Boston: James R. Osgood, 1881), Esther Annie Brown's copy, Arthur Y. Ford donation, University of Louisville Library, PS 1999 .H415G3 1881, barcode U005 00495339 4.

8. Arthur Younger Ford (1861–1926) was a journalist and banker who served as the seventh president of the University of Louisville from 1914 to 1926. See *The Kentucky Encyclopedia,* ed. John E. Kleber (Lexington: University Press of Kentucky, 1992), 341.

9. For historical background on book clubs of this era, which might have given rise to the kind of group reading practiced by Brown and her friends, see Simon Eliot, "Bookselling by the Backdoor: Circulating Libraries, Booksellers and Book Clubs, 1870–1906," in *A Genius for Letters: Bookselling from the Sixteenth to the Twentieth Century*, ed. M. Harris and R. Myers (New Castle, DE: Oak Knoll, 1995), 145–66.

10. One reader notes the similarity of a passage to Meredith's blockbuster: "Does not this remind you of Lucile—'We may live &c.'" (131; *Lucile*, II.24); another quotes the opening

four lines of Thomas Moore's "Oh! 'Tis sweet to think" after lines in *Geraldine* that are reminiscent of that poem (185).

11. On marginalia as interactivity, see "Marking" and other chapters in the Multigraph Collective's *Interacting with Print: Elements of Reading in the Era of Print Saturation* (Chicago: University of Chicago Press, 2018). Deborah Lupton's *The Quantified Self: Social Media and the Accounting of Everyday Life* (Cambridge, UK: Polity, 2016) offers a technologically updated account of how identity develops via media interactions of a similar kind.

12. The formulation linking poetry to an "operating system" of a life is Jonathan Mulrooney's.

13. Kathryn M. Rudy, *Postcards on Parchment: The Social Lives of Medieval Books* (New Haven, CT: Yale University Press, 2015); William H. Sherman, *Used Books: Marking Readers in Renaissance England* (Philadelphia: University of Pennsylvania Press, 2007); Stephen Orgel, *The Reader in the Book: A Study of Spaces and Traces* (Oxford: Oxford University Press, 2018); Leah Knight, Micheline White, and Elizabeth Sauer, eds., *Women's Bookscapes in Early Modern Britain: Reading, Ownership, Circulation* (Ann Arbor: University of Michigan Press, 2018); and Abigail Williams, *The Social Life of Books: Reading Together in the Eighteenth-Century Home* (New Haven, CT: Yale University Press, 2017). Williams writes, "A history of sociable reading puts books back into lives and homes, enabling us to see literature in the round. . . . We can see the way readers' hopes, choices, constraints, and concerns form part of the history of meanings of the book we hold before us three centuries later" (3). Near the headwaters of this critical trend is Anthony Grafton, "Is the History of Reading a Marginal Enterprise? Guillaume Budé and His Books," *Papers of the Bibliographical Society of America* 91, no. 2 (1997): 139–57. See also Andrew Taylor, *Textual Situations: Three Medieval Manuscripts and Their Readers* (Philadelphia: University of Pennsylvania Press, 2002); Heidi Brayman Hackel, *Reading Material in Early Modern England: Print, Gender, and Literacy* (Cambridge: Cambridge University Press, 2009); Jennifer Andersen and Elizabeth Sauer, eds., *Books and Readers in Early Modern England: Material Studies* (Philadelphia: University of Pennsylvania Press, 2001); Sylvia Brown and John Considine, *Marginated: Seventeenth-Century Printed Books and the Traces of Their Readers* (Edmonton: University of Alberta Press, 2010); Robin Myers, Michael Harris, and Giles Mandelbrote, eds., *Owners, Annotators, and the Signs of Reading* (New Castle, DE / London: Oak Knoll / British Library, 2005); Barbara M. Benedict et al., *Annotation in Eighteenth-Century Poetry*, ed. Michael Edson (Bethlehem, PA: Lehigh University Press, 2017); and Seth Lerer, "Devotion and Defacement: Reading Children's Marginalia," *Representations* 118, no. 1 (2012): 126–53.

14. Heather Jackson, *Romantic Readers: The Evidence of Marginalia* (New Haven, CT: Yale University Press, 2005), 300. See also Jackson's groundbreaking study *Marginalia: Readers Writing in Books* (New Haven, CT: Yale University Press, 2001).

15. For work along these lines, see Lisa Spiro, "Reading with a Tender Rapture: 'Reveries of a Bachelor' and the Rhetoric of Detached Intimacy," *Book History* 6 (2003): 57–93; and Mats Dahlström, "A Book of One's Own: Examples of Library Book Marginalia," in *The History of Reading*, vol. 3, *Methods, Strategies, Tactics*, ed. Rosalind Crone and Shafquat Toweed (New York: Palgrave Macmillan, 2011), 115–31.

16. Richard Daniel Altick's *The English Common Reader: A Social History of the Mass Reading Public, 1800–1900* (Chicago: University of Chicago Press, 1957) is the foundational text on middle-class reading in the nineteenth century. Also important are James Raven, *The Business of Books: Booksellers and the English Book Trade 1450–1850* (New Haven, CT: Yale University Press, 2007); and David Vincent, *Literacy and Popular Culture: England 1750–1914* (Cambridge: Cambridge University Press, 1993). For work that is more recent, see Michael C. Cohen, *The Social Lives of Poems in Nineteenth-Century America* (Philadelphia: University of Pennsylvania Press, 2015); Ina Ferris and Paul Keen, eds., *Bookish Histories: Books, Lit-*

erature and Commercial Modernity 1700–1850 (New York: Palgrave Macmillan, 2009); David McKitterick, ed., *The Cambridge History of the Book in Britain*, vol. 6, *1830–1913* (Cambridge: Cambridge University Press, 2009); William St. Clair, *The Reading Nation in the Romantic Period* (Cambridge: Cambridge University Press, 2004); and Alexis Weedon, *Victorian Publishing: The Economics of Book Production for a Mass Market, 1836–1916* (Aldershot, UK: Ashgate, 2003).

17. Sources for the history of nineteenth-century papermaking include Donald Cuthbert Coleman, *The British Paper Industry, 1495–1860: A Study in Industrial Growth* (Oxford: Clarendon Press, 1958); Richard Leslie Hills, *Papermaking in Britain, 1488–1988: A Short History* (London: Athlone Press, 1988); Dard Hunter, *Papermaking: The History and Technique of an Ancient Craft* (New York: Dover Publications, 2011); and Lyman Horace Weeks, *A History of Paper-Manufacturing in the United States, 1690–1916* (New York: Lockwood Trade Journal Company, 1916). In *Double Fold: Libraries and the Assault on Paper* (New York: Random House, 2001), Nicholson Baker offers a thorough survey and sharp critique of library preservation policies regarding items with brittle paper, especially nineteenth-century newspapers.

18. A recent exception is Tom Mole's *What the Victorians Made of Romanticism: Material Artifacts, Cultural Practices, and Reception History* (Princeton: Princeton University Press, 2017). Mole moves beyond the "punctual historicism" of first and early editions and their readers to pay attention to things frequently dismissed as belated and irrelevant, like reprints of Romantic poems in Victorian-era anthologies.

19. On the rise of the modern university and its relation to information culture, see Chad Wellmon, *Organizing Enlightenment: Information Overload and the Invention of the Modern Research University* (Baltimore: Johns Hopkins University Press, 2016).

20. Leah Price, *How to Do Things with Books in Victorian Britain* (Princeton: Princeton University Press, 2012); Andrew Piper, *Dreaming in Books: The Making of the Bibliographic Imagination in the Romantic Age* (Chicago: University of Chicago Press, 2013).

21. On various aspects of books as objects in process and in time, see Alexandra Gillespie and Deidre Lynch, eds., *The Unfinished Book* (Oxford: Oxford University Press, 2020).

22. The annotator of this book was Miriam Adelaide Trowbridge Osborn (1840–91); see Mark R. Zwerger et al., *The Osborn* (Charleston, SC: Arcadia Publishing, 2008), 7–9. Their teacher was Heloise Chegary (1797–1889), who ran a famous school for girls on Madison Avenue in New York City; Constance Fenimore Woolson graduated in 1858 and was a classmate of Miriam's and Ruth Whitehead's. For a reminiscence of Madame Chegary's school, see Emma Benedict Knapp and Shepherd Knapp, *Hic Habitat Felicitas: A Volume of Recollections and Letters* (Boston: W. B. Clarke, 1910), 12–14. For more on the Trowbridge family and their books, see James Rathjen's blog post, https://booktraces.library.virginia.edu/book-find-the-poets-are-human/.

23. George Eliot, *The Mill on the Floss*, ed. Oliver Lovesey (Peterborough, ON: Broadview Press, 2007), 309, quoted in Price, *How to Do Things with Books*, 229.

24. Algernon Charles Swinburne, "Ave atque Vale," in *The Poems of Algernon Charles Swinburne*, 6 vols. (London: Chatto & Windus, 1904), 3:54.

25. Walt Whitman, "So Long!," in *Leaves of Grass* (Boston: Thayer and Eldridge, 1860), 455.

26. Gillian Silverman, *Bodies and Books: Reading and the Fantasy of Communion in Nineteenth-Century America* (Philadelphia: University of Pennsylvania Press, 2012).

27. Stephen Greenblatt, *Shakespearean Negotiations: The Circulation of Social Energy in Renaissance England* (Berkeley: University of California Press, 1988), 1.

28. Alan Liu, "Local Transcendence: Cultural Criticism, Postmodernism, and the Romanticism of Detail," *Representations* 32, no. 1 (1990): 91.

29. W. K. Wimsatt, *The Verbal Icon: Studies in the Meaning of Poetry* (Lexington: University Press of Kentucky, 1954), 21–39.

30. See Ted Underwood, "A Genealogy of Distant Reading," *Digital Humanities Quarterly* 11, no. 2 (2017), http://www.digitalhumanities.org/dhq/vol/11/2/000317/000317.html. Recent examples of the power of distant reading and computational text analysis, and of the limits of these methods in accounting for publication and reception history, include Daniel Shore, *Cyberformalism: Histories of Linguistic Forms in the Digital Archive* (Baltimore: Johns Hopkins University Press, 2018); and Andrew Piper, *Enumerations: Data and Literary Study* (Chicago: University of Chicago Press, 2018). Katherine Bode calls for computational analytics to pay more attention to the details of publication and circulation in *A World of Fiction: Digital Collections and the Future of Literary History* (Ann Arbor: University of Michigan Press, 2018).

31. See Mary Louise Kete's groundbreaking *Sentimental Collaborations: Mourning and Middle-Class Identity in Nineteenth-Century America* (Durham, NC: Duke University Press, 2000); and Faye Halpern, *Sentimental Readers: The Rise, Fall, and Revival of a Disparaged Rhetoric* (Iowa City: University of Iowa Press, 2013). In *Dickinson's Misery: A Theory of Lyric Reading* (Princeton: Princeton University Press, 2005), Virginia Jackson writes, "None of the influential treatments of sentimentalism and gender in nineteenth-century culture has much to say about poetry" (270). For a more recent account, see Wendy Dasler Johnson, *Antebellum American Women's Poetry: A Rhetoric of Sentiment* (Carbondale: Southern Illinois University Press, 2016).

32. Robyn R. Warhol, *Having a Good Cry: Effeminate Feelings and Pop-Culture Forms* (Columbus: Ohio State University Press, 2003), 33.

33. James Chandler, *An Archaeology of Sympathy: The Sentimental Mode in Literature and Cinema* (Chicago: University of Chicago Press, 2013).

34. Rita Felski, *The Uses of Literature* (Oxford: Wiley-Blackwell, 2008), 20. Felski believes that, overcommitted to the idea of the decentered or illusory subject (the fables of Lacan and Althusser), we have been embarrassed to consider ourselves as such, as "embodied and embedded beings" capable of recognitions that might aid our self-formation within the discursive webs we inhabit (31).

35. Pierre Nora, "Between Memory and History: Les Lieux de Mémoire," *Representations* 26, no. 1 (1989): 8.

36. See Patricia Crain, *Reading Children: Literacy, Property, and the Dilemmas of Childhood in Nineteenth-Century America* (Philadelphia: University of Pennsylvania Press, 2016): "the affective expressiveness of these artifacts has been largely sidelined as somewhat infra dig for literary historical scholarship, belonging instead to the book-fetish shelf in the belle lettres case" (111). For a critical experiment in confronting such affect, see Brent Hayes Edwards, "The Taste of the Archive," *Callaloo* 35, no. 4 (Fall 2012): 944–72. I take the metaphor of the "constellation" in relation to the anachronic or heterochronic nature of books from Jacques Khalip and Forest Pyle, eds., *Constellations of a Contemporary Romanticism* (New York: Fordham University Press, 2016).

37. Michael C. Cohen, "Reading the Nineteenth Century," *American Literary History* 26, no. 2 (Summer 2014): 408.

38. Leah Price, "Reading: The State of the Discipline," *Book History* 7 (2004): 312–13.

39. Book artists who have engaged with the creative possibilities of marginalia and marks found in library books include Amelia Bird, *Walden Marginalia; or, The Contents of a Dozen Shanties* (Kingston, NY: Women's Studio Workshop, 2012); Mariana Castillo Deball, *Interlude: The Reader's Traces* (Maastricht: Jan van Eyck Academie, 2005); and Kerry Mansfield, *Expired* (San Francisco: Modernbook Editions, 2017).

40. Lisa Gitelman, *Paper Knowledge: Towards a Media History of Documents* (Durham, NC: Duke University Press, 2014), 18.

41. Theodore M. Porter, *Trust in Numbers* (Princeton: Princeton University Press, 1996), ix. Relevant here is Ted Underwood, "Why Literary Time Is Measured in Minutes," *ELH* 85, no. 2 (June 6, 2018): "The timeline and the anecdote are not just compatible, but complementary ways of thinking about the past" (363).

42. John Plotz, review of *Practicing New Historicism*, *Modern Language Quarterly* 62, no. 3 (September 2001): 286.

43. Ralph Waldo Emerson, "Self-Reliance," in *The Essential Writings of Ralph Waldo Emerson* (New York: Modern Library, 2000), 132.

44. Nicholas Dames, "Seventies Throwback Fiction," *N+1* (December 10, 2014), https://nplusonemag.com/issue-21/reviews/seventies-throwback-fiction/.

45. Svetlana Boym, *The Future of Nostalgia* (New York: Basic Books, 2002), 49–50.

46. On this theme, see my article "Ruins of Paper: Dickens and the Necropolitan Library," *Romanticism and Victorianism on the Net* 47 (August 2007), https://doi.org/10.7202/016700ar.

47. Christina Lupton, *Reading and the Making of Time in the Eighteenth Century* (Baltimore: Johns Hopkins University Press, 2018), 8.

48. Nicholas Carr, *The Shallows: What the Internet Is Doing to Our Brains* (New York: W. W. Norton, 2011); Sven Birkerts, *The Gutenberg Elegies: The Fate of Reading in an Electronic Age* (New York: Farrar, Straus and Giroux, 2006) and *Changing the Subject: Art and Attention in the Internet Age* (Minneapolis: Graywolf Press, 2015).

49. For more on the (nonpoetic) Victorian uses of nostalgia in literature, see Anne C. Colley, *Nostalgia and Recollection in Victorian Culture* (New York: Palgrave Macmillan, 1998).

50. Natalie Houston has studied the typographic layout of nineteenth-century poems in relation to the white space of the page in her project *The Visual Page as Interface*; for an introduction to this project, see Natalie Houston and Neal Audenaert, "VisualPage: Towards Large Scale Analysis of Nineteenth-Century Print Culture," *2013 IEEE International Conference on Big Data* (October 2013): 9–16.

51. This particular copy is accessible in digital form at the *Walt Whitman Archive*, ed. Kenneth M. Price and Ed Folsom, https://whitmanarchive.org/manuscripts/marginalia/transcriptions/loc.03445.html.

52. John Higham, "The Matrix of Speculation," *Bulletin of the American Academy of Arts and Sciences* 33, no. 5 (February 1980): 9.

53. Phyllis Dain, "Scholarship, Higher Education, and Libraries in the United States: Historical Questions and Quests," in *Libraries and Scholarly Communication in the United States: The Historical Dimension*, ed. Phyllis Dain and John Y. Cole (New York: Greenwood Press, 1990), 8.

54. Hendrik Edelman and G. Marvin Tatum Jr., "The Development of Collections in American University Libraries," *College and Research Libraries* 37, no. 3 (May 1976): 222–45. Among research universities, "The scramble to develop scholarly library collections on short notice brought about an all-out effort to acquire small and large private collections of books" (224). The University of Virginia collection, for example, went from about 70,000 books in 1900 to almost 600,000 by 1950; in the same period the University of Illinois collection went from 47,000 to over 2,000,000 (242, 239).

55. As background, see David McKitterick, *The Invention of Rare Books: Private Interest and Public Memory, 1600–1840* (Cambridge: Cambridge University Press, 2018).

56. Neil Harris, "Special Collections and Academic Scholarship: A Tangled Relationship," in *Libraries and Scholarly Communication in the United States: The Historical Dimension*, ed. Phyllis Dain and John Y. Cole (New York: Greenwood Press, 1990), 67. As Sharon Gray Weiner writes, "Competitive collection-building was characteristic of academic libraries

of the late nineteenth and early twentieth centuries." Weiner, "The History of Academic Libraries in the United States: A Review of the Literature," *Library Philosophy and Practice* 7, no. 2 (Spring 2005), http://www.webpages.uidaho.edu/~mbolin/weiner.htm.

57. On book production in this era in the United States, see Scott E. Casper et al., eds., *A History of the Book in America*, vol. 3, *The Industrial Book 1840–1880* (Chapel Hill: Univeristy of North Carolina Press, 2007). Particlarly relevant for my purposes is Louise Stevenson's chapter, "Homes, Books, and Reading" (319–31).

58. In the Book Traces @ UVA survey of the stack collections, approximately 13 percent of all pre-1923 books had some marking traceable to an original owner or reader. My estimate here is a conservative one, based on assumed differences among institutions and collections.

59. For example, the Book Traces project has discovered, on the shelves of Virginia Union University, a number of books owned and inscribed by Rev. Dr. O. Clay Maxwell (1885–1973), an African American Baptist pastor and associate of Dr. Martin Luther King, Jr. More work needs to be done on the collections at historically black colleges and universities and other minority-serving institutions.

60. Admirable instances of the "new sentimentalism" in book history are Crain, *Reading Children*; Silverman, *Bodies and Books*; and Maria Zytaruk, "Caught in the Archive: Unruly Objects at the Foundling Hospital," *Studies in Romanticism* 57, no. 1 (Spring 2018): 39–65.

61. Felicia Hemans, "The Image in Lava," in *Felicia Hemans: Selected Poems, Prose and Letters*, ed. Gary Kelly (Peterborough, ON: Broadview Press, 2002), 348–50, lines 1, 7.

Chapter 1

1. On Hemans's popularity and the development of her reputation, see Susan J. Wolfson, "Felicia Hemans and the Revolving Doors of Reception," in *Romanticism and Women Poets: Opening the Doors of Reception*, ed. Harriet Kramer Linkin and Stephen Behrendt (Lexington: University Press of Kentucky, 1999), 214–41; Paula R. Feldman, "Endurance and Forgetting: What the Evidence Suggests," in Linkin and Behrendt, *Romanticism and Women Poets*, 15–21; Gary Kelly, "Introduction," in *Felicia Hemans: Selected Poems, Prose and Letters*, ed. Gary Kelly (Peterborough, ON: Broadview Press, 2002), 15–85; and Nanora Sweet and Julie Melnyk, eds., *Felicia Hemans: Reimagining Poetry in the Nineteenth Century* (New York: Palgrave Macmillan, 2001), 1–10.

2. "The Nightingale's Death-Song" begins with "Mournfully, sing mournfully, / And die away, my heart!" (333, lines 1–2) and continues later with "Mournfully, sing mournfully / The royal rose is gone" (333, lines 21–22). In "The Burial of an Emigrant's Child in the Forests," the mother Agnes laments, "My gentle son! / Th' affectionate, the gifted!" (358, lines 93–94).

3. Abbot Low Moffat, *The Pierreponts, 1802–1962: The American Forebears and the Descendants of Hezekiah Beers Pierpont and Anna Maria Constable* (Washington, DC: Privately printed, 1962), 40.

4. On this issue, see my essay "The Nineteenth-Century Archive in the Digital Age," *European Romantic Review* 23, no. 3 (June 2012): 335–41.

5. An exception is Paula R. Feldman, "Women, Literary Annuals, and the Evidence of Inscriptions," *Keats-Shelley Journal* 55 (2006): 54–62.

6. Felicia Hemans, "The Image in Lava," in Kelly, *Felicia Hemans*, 348–50, lines 1–12.

7. As Patricia Crain writes, "Old books and dead children make a perfect storm for the access of emotions" (*Reading Children: Literacy, Property, and the Dilemmas of Childhood in Nineteenth-Century America* [Philadelphia: University of Pennsylvania Press, 2016], 111).

8. Brian P. Elliott, "'Nothing Beside Remains': Empty Icons and Elegiac Ekphrasis in Felicia Hemans," *Studies in Romanticism* 51, no. 1 (2012): 26. Elliott argues that in "The Image in Lava" the monument becomes "the mold into which [Hemans's] thoughts flow and solidify into verse" via her "projected affective materials" (29–30).

9. According to Rebecca Mead in a trenchant critique, "the notion of relatability implies that the work in question serves like a selfie: a flattering confirmation of an individual's solipsism" ("The Scourge of 'Relatability,'" *New Yorker* [August 1, 2014], https://www.newyorker.com/culture/cultural-comment/scourge-relatability).

10. Jonathan Culler, *Theory of the Lyric* (Cambridge, MA: Harvard University Press, 2017), 5.

11. Mary Louise Kete, *Sentimental Collaborations: Mourning and Middle-Class Identity in Nineteenth-Century America* (Durham, NC: Duke University Press, 2000), xiv.

12. Karen Sánchez-Eppler, *Dependent States: The Child's Part in Nineteenth-Century American Culture* (Chicago: University of Chicago Press, 2005), 101–2.

13. Karen Sánchez-Eppler, "In the Archives of Childhood," in *The Children's Table: Childhood Studies and the Humanities*, ed. Anne Mae Duane (Athens: University of Georgia Press, 2013), 177.

14. Susan J. Wolfson, ed., *Felicia Hemans: Selected Poems, Letters, Reception Materials* (Princeton: Princeton University Press, 2001), xiv.

15. Steven C. Behrendt, review of *Felicia Hemans: Selected Poems, Letters, Reception Materials, Criticism* 44, no. 2 (2002): 218. Anthony Harding writes, "One embarrassing fact to be faced—embarrassing at least for those feminists who consider the recuperation of previously ignored or marginalized texts to be an important part of the feminist project—is that Hemans, while marginal to the Romantic canon of today, was not exactly marginal in her time. Hemans was destined to be read as not a margin but a center, the embodiment of that hearth and home. . . . And yet, of course, this center was not a center of power" ("Felicia Hemans and the Effacement of Woman," in *Romantic Women Writers: Voices and Countervoices*, ed. Paula R. Feldman and Theresa M. Kelley [Hanover, NH: University Press of New England, 1995], 147–48). Kathleen Lundeen comments along similar lines: "The difficulty of reconciling the philosophical strength of her poems with their sentimental trappings tempts one to ask, What's a smart poet like her doing in a genre like this?" ("'When Life Becomes Art'—on Hemans's 'Image in Lava,'" *Romanticism on the Net*, nos. 29–30 [2003], https://doi.org/10.7202/007716ar).

16. Antidomestic readings of Hemans include Tricia Lootens, "Hemans and Home: Victorianism, Feminine 'Internal Enemies,' and the Domestication of National Identity," *PMLA* 109, no. 2 (1994): 238–53; Sharifah Osman, "'Mightier Than Death, Untamable by Fate': Felicia Hemans's Byronic Heroines and the Sorority of the Domestic Affections," *Romanticism on the Net: An Electronic Journal Devoted to Romantic Studies* 43 (August 2006), https://doi.org/10.7202/013590ar; and Susan J. Wolfson, "'Something Must Be Done': Shelley, Hemans, and the Flash of Revolutionary Female Violence," in *Fellow Romantics: Male and Female British Writers, 1790–1835*, ed. Beth Lau (Surrey, UK: Ashgate, 2009), 199–222.

17. David E. Latané, "Who Counts? Popularity, Modern Recovery, and the Early Nineteenth-Century Woman Poet," in *Teaching British Women Writers 1750–1900*, ed. Jeanne Moskal and Shannon R. Wooden (New York: Peter Lang, 2005), 214.

18. As Marlon B. Ross writes, "Bringing her readers to tears is not simply a way of sensitizing them individually; it is more importantly a way of transforming them collectively into a community of shared desire" (*The Contours of Masculine Desire: Romanticism and the Rise of Women's Poetry* [Oxford: Oxford University Press, 1990], 292). For more on this aspect of Hemans's work, see my essay "Hemans by the Book," *European Romantic Review* 22, no. 3 (2011): 373–80.

19. Philadelphia editions appeared in 1836–37, 1839, 1841–49, 1851–52, 1854–57, 1859–60, and 1867. The book expanded from 444 pages (1836) to 559 pages (1839 and after). Grigg & Elliot was succeeded by Lippincott, Grambo, and Co. as the publisher of this edition around 1851.

20. *The Poetical Works of Mrs. Felicia Hemans* (Philadelphia: Grigg & Elliot, 1839), Charlotte M. Cocke's copy, Albert and Shirley Small Special Collections Library, University of Virginia, PR 4780 .A1 1839, barcode 030434848.

21. Alfred Tennyson, "Locksley Hall," in *The Poems of Tennyson*, ed. Christopher B. Ricks (London: Longmans, 1969), 697, line 155.

22. Information on the Gordons can be found in their family papers held by the Albert and Shirley Small Special Collections Library at the University of Virginia, Papers of the Gordon Family 1744–1905, MSS 9553. This collection includes a nine-volume diary and a family genealogy written by William Gordon (Charlotte's husband), as well as a photograph of William Fitzhugh Gordon taken in 1872. The elder Gordon's laconic diary entry for Saturday, January 10, 1880, reads in part, "In evening heard of the death of our dear son William, near Fort Concho" in western Texas (vol. 8, p. 264).

23. Here I follow Ross: "Upon finishing one of Hemans's romances—or lyrics, for that matter—the reader discovers the deepness and broadness of her own heart in the guise of another's suffering or joy (though usually it is suffering)" (*Contours of Masculine Desire*, 275).

24. *The Poetical Works of Mrs. Felicia Hemans* (Philadelphia: Grigg & Elliot, 1836), iv.

25. Rachel Ablow, ed., "Introduction," in *The Feeling of Reading: Affective Experience and Victorian Literature* (Ann Arbor: University of Michigan Press, 2010), 2. See also Mary Favret, "The Pathos of Reading," *PMLA* 130, no. 5 (October 2015): 1318–31.

26. Charles Lamb, "Detached Thoughts on Books and Reading," *London Magazine* 6 (July 1822): 33.

27. Jerome McGann, *The Poetics of Sensibility: A Revolution in Literary Style* (Oxford: Oxford University Press, 1998), 137; Jerome McGann, "Private Enigmas and Critical Functions, with Particular Reference to the Writing of Charles Bernstein," *New Literary History* 22, no. 2 (1991): 461.

28. Indeed, such a miscellaneous arrangement seems to have confused the publishers themselves, who insert the poem "The Spells of Home" twice, on pages 316 and 429 in editions from 1839 onward.

29. For more on Hemans and the male Romantics, see Michael O'Neill, "A Deeper and Richer Music: Felicia Hemans in Dialogue with Wordsworth, Byron, and Shelley," *Charles Lamb Bulletin* 145 (2009): 3–12.

30. Thanks to Andrew Elfenbein and Dennis Denisoff for helping me decipher this annotation.

31. Moffat, *Pierreponts*, 45–46; Henry Evelyn Pierrepont, *Historical Sketch of the Fulton Ferry, and Its Associated Ferries* (Brooklyn: Eagle Job and Book Printing Department, 1879), 57–60.

32. She makes a similar note on Mary's death in the other family Bible that originally belonged to her husband: "Mary Montague Minor—died Saturday Oct 4th 1862 5 ½ p.m.—at 100 Willow St. Brooklyn of Diptheria—aged seven years, five months & 4 days" (*The Illuminated Bible* [New York: Harper and Brothers, 1846], Papers of the Pierrepont and Minor Families, 7286-c, Box 1, Albert and Shirley Small Special Collections Library, University of Virginia).

33. Before vaccines and antibiotics, diphtheria was a common killer. Queen Victoria's daughter, Princess Alice, lost a four-year-old child, Marie, to the disease in 1878 and then died of it herself the following month.

34. On the verso of this page, Pierrepont has written, "On Sunday March 23, 1879 / of pneumonia, my / beloved husband / James M. Minor, in / his 63d year," this time inking a

black border of emphasis all the way around it. And just after that, in a different hand, we read, "On May 4 1879 / of pneumonia my / dear mother Ellen I. / Minor in her 50th / year—C. L. Minor / 'Blessed are the dead which / die in the Lord.'" She lived only six weeks longer than her husband, both carried off by pneumonia, and, as Charles L. Minor (her youngest child, who was to become the recordkeeper for the family, and whose books were eventually donated to the University of Virginia, where he had been a student) writes in the Bible, "aided by a broken heart over the loss of her devotedly loved husband."

35. One might also, following George Santayana, dismiss such poetry as merely "genteel," associating it with the nineteenth century's "complacency and intellectual vapidity," but that view is changing; see Elizabeth Renker, "The 'Genteel Tradition' and Its Discontents," in *The Cambridge History of American Poetry*, ed. Alfred Bendixen and Stephen Burt (Cambridge: Cambridge University Press, 2014), 403. Renker concludes, "The genteel tradition is an ideology that has been mistaken for a history. The era was not a barren one, awaiting later modernist redemption. An imprecise generalization even when Santayana coined the term, its repeated invocation has served to obscure the complexity of actual poetic practices during the decades in question" (421).

36. Christina Lupton, *Reading and the Making of Time in the Eighteenth Century* (Baltimore: Johns Hopkins University Press, 2018), 25.

37. Herbert F. Tucker, "House Arrest: The Domestication of English Poetry in the 1820s," *New Literary History* 25, no. 3 (1994): 524.

38. Walter Pater, *The Renaissance: Studies in Art and Poetry, the 1893 Text*, ed. Donald L. Hill (Berkeley: University of California Press, 1980), 236.

Chapter 2

1. Quoted in Hermione Lee, *Virginia Woolf* (London: Vintage, 1999), 406.

2. See Theresa M. Kelley, *Clandestine Marriage: Botany and Romantic Culture* (Baltimore: Johns Hopkins University Press, 2012), on the cultural significance of botany and the popularity of amateur botanizing during the Romantic era.

3. As Katherine D. Harris writes, "With flowers referenced in British literary annual titles, . . . poetry that meditates on flowers, and engravings that reproduce bouquets of flowers, . . . the literary annual represents a metaphorical bouquet of poetry and prose—an 'anthology' of sorts, which is traditionally defined as 'a collection of flowers of verse'" (*Forget Me Not: The Rise of the British Literary Annual, 1823-1835* [Athens: Ohio University Press, 2015], 105).

4. Dahlia Porter, "Specimen Poetics: Botany, Reanimation, and the Romantic Collection," *Representations* 139, no. 1 (Summer 2017): 61, 89n4.

5. See Beverly Seaton, "Miscellaneous Flower Books: A Bibliography," in *The Language of Flowers: A History* (Charlottesville: University of Virginia Press, 2012), 211–17; and Fabienne Moine, *Women Poets in the Victorian Era: Cultural Practices and Nature Poetry* (New York: Routledge, 2016), 63. Many of these floral poetry volumes went through multiple editions or appeared under altered titles after they were published.

6. Matthias Koops, *Historical Account of the Substances Which Have Been Used to Describe Events and to Convey Ideas from the Earliest Date to the Invention of Paper*, 2nd ed. (London: Jacques and Co., 1801). Joshua Calhoun has written about the presence of flax and other cheapening materials in Renaissance England, in "The Word Made Flax: Cheap Bibles, Textual Corruption, and the Poetics of Paper," *PMLA* 126, no. 2 (March 2011): 327–44. On the material composition of nineteenth-century paper, see also Jonathan Senchyne, "Vibrant Material Textuality: New Materialism, Book History, and the Archive in Paper,"

Studies in Romanticism 57, no. 1 (Spring 2018): 67–85. Thora Brylowe is at work on a book entitled "Impressions and Folds: The Ecology of Romantic-Era Paper," which will discuss paper's organic prehistory.

7. Donald Cuthbert Coleman, *The British Paper Industry, 1495–1860: A Study in Industrial Growth* (Oxford: Clarendon Press, 1958), 344: "The decades of the 1860s and 1880s are a true dividing line in the history of paper-making. They mark the creation of what is in some senses, though only in some senses, a new industry. After eighteen centuries of existence as a manufacture based on rags and nearly four hundred years of existence in Britain, it found a major new raw material. It has continued to use the old in relatively small quantities; but it is wood pulp that has made possible the many and diverse guises in which paper appears in modern life and which has formed the rationale of the modern international pulp and paper industry."

8. On the relationship between reading and trees, see Andrew Piper's chapter, "Among the Trees," in *Book Was There: Reading in Electronic Times* (Chicago: University of Chicago Press, 2013), 109–30.

9. On contemporary practices of botanical insertion, see Alison Syme, "Pressed Flowers: Burne-Jones, *The Romaunt of the Rose*, and the Kelmscott Chaucer," *Journal of Pre-Raphaelite Studies* 28 (Fall 2019): 42–70; and Cindy Dickinson, "Creating a World of Books, Friends, and Flowers: Gift Books and Inscriptions, 1825–60," *Winterthur Portfolio* 31, no. 1 (Spring 1996): 53–66.

10. William Wordsworth, "I wandered lonely as a cloud," in *Wordsworth's Poetry and Prose*, ed. Nicholas Halmi (New York: W. W. Norton, 2013), lines 21–22; Alfred, Lord Tennyson, "Flower in the crannied wall," in *Tennyson: A Selected Edition*, ed. Christopher Ricks, rev. ed. (London: Routledge, 2007), 349.

11. *The Language and Poetry of Flowers* (London: George Routledge and Sons, 1860), 21, 31.

12. This figuration of poems as flowers also informs the lyric that concludes A. E. Housman's *A Shropshire Lad* (1896): "I hoed and trenched and weeded."

13. Maria Zytaruk has shown how Victorian printed books of botany with published specimen plants as natural illustrations "adhere to and resist the logic of both the specimen and the souvenir" ("Preserved in Print: Victorian Books with Mounted Natural History Specimens," *Victorian Studies* 60, no. 2 ([Winter 2018]: 187). These were too unscientific for true specimens, too mass-produced for the logic of the personal souvenir. As Susan Stewart has written in her work on the souvenir, "Pressed flowers under glass speak to the significance of their owner in nature and not to themselves in nature. They are a sample of a larger and more sublime nature . . . differentiated by human experience, by human history" (*On Longing: Narratives of the Miniature, the Gigantic, the Souvenir, the Collection* [Durham, NC: Duke University Press, 1993], 151).

14. Stewart, *On Longing*, xii.

15. "The Dead Flower," *Chambers's Journal of Popular Literature, Science, and Art*, no. 149 (November 3, 1866): 704.

16. Letitia E. Landon, "The Basque Girl and Henri Quatre," *Literary Gazette and Journal of the Belle Lettres* (October 12, 1822): 648–49, lines 48–53.

17. Julia Ward Howe, "What I Said to the Dying Rose, and What She Said to Me," in *Passion Flowers* (Boston: Ticknor, Reed, and Fields, 1854), 179. On the rhetoric and reception of Howe's *Passion Flowers*, see Wendy Dasler Johnson, *Antebellum American Women's Poetry: A Rhetoric of Sentiment* (Carbondale: Southern Illinois University Press, 2016). For more on nineteenth-century sentimental rhetoric (focusing on novels), see Faye Halpern, *Sentimental Readers: The Rise, Fall, and Revival of a Disparaged Rhetoric* (Iowa City: University of Iowa Press, 2013); and Mary Loeffelholz, *From School to Salon: Reading Nineteenth-Century*

American Women's Poetry (Princeton: Princeton University Press, 2004). See also Cheryl Walker, *The Nightingale's Burden: Women Poets and American Culture Before 1900* (Bloomington: Indiana University Press, 1983).

18. As Moine writes, "The Victorian cult of domesticity and femininity was also often reflected in poems about dried flowers pressed between the pages of a book. . . . For Victorian women poets, dried flowers or herbariums represented all-encompassing symbols of womanhood since they tapped into images of beauty and frailty as well as those of femininity and death" (58).

19. Mary A. Coffin, "Pressed Flowers and Their Associations," *Ladies' Companion: A Monthly Magazine Devoted to Literature and the Fine Arts* (August 1841): 203. I am indebted to Jackie Morrogh, whose thesis "Poetry and the Evidence of Nineteenth-Century Reading" contains this reference and a discussion of Coffin.

20. Virginia Jackson, *Dickinson's Misery: A Theory of Lyric Reading* (Princeton: Princeton University Press, 2005), 11, 12.

21. Emily Dickinson, "Whose cheek is this?," in *The Poems of Emily Dickinson*, Variorum ed., 3 vols. (Cambridge, MA: Belknap Press of Harvard University Press, 1999), F48.

22. Letitia Landon, "The Lost Pleiad," in *"The Venetian Bracelet," "The Lost Pleiad," "A History of the Lyre" and Other Poems* (London: Longman, Rees, Orme, Brown, and Green, 1829), 67.

23. "Aster hybridus nanus," *Garden* 40 (December 26, 1891): 580.

24. Letitia E. Landon, "The Michaelmas Daisy," *Literary Gazette* (March 18, 1820): 190.

25. Gerard Manley Hopkins, "Spring and Fall: To a Young Child," in *Gerard Manley Hopkins: The Major Works*, ed. Catherine Phillips (Oxford: Oxford University Press, 2009), 152.

26. W. E. B. Du Bois, *The Souls of Black Folk*, ed. Brent Hayes Edwards (Oxford: Oxford University Press, 2009), 178.

27. Henry Wadsworth Longfellow, *The Waif: A Collection of Poems* (Cambridge, MA: J. Owen, 1845). Also in *The Waif* is the poem by Jones Very, "Lines to a Withered Leaf Seen upon a Poet's Table," which refers to the leaf as "Autumn's brown and withered scroll." The poet claims that "Though no human pen has traced / On that leaf its learned lore," "Echoes from yon tablet sere:—/ Distant music of the past / Steals upon the poet's ear" (139–40).

28. Patricia Crain observes a similar phenomenon in an 1872 botany book: the pressed flowers "are long gone but have left their photograph-like shadows," which "seem to emanate from the book, adding fullness or presence to the abstraction of words" (*Reading Children: Literacy, Property, and the Dilemmas of Childhood in Nineteenth-Century America* [Philadelphia: University of Pennsylvania Press, 2016], 135–36).

29. Compare Felicia Hemans's poem "The Wanderer and the Night-Flowers" (from *National Lyrics and Songs for Music*, 1834), in which the flowers speak: "And love us as emblems, night's dewy flowers, / Of hopes unto sorrow given, / That spring through the gloom of darkest hours, / Looking alone to Heaven!" (lines 29–32). Reprinted in *The Poetical Works of Mrs. Felicia Hemans* (Philadelphia: Grigg & Elliot, 1843), 393.

30. "Charles Deering," *Wikipedia* (June 15, 2018), https://en.wikipedia.org/wiki/Charles_Deering. I believe the gift inscription refers to Mary Ellen Burleigh Deering (1831–1924), a cousin or aunt married to Robert Deering, part of the extended family in Maine.

31. The son was Charles William Case Deering (1876–1924). See Walter Dill Scott and Robert B. Harshe, *Charles Deering, 1852–1927: An Appreciation* (Boston: Privately printed, 1929).

32. For more on this particular book, see Jamie Rathjen, "Book Find: The Partridges Live On | Book Traces @ UVA," Book Traces, https://booktraces.library.virginia.edu/book-find-the-partridges-live-on/.

33. Lord Byron, *Don Juan*, vol. 5 of *The Complete Poetical Works*, ed. Jerome J. McGann, 7 vols. (Oxford: Clarendon Press, 1980–93), canto 1, line 745.

34. After Wordsworth, this flower (the violet-pansy) became associated with the loss of childhood pleasures, as Romanticism evolved into the sentimental verse of the 1820s and later. See, for example, Letitia Elizabeth Landon, "The Violet," originally published in *The Literary Souvenir* for 1831 and reprinted in (among other places) *Flora and Thalia, or Gems of Flowers and Poetry: Being an Alphabetical Arrangement of Flowers, with Appropriate Poetical Illustrations, Embellished with Coloured Plates* (Philadelphia: Carey, Lea, and Blanchard, 1836), 124; and Alfred A. Phillips, ed., *The Bouquet for 1847* (New York: Nafis & Cornish, 1847), 104: "Because its fragrant leaves are those / I loved in childhood's hour" (lines 3–4). Compare the anonymous "Heartsease," *London Magazine* 10 (September 1824): 308: "I used to love thee, simple flow'r / To love thee dearly when a boy, / For thou did'st seem, in childhood's hour, / The smiling type of childhood's joy."

35. William Wordsworth, *Ode on Immortality, and Lines on Tintern Abbey* (London: Cassell and Company, 1885).

36. For another example, see Tennyson's *The Song of the Brook*, illus. William J. Mozart (Troy, NY: Nims and Knight, 1886).

37. Deidre Shauna Lynch describes a similar trompe l'oeil effect in an 1815 scrapbook album in "Paper Slips: Album, Archiving, Accident," *Studies in Romanticism* 57, no. 1 (Spring 2018): 99–101.

38. The 1881 edition reports the following about its illustrative matter: "The full-page illustrations are designed by Miss C.A. Northam and J. Francis Murphy, and those in the text, by Edmund H. Garrett. The book is prepared and the illustrations engraved by Geo. T. Andrew."

39. Amy M. King has written about this culture of botanical metaphors for female development in *Bloom: The Botanical Vernacular in the English Novel* (Oxford: Oxford University Press, 2003). See also Seaton, *Language of Flowers*, 168–69, 178–79.

40. Eulalie, *Buds, Blossoms, and Leaves: Poems* (Cincinnati, OH: Moore, Wilstach and Keys, 1854).

41. The sequence recalls Tennyson in other ways as well. The waiting speaker of Ingelow's "Romance" is rather like Mariana in her moated grange, and the lover leaning out the window into a dark garden in Ingelow's "Love" is indebted to that most floral of popular Victorian lyrics, "Come into the Garden, Maud."

42. Thanks to Deidre Shauna Lynch and Megan O'Donnell for assistance with this particular copy, a scanned version of which can be found via HathiTrust: https://babel.hathitrust .org/cgi/pt?id=hvd.hn3jza;view=2up;seq=8.

43. "Miss Florence McKeehan . . . and Capt. Louis John Magill, of the U.S.M.C., were quietly married at the home of the bride's mother, 2116 Chestnut Street, Philadelphia, May 17. . . . A wedding breakfast, attended by members of the two families and a few intimate friends, followed" ("Service Weddings," *United States Army and Navy Journal and Gazette* [May 24, 1902]: 951).

44. "Col. Louis J. Magill, assistant adjutant and inspector of the U.S. Marine Corps, died suddenly at his home in the navy yard, Philadelphia, Pa., Feb. 20, 1921. He was out shoveling snow in the morning, apparently in the best of health. About noon he complained of indigestion and at five o'clock collapsed and died. Death was attributed to an acute heart attack. . . . Colonel Magill married Florence McKeehan. . . . She survives him, together with one son" ("Deaths," *United States Army and Navy Journal* 58, pt. 1 [February 26, 1921]: 718).

45. Bartholomew Brinkman, *Poetic Modernism in the Culture of Mass Print* (Baltimore: Johns Hopkins University Press, 2016), 15.

46. Carolyn Steedman tells of her young obsessive reading of Stevenson's collection and her liking this poem best, remarking that we are "already nostalgic for childhood whilst it

happens" (*Past Tenses: Essays on Writing, Autobiography and History* [London: Rivers Oram Press, 1992], 40). See also Patricia Crain's reading of this poem: "Stevenson . . . articulates a disconcerting, displacing condition of bookness, or in-bookness, of children" (*Reading Children*, 174–76).

47. Walter Benjamin, "On the Concept of History," trans. Edmund Jephcott, in *Walter Benjamin: Selected Writings*, vol. 4, *1938–1940*, ed. Howard Eiland and Michael W. Jennings (Cambridge, MA: Harvard University Press, 2003), 397.

Chapter 3

1. John Keats, "On First Looking into Chapman's Homer," in *Complete Poems*, ed. Jack Stillinger (Cambridge, MA: Belknap Press, 1991), 34.

2. Emily Rohrbach has located the Romantic subject at the intersection of such imaginative postures toward historical events: the anticipation of the backward look was crucial to the imagination of the self in time (*Modernity's Mist: British Romanticism and the Poetics of Anticipation* [New York: Fordham University Press, 2015]).

3. William Wordsworth, "Lines Written a Few Miles Above Tintern Abbey," in *Wordsworth's Poetry and Prose*, ed. Nicholas Halmi (New York: W. W. Norton, 2013), 65–70, lines 61 and 85–86.

4. Samuel Taylor Coleridge, "Frost at Midnight," in *Coleridge's Poetry and Prose*, ed. Nicholas Halmi et al. (New York: W. W. Norton, 2003), 120–23, line 15.

5. On various aspects of this cultural transmission, see Tom Mole, *What the Victorians Made of Romanticism: Material Artifacts, Cultural Practices, and Reception History* (Princeton: Princeton University Press, 2017).

6. I borrow the phrase "slow time" from Jonathan Sachs, who uses it to refer to "human attempts to grasp imaginatively a pace of change that cannot be seen and that leaves few if any visible traces" (*The Poetics of Decline in British Romanticism* [Cambridge: Cambridge University Press, 2018], 164). Here I am emphasizing the traces. See also Sachs, "Slow Time," *PMLA* 134, no. 2 (March 2019): 315–31.

7. Catherine Robson, *Heart Beats: Everyday Life and the Memorized Poem* (Princeton: Princeton University Press, 2015); Deidre Shauna Lynch, *Loving Literature: A Cultural History* (Chicago: University of Chicago Press, 2015); Meredith L. McGill, *American Literature and the Culture of Reprinting, 1834–1853* (Philadelphia: University of Pennsylvania Press, 2007).

8. Wordsworth, *The Prelude*, in *Wordsworth's Poetry and Prose*, Book 11, lines 258–59, 353.

9. Hardy, "Her Initials," in *Wessex Poems and Other Verses* (New York: Harper and Brothers, 1898), 21.

10. Between 1860 and 1869, Bell and Daldy published a number of books with similar layouts in their series Aldine Poets, including volumes by Spenser, Wyatt, Surrey, and Burns—all of which contain plenty of poems about love.

11. Written in 1891 and first published in *The Countess Kathleen and Various Legends and Lyrics*, ed. John T. Nettleship (London: T. F. Unwin, 1892).

12. Rohrbach, *Modernity's Mist*; Sachs, *Poetics of Decline*.

13. See Andrew Piper, *Dreaming in Books: The Making of the Bibliographic Imagination in the Romantic Age* (Chicago: University of Chicago Press, 2013), 121–52, on the complex semiotics of inscription in Romantic-era gift books and annuals, which were printed to invite readers to personalize them.

14. Kevin McLaughlin, *Paperwork: Fiction and Mass Mediacy in the Paper Age* (Philadelphia: University of Pennsylvania Press, 2011). See, in particular, "Introduction: Apparitions in Paper," 1–28.

15. Letitia Landon, "Emily," *Finden's Gallery of the Graces* (London: Charles Tilt, 1834), n.p. lines 1–4. This poem also appeared anonymously under the title "The Wandering Thought," illustrating a different engraving of a paused female reader, in *The Amulet: A Christian and Literary Rembrancer*, ed. S. C. Hall (London: Frederick Westley and A. H. Davis, 1834), 172–75. In this printing, the poem is signed "Æ," and the female reader's book is open, rather than closed, in both the engraving and the second line of the poem. It is possible that Finden attributed the poem to Landon without justification or that Landon submitted to both venues at the same time. The best critical work on Landon's complexities of this kind is that of Sarah A. Storti: see "Letitia Landon: Still a Problem," *Victorian Poetry* 57, no. 4 (Winter 2019): 533–56.

16. On these phenomena, see David Allan, *Commonplace Books and Reading in Georgian England* (Cambridge: Cambridge University Press, 2010); Michael C. Cohen, "Album Verse and the Poetics of Scribal Circulation," in *A History of Nineteenth-Century American Women's Poetry*, ed. Jennifer Putzi and Alexandra Socarides (Cambridge: Cambridge University Press, 2016), 68–86; and Deidre Shauna Lynch, "Paper Slips: Album, Archiving, Accident," *Studies in Romanticism* 57, no. 1 (Spring 2018): 87–119.

17. The poem was first collected in Taylor's *Poet's Journal* (Boston: Ticknor and Fields, 1863), 146–48, but had first appeared a few years earlier. For example, it was printed in the *Southern Literary Messenger* in August 1856 with the note that many readers "have perhaps seen it already in the newspapers" (156). It also seems to have had rather wide circulation during, and in reference to, the American Civil War.

18. "Annie Laurie," in *The Songs of Scotland, Ancient and Modern*, ed. Allan Cunningham, 4 vols. (London: John Taylor, 1825), 3:256.

19. Robert Browning, "By the Fire-Side," in *Robert Browning's Poetry*, ed. James F. Loucks and Andrew M. Stauffer (New York: W. W. Norton, 2007), 160–69, lines 6–7, 258.

20. William Wordsworth, "Resolution and Independence," in *Wordsworth's Poetry and Prose*, ed. Nicholas Halmi (New York: W. W. Norton, 2013), 397–401, lines 87–88.

21. This was most likely *Picturesque America*, a large-format, copiously illustrated book edited by William Cullen Bryant and published in 1872. He could also have seen a reproduction of the same engraving in the November 1878 issue of *Potter's American Monthly*. See William Cullen Bryant and Oliver Bell Bunce, eds., *Picturesque America; or, The Land We Live In. A Delineation by Pen and Pencil of the Mountains, Rivers, Lakes, Forests, Water-Falls, Shores, Cañons, Valleys, Cities, and Other Picturesque Features of Our Country, With Illustrations on Steel and Wood* (New York: D. Appleton, 1872), 501; and *Potter's American Monthly* 11, no. 83 (November 1878): 327.

22. Charles C. Calhoun, *Longfellow: A Rediscovered Life* (Boston: Beacon Press, 2005), 217–20.

23. "The Cross of Snow," in *Life of Henry Wadsworth Longfellow*, ed. Samuel Longfellow, vol. 2 (Boston: Ticknor and Co., 1886), 373.

24. Mary Fontaine Cosby (1833–81) was born in Louisville, Kentucky; she married Lucius Loomis Rich (born in 1830 in Missouri) in April 1859. They had two children, both of which died young; he became a Confederate colonel in 1861 and served in the 1st Missouri infantry. He was wounded at Shiloh, Tennessee, on April 6, 1862, and never recovered, dying at Okalona, Mississippi, on August 9, 1862 (Mary was twenty-nine). Her father died in 1871. In 1872—the same year that her son Bradley died (June 4), at the approximate age of twelve—she married Thomas A. Bradley (on July 25); they had one child, Thomas Jr., born in the Washington, DC, area in 1873. Mary died in Nantucket, Massachusetts, in 1881 at the age of forty-eight. Mary's father was Fortunatus Cosby Jr., a poet, writer, and the superintendent of Louisville public schools. She was one of seven children. Her mother, Ellen Mary Jane Blake, died in 1848 (when Mary was fifteen), and Fortunatus remarried in 1854 to Anna T. Mills,

who died in 1864. See *The Encyclopedia of Louisville*, ed. John E. Kleber (Lexington: University Press of Kentucky, 2001), 223. For more on Fortunatus Cosby Jr., and the family, see Josiah Stoddard Johnston, *Memorial History of Louisville from Its First Settlement to the Year 1896*, vol. 2 (Chicago: American Biographical Publishing Company, 1896), 484–86. You can find some of Fortunatus's poems in M. Joblin and Co., *Louisville Past and Present* (Louisville, KY: John P. Morton and Co., 1875). See also Walter Garland Duke, *Henry Duke, Councilor: His Descendants and Connections Comprising Partial Records of Many Allied Families* (Richmond, VA: Dietz Press, 1949), 308–9. Catherine Smith Caldwell (1838–82) married Isaac Caldwell on January 20, 1857. He became the president of the University of Louisville in 1868. See *Encyclopedia of Louisville*, 155. They resided at 427 West Green Street, which is now West Liberty Street (Henry Tanner, *The Louisville Directory and Business Advertiser for 1861* [Louisville, KY: Louisville Directory, Printing and Binding Establishment, 1861], 49).

25. Denise Gigante, *The Keats Brothers: The Life of John and George* (Cambridge, MA: Harvard University Press, 2013), 398. Georgiana was widowed by this time and living at "The Englishman's Palace" (on Walnut Street between Third and Fourth Streets) with her six children.

26. Johnston, *Memorial History of Louisville*, 485, 603.

27. W. Gordon McCabe, "Graduates of West Point Serving in the CSA Army," *Southern Historical Society Papers* 30 (1902): 34–76.

28. Tanner, *Louisville Directory*, 197.

29. "Extensive Robbery—Ten Thousand Dollars Worth of Opium Stolen," *Daily Dispatch* 35, no. 63 (September 11, 1868): 3.

30. J. W. Simmons, *The Greek Girl: A Tale, in Two Cantos* (Boston: James Munroe and Company, 1852). Echoing canto 2 of *Childe Harold*, Simmons writes, "Alas, the broken image multiplies, / In ev'ry shatter'd fragment still the same" (41, canto 1, stanza 61); and thinking of Byron's "On This Day I Complete My Thirty-Sixth Year," he proclaims that passion "like the fires of some volcanic isle . . . lights the flames of its own funeral pile" (46, canto 1, stanza 69). Simmons also borrows Byron's jokes, saying that "th' unhappy Bard is doom'd to draw / Upon his brain, extracting it on paper, / To furnish forth, perhaps, a dirty wrapper!" (113, canto 2, stanza 92). In another publication, Simmons calls *Don Juan* "the most remarkable record of human feelings and human frailties, that Genius ever prepared for the moral instruction of mankind" (*An Inquiry into the Moral Character of Lord Byron* [London: Ibotson and Palmer, 1826], 73).

31. George B. Kulp, "George Butler Griffin," in *Families of the Wyoming Valley: Biographical, Genealogical and Historical Sketches of the Bench and Bar of Luzerne County, Pennsylvania* (Wilkes-Barre, PA: E. B. Yordy, 1885), 1070–72; *New York Genealogical and Biographical Record* 22, no. 1 (January 1891): 202–3. A tribute obituary for Griffin appeared in the *Los Angeles Herald* 40, no. 54 (June 4, 1893). See also Clementina de Forest Griffin, "A Sketch of the Life of George Butler Griffin," *Annual Publication of the Historical Society of Southern California* 14, no. 2 (January 1, 1929): 208–13.

32. Adela Pinch, *Strange Fits of Passion: Epistemologies of Emotion, Hume to Austen* (Stanford, CA: Stanford University Press, 1996), 166–67.

33. Similarly, regarding the line "And the sun that has set, shall rise never for *thee*," someone (likely George) has crossed out "thee" and inserted "me," and Fred has written beneath it, "it has risen—not so? Fred" (95, stanza 57).

34. It eventually joined him in Southern California, whence he returned with a second wife, Eva Guadelupe. In addition to being a surveyor, Griffin was also a historian and a translator. See Griffin, "Sketch."

35. *The Poetical Works of Thomas Moore* (Buffalo, NY: George H. Derby and Co., 1852), Juliana Shields Haskell's copy, Butler Library, Columbia University, PR5054 .P6 1852g. This copy

was found in the stacks, and it has since been moved to Columbia Rare Books. A close friend and biographer of Lord Byron, Moore was popular throughout the century, particularly because of his *Irish Melodies*, whose poems and parlor songs circulated widely on both sides of the Atlantic. Publishers issued many editions of his collected works, including his well-loved Middle Eastern fantasy epic *Lalla Rookh* and his other lyrics, including his "Odes from Anacreon."

36. Thanks to Fred Burwick for deciphering the German marginalia.

37. Compare the poem "Lines Written in a Copy of Lalla Rookh, Presented to——," which appeared in *The Keepsake* for 1828, another sign that books of Moore's poetry were used as remembrancers of this kind: "With wishes fond, and vows that burn, / I bless the gift I send to thee; / . . . Think that my spirit, 'mid the leaves, / Breathes through the poet's words to thee!" (1–2, 15–16). That such lyrics were already being written and printed by 1827 suggests a recognizable set of associations and inscriptive practices across the century.

38. *Transactions of the Medical Association of Georgia: Forty-Fourth Annual Session* (Atlanta: Medical Association of Georgia, 1893), 25.

39. L. V. Bertarelli, *L'Italie en un volume* (Paris: Hachette, 1932), 605, Columbia University Library copy, DG416 .T6 1932g. This book was found in the Butler Library stacks and since has been moved to Special Collections.

40. Henry Wadsworth Longfellow, *Poems and Ballads* (New York: Worthington Company, 1891), University of Virginia, Alderman Library copy, PS2252 .W6 1891.

41. The Alexandria Infirmary was founded in 1872 by Julia Jones. It had some direct relation to the Alexandria Hospital School of Nursing, founded in 1894 by Marjorie Adamson, mother of John Adamson. A physician and a nurse, she was a graduate of the Glasgow Royal Infirmary. "The Alexandria School of Nursing Collection 1894–1987" can be found in the Historical Collections of the Claude Moore Health Sciences Library at the University of Virginia, accession number MS-14.

42. Thomas Moore, "Oft, in the Stilly Night," in *The Poetical Works of Thomas Moore, Collected by Himself*, 10 vols. (London: Longmans, 1840–41), 4:167.

43. Edgar Allan Poe, "The Raven," in *The Collected Works of Edgar Allan Poe*, vol. 1, *Poems*, ed. T. O. Mabbott (Cambridge, MA: Harvard University Press, 1998), 460. On the search for the origins of "The Raven," see Eliza Richards, "Outsourcing 'The Raven': Retroactive Origins," *Victorian Poetry* 43, no. 2 (Summer 2005): 205–21.

44. D. Elwood Dunn, "The Episcopal Church in Liberia Under Experimental Liberian Leadership: 1884–1916," *Anglican and Episcopal History* 58, no. 1 (March 1989): 3–36.

45. Katherine E. Slaughter, "Jane Chapman Slaughter: Virginia's Daughter of the Modern Era," *Central Virginia Heritage* 18, no. 2 (Spring 2001). Her papers are in Special Collections at the University of Virginia. Ironically, her Longfellow book with its fascinating marginalia ended up in the circulating stacks.

46. Christina Lupton, *Reading and the Making of Time in the Eighteenth Century* (Baltimore: Johns Hopkins University Press, 2018), 152.

47. Letitia Landon, epigraph to "Sonnets for Pictures," *New Monthly Magazine* 47 (1838): 175, lines 1–4. My thanks to Sarah Storti for pointing me to this poem.

48. Samuel Taylor Coleridge, "Frost at Midnight," in *The Collected Works of Samuel Taylor Coleridge*, vol. 16, *Poetical Works, Part I*, ed. J. C. C. Mays (Princeton: Princeton University Press, 2001), 456, lines 75–76 (with an evocation of Coleridge's "eave-drops" from this poem).

Chapter 4

1. Maurice Halbwachs, *On Collective Memory*, trans. Lewis A. Coser (Chicago: University of Chicago Press, 1992), 46.

2. Wolfgang Iser predicts the opposite result of a second encounter with a text, but he is using novel reading done by adults as his model: "It is a common enough experience for a person to say that on a second reading he noticed things he had missed when he read the book for the first time, but this is scarcely surprising [since] he is looking at the text from a different perspective" (*The Implied Reader: Patterns of Communication in Prose Fiction from Bunyan to Beckett* [Baltimore: Johns Hopkins University Press, 1978], 281).

3. Patricia Meyer Spacks registers a wider range of response to books read as a child. As she writes of her rereading of *Alice in Wonderland*, "The sense of having it both ways, of preserving the joy that is the object of nostalgia while possessing new powers of understanding, makes the rereading of treasures from long ago especially satisfying" (*On Rereading* [Cambridge, MA: Belknap Press, 2011], 46).

4. David Simpson, *Wordsworth, Commodification, and Social Concern: The Poetics of Modernity* (Cambridge: Cambridge University Press, 2009), 221–22.

5. Benjamin refers specifically to A. L. Grimm's *Linas Marchenbuch*, a nineteenth-century children's book published in 1837, as well as other volumes from that century, including his 1838 Paris edition of Balzac's *La peau de chagrin* ("Unpacking My Library," in *Illuminations: Essays and Reflections*, ed. Hannah Arendt, trans. Harry Zohn [New York: Schocken, 1969], 59–67).

6. A. E. Housman, "40: Into my heart an air that kills," in *A Shropshire Lad* (London: Kegan Paul, 1896), lines 5, 8.

7. Deidre Shauna Lynch, *Loving Literature: A Cultural History* (Chicago: University of Chicago Press, 2015), 236.

8. See Patricia Crain, *Reading Children: Literacy, Property, and the Dilemmas of Childhood in Nineteenth-Century America* (Philadelphia: University of Pennsylvania Press, 2016); and Kathleen McDowell, "Toward a History of Children as Readers, 1890–1930," *Book History* 12, no. 1 (2009): 240–65, for more on actual childhood reading practices of this era, which seem to have heavily favored the reading of novels (such as *Robinson Crusoe* and *Little Women*).

9. Nicholson Baker, "Discards," *New Yorker* (April 4, 1994): 64–86. Retelling the story of the Velveteen Rabbit, Baker remarks, "This may or may not be a sappy story, but as an allegory of card catalogues it works fairly well" (85).

10. Margery Williams, *The Velveteen Rabbit; or, How Toys Become Real*, illus. William Nicholson (New York: Doubleday, Doran, and Co., 1922), 14.

11. Jacques Derrida, *Archive Fever: A Freudian Impression* (Chicago: University of Chicago Press, 1996).

12. On dated nineteenth-century inscriptions and annotations, see my essay "The Date-Stamped Book," in *The Unfinished Book*, ed. Alexandra Gillespie and Deidre Shauna Lynch (Oxford: Oxford University Press, forthcoming 2020).

13. William H. Sherman, *Used Books: Marking Readers in Renaissance England* (Philadelphia: University of Pennsylvania Press, 2009), 151.

14. Charles Lamb, "Detached Thoughts on Books and Reading," *London Magazine* 6 (July 1822): 33–36.

15. On daydreaming and nineteenth-century reading, see Debra Gettelman, "Reading Ahead in George Eliot," *Novel: A Forum on Fiction* 39, no. 1 (Fall 2005): 25–47. When attention turns to an older physical book itself, speculative reveries often hold sway. The twentieth-century collector Charles G. Osgood wrote (in a passage partially quoted by Sherman) of his admiration for "the man who could luxuriate in sentiment over a rare old book; such as loves to ask himself: who in all the centuries have touched this book as I am touching it now? . . . [P]erhaps with some hunted or overwrought figure in periwig or farthingale, it has withdrawn behind the panel of an old country house, and in one of those intervals of silent eternity that

point the lives of troubled men and women, transmitted a flash of the eternal to show them their way through the night. . . . From all its previous owners and readers, known or unknown, it has accrued to it a certain potential of humanity which is more than a mere matter of sentiment" ("Library Notes and Queries," *Princeton University Library Chronicle* 2, no. 3 [April 1941]: 112).

16. Walter Learned, "On the Fly-Leaf of a Book of Old Plays," in *Ballads of Books*, ed. Brander Matthews (New York: George J. Coombes, 1887), 93–94.

17. The scene recalls Wordsworth's "The Solitary Reaper," another poem of erotically charged speculation, in which the poet remembers, "I saw her singing at her work, / And o'er the sickle bending." Michael Fried analyzes the appeal of observing such postures of sincere absorption in *Absorption and Theatricality: Painting and Beholder in the Age of Diderot* (Chicago: University of Chicago Press, 1980).

18. On this theme, see Billy Collins's poem "Marginalia," in which the narrator imagines a "beautiful girl . . . whom I would never meet" after finding her marginal note—"the one that dangles from me like a locket"—in a copy of *Catcher in the Rye*. As he says of his discovery, "I cannot tell you / how vastly my loneliness was deepened, / how poignant and amplified the world before me seemed" (*Sailing Alone Around the Room: New and Selected Poems* [New York: Penguin, 2002], 94–96).

19. Frank L. Stanton, "Annetta Jones—Her Book," *Current Opinion* 10 (August 1892): 126'–27.

20. Frank L. Stanton, "A Little Book," *Current Opinion* 10 (August 1892): 383.

21. Robert Browning, "A Toccata of Galuppi's," in *Robert Browning's Poetry*, ed. James F. Loucks and Andrew M. Stauffer (New York: W. W. Norton, 2007), 157–60, lines 44–45.

22. *The Dramatic Works of William Shakespeare* (Philadelphia: J. B. Lippincott, 1847), Alderman Library, University of Virginia, PR2752 . J7 1847 copy 2.

23. Pendleton Family Papers 1830–1929, Special Collections Department, Albert and Shirley Small Special Collections Library, University of Virginia, accession number 415, box 1.

24. Leah Price, *How to Do Things with Books in Victorian Britain* (Princeton: Princeton University Press, 2012), 130.

25. Sara Ahmed, *The Cultural Politics of Emotion* (New York: Routledge, 2014), 11–16.

26. Felicia Hemans, "To a Family Bible," in *The Poetical Works of Mrs. Felicia Hemans* (Philadelphia: Grigg & Elliot, 1839); Eliza Cook, "The Old Arm-Chair," in *The Poems of Eliza Cook* (New York: Leavitt & Co., 1850), 85–86.

27. Cook wrote a number of poems along similar lines, based on sentimental investments made in objects: "The Old Clock," "The Grandfather's Stick," "My Old Straw Hat"—and also "Old Story Books" and the prefatory poem about reading, "The Babes in the Wood." See Lorraine Janzen Kooistra, *Poetry, Pictures, and Popular Publishing: The Illustrated Gift Book and Victorian Visual Culture, 1855–1875* (Athens: Ohio University Press, 2011): "Cook deliberately connects the effect that picture and story had on her imagination with the hoped-for effect of her illustrated collection on her readers" (138).

28. Abigail Williams has shown that this process of bibliographic expansion and diversification in the home in fact began in earnest in the eighteenth century, so it might be more accurate to say that the Victorians merely amplified the phenomena, albeit to levels that would have staggered earlier generations (*The Social Life of Books: Reading Together in the Eighteenth-Century Home* [New Haven, CT: Yale University Press, 2017]).

29. Henry Wadsworth Longfellow, "Dedication," in *The Seaside and the Fireside* (Boston: Ticknor, Reed, and Fields, 1850), 2.

30. John Keats, "Lines Supposed to Have Been Addressed to Fanny Brawne ['This Living Hand']," in *The Poetical Works of John Keats*, ed. H. B. Forman, 6th ed. (London: printed for Reeves and Turner, 1898), 417.

31. John Plotz, "Out of Circulation: For and Against Book Collection," *Southwest Review* 84, no. 4 (1999): 462–78, 472.

32. George Poulet, "Phenomenology of Reading," *New Literary History* 1, no. 1 (1969): 54, 55.

33. Roman Ingarden is quoted in Wolfgang Iser, "The Reading Process: A Phenomenological Approach," *New Literary History* 3, no. 2 (1972): 284; Kevin McLaughlin, *Paperwork: Fiction and Mass Mediacy in the Paper Age* (Philadelphia: University of Pennsylvania Press, 2011), 6.

34. Christina Lupton, *Knowing Books: The Consciousness of Mediation in Eighteenth-Century Britain* (Philadelphia: University of Pennsylvania Press, 2011); Williams, *Social Life of Books*; Gillian Silverman, *Bodies and Books: Reading and the Fantasy of Communion in Nineteenth-Century America* (Philadelphia: University of Pennsylvania Press, 2012).

35. Joshua Calhoun, "The Word Made Flax: Cheap Bibles, Textual Corruption, and the Poetics of Paper," *PMLA* 126, no. 2 (March 2011): 327–44; Jonathan Senchyne, "Vibrant Material Textuality: New Materialism, Book History, and the Archive in Paper," *Studies in Romanticism* 57, no. 1 (Spring 2018): 67–85.

36. Lisa Gitelman, *Paper Knowledge: Towards a Media History of Documents* (Durham, NC: Duke University Press, 2014); Ben Kafka, *The Demon of Writing: Powers and Failures of Paperwork* (New York: Zone Books, 2012).

37. Eric Livingstone, "The Textuality of Pleasure," *New Literary History* 37, no. 3 (Summer 2006): 655.

38. Herbert F. Tucker, "Over Worked, Worked Over: A Poetics of Fatigue," in *The Feeling of Reading: Affective Experience and Victorian Literature*, ed. Rachel Ablow (Ann Arbor: University of Michigan Press, 2010), 117.

39. Deborah Lutz, "The Dead Are Still Among Us: Victorian Secular Relics, Hair Jewelry, and Death Culture," *Victorian Literature and Culture* 39, no. 1 (2011): 135. Lutz also observes that locks of hair are "traces of a life and body completed and disappeared . . . but they also serve as frames or fragments of the moment of loss" (127).

40. John Keats, "Lines on Seeing a Lock of Milton's Hair," in *Complete Poems*, ed. Jack Stillinger (Cambridge, MA: Belknap Press, 1991), 165.

41. Elizabeth Barrett Browning, "Sonnets from the Portuguese," *Selected Writings*, 117–35, ed. Josie Billington and Philip Davis (Oxford: Oxford University Press, 2014).

42. Alfred, Lord Tennyson, "Ring Out, Wild Bells, to the Wild Sky," in *In Memoriam (1850)*, ed. Matthew Rowlinson (Peterborough, ON: Broadview Press, 2014), 122–23.

43. Crain, *Reading Children*, 176. Crain cites Judith Plotz, *Romanticism and the Vocation of Childhood* (New York: Palgrave Macmillan, 2001), 3.

44. D. W. Winnicott, *Playing and Reality* (1971; New York: Routledge Classics, 2005), 19.

45. Wordsworth, "Ode: Intimations of Immortality," 297–302, in *William Wordsworth: The Major Works Including "The Prelude,"* ed. Stephen Gill (Oxford: Oxford University Press, 2008), lines 151, 155.

46. Samuel Taylor Coleridge, "Dejection: An Ode," in *Coleridge's Poetry and Prose*, ed. Nicholas Halmi et al. (New York: W. W. Norton, 2003), 155–58, lines 54–56, 47–48.

47. William Wordsworth, "Resolution and Independence," in *William Wordsworth: The Major Works Including "The Prelude,"* ed. Stephen Gill (Oxford: Oxford University Press, 2008), 260–64, lines 11–14.

48. Crain found doll clothes, too, in a copy of *Mamma's Gift Book* (Philadelphia, 1854), owned by one Kate Anthony and now, like most of Crain's examples, held at the American Antiquarian Society (*Reading Children*, 135).

49. Emily Tapscott Clark went on to become a significant figure in the Richmond literary scene in the 1920s, as a writer and the founding editor of *The Reviewer*. See her entry in

Encyclopedia Virginia, https://www.encyclopediavirginia.org/Clark_Emily_Tapscott_ca _1890-1953.

50. Seth Lerer, "Devotion and Defacement: Reading Children's Marginalia," *Representations* 118, no. 1 (2012): 128.

51. Anne-Lise François, "Ungiving Time: Reading Lyric by the Light of the Anthropocene," in *Anthropocene Reading: Literary History in Geologic Times*, ed. Tobias Menely and Jesse Oak Taylor (State College: Pennsylvania State University Press, 2017), 256.

52. Geoffrey Nunberg, "Google's Book Search: A Disaster for Scholars," *Chronicle of Higher Education* (August 31, 2009), https://www.chronicle.com/article/Googles-Book -Search-A/48245. For myriad examples of distorted scans of pages, see Krissy Wilson, *The Art of Google Books*, http://theartofgooglebooks.tumblr.com.

53. Lady Morgan, *Florence Macarthy: An Irish Tale* (Philadelphia: M. Carey and Son, 1819), Alderman Library copy, University of Virginia, PR 5059 .M3F5 1819a copy 2, barcode X030703492. The book was formerly owned by Charles Cocke (1784–1861) at the Esmont plantation near Charlottesville. It has a note dated November 13, 1850, about giving clothes to a list of men named "Old Billy," "Church," "Wilson," "Little Billy," "Israel," and "Joe," among others. Charlotte Mary Cocke Gordon, whom we met in Chapter 1, and who mourned the death of her son in her copy of Hemans, was Charles Cocke's daughter and had grown up at Esmont.

54. Irene Owens outlines the difficulties that libraries at historically black colleges and universities face in the article "Stories Told but Yet Unfinished: Challenges Facing African-American Libraries and Special Collections in Historically Black Colleges and Universities," *Journal of Library Administration* 33, nos. 3 and 4 (April 2001): 165–81.

55. Alfred Tennyson, *Henoch Arden naar het Engelsch*, trans. S. J. van den Bergh (The Hague, 1869), Thomas Randolph Price's copy, Alderman Library, University of Virginia, PR 5556 .A63 1869, barcode X030702646.

56. "Presentation of the Thomas Price Memorial Library," *University of Virginia Bulletins*, New Series, 5, no. 1 (January 1905): 1–17.

57. Charles Sears Baldwin, "Thomas Randolph Price (March 18, 1839–May 7, 1903)," *Journal of English and Germanic Philology* 5, no. 2 (December 1903): 239–52, 255–59.

58. Qtd. in "Presentation of the Thomas Price Memorial Library," 11–12.

59. Mary J. Morrogh suggests one James Richards, who was, like Price, in the Corps of Engineers in the Confederate army at this time ("Poetry and the Evidence of Nineteenth-Century Reading" [MA thesis, University of Virginia, 2017], 19).

60. The lines James remembers Tom reading aloud are the ones that describe Enoch's isolated sojourn on his tropical island, listening to "[t]he league-long roller thundering on the reef." Perhaps recalling this passage, Price published a poem of his own in 1871 entitled "The Breakers Broken" (*Southern Magazine* 8 [1871]: 564). In it, he compares the striving of men to the waves of the ocean, asking "shall brave endeavor / Fall back in froth and foam forever?" (lines 3–4). Observing the "eager crests" (line 5) that "perish on the beach" (line 9), the poem concludes that "[t]o strive is but to fail" (line 12) and praises "A lowly life where love and rest / House in the chambers of the breast" (lines 17–18).

61. Kirstie Blair, "'Thousands of Throbbing Hearts': Sentimentality and Community in Popular Victorian Poetry: Longfellow's *Evangeline* and Tennyson's *Enoch Arden*," *19: Interdisciplinary Studies in the Long Nineteenth Century* 4 (April 2007), http://doi.org/10.16995 /ntn.455.

62. Pierre Nora, "Between Memory and History: Les Lieux de Mémoire," *Representations* 26, no. 1 (1989): 13–14.

63. Amelia Bird, *Walden Marginalia; or, The Contents of a Dozen Shanties* (Kingston, NY: Women's Studio Workshop, 2012). Bird writes, "Writing in the margins of a book is

similar to writing in a diary. The notes may be intended for your eyes only, but you can't help but imagine a stranger or the stranger of your older self re-reading them" (n.p.).

64. Byron, "Written Beneath a Picture," in *Lord Byron: The Complete Poetical Works*, vol. 7, 287, ed. Jerome J. McGann, 7 vols. (Oxford: Clarendon Press, 1980–93), line 1.

Chapter 5

1. On the origin and goals of NINES, see Jerome McGann, "The Way We Live Now, What Is to Be Done?" *Electronic Book Review* (January 3, 2007), https://electronicbookreview.com/essay/the-way-we-live-now-what-is-to-be-done/.

2. Data from the Book Traces @ UVA project can be found in the 2018 final report white paper, available at https://booktraces.library.virginia.edu/white-paper/.

3. Stack searches, some formal and some informal and typically involving students, faculty members, and librarians, have been organized at Appalachian State University, Arizona State University, Brandeis University, Bryn Mawr College, Columbia University, Eastern Mennonite University, the University of Connecticut, Emory and Henry College, the University of Georgia, Harvard University, the College of the Holy Cross, the University of Iowa, James Madison University, Lafayette College, Lehigh University, Louisiana State University, the University of Louisville, Loyola University New Orleans, Mary Baldwin College, Millsaps College, the University of Nebraska, the University of Nevada at Las Vegas, the University of North Carolina at Chapel Hill, the University of North Carolina at Pembroke, Old Dominian University, Randolph College, Roanoke College, Richmond University, Simon Fraser University, the University of South Carolina, Stevenson University, Texas A&M University, the University of Victoria, Virginia Commonwealth University, Virginia Military Institute, Virginia Tech University, Virginia Union University, the University of Washington, Washington and Lee University, the College of William and Mary, and Yale University.

4. Stephen G. Nichols and Abby Smith, "The Evidence in Hand: Report of the Task Force on the Artifact in Library Collections," *Council on Library and Information Resources* (November 2001), https://clir.wordpress.clir.org/wp-content/uploads/sites/6/pub103_57d70f70 19307.pdf, p. 71. Meredith Griffin of Concordia Library reports that "concerns had . . . been voiced by some faculty in the humanities about the deselection process" so that "any weeding of unique titles in these subject areas" was "limited in scope and required careful review by librarians and faculty"; but she also notes that "the proposal to remove duplicate copies, however, did not elicit any negative reactions from these stakeholders" ("High-Yield, Low-Risk Deselection in an Academic Library," International Federation of Library Associations World Library and Information Conference [2016], http://library.ifla.org/1571/).

5. Jerome McGann, "Philology in a New Key," *Critical Inquiry* 39, no. 2 (2013): 327–46.

6. OCLC, "Shared Print Management," https://www.oclc.org/en/services/shared-print-management.html.

7. OCLC, "Shared Print Strategy," https://www.oclc.org/en/shared-print.html.

8. Alex D. McAllister and Allan Scherlen, "Weeding with Wisdom: Tuning Deselection of Print Monographs in Book-Reliant Disciplines," *Collection Management* 42, no. 2 (April 3, 2017): 76. For a bracing overview of recent library weeding projects, see Victor T. Oliva, "Deselection of Print Monographs in the Humanities and Social Sciences in the Digital Age," *Collection Building* 35, no. 2 (2016): 37–47.

9. McAllister and Scherlen, "Weeding with Wisdom," 76. A 2009 ITHAKA Strategy and Research report noted that "numerous libraries would . . . like to reassign the space occupied by print collections towards higher-value uses" (2), and, since 2009, many have been doing just that.

10. For an analytical review of the conversation about print circulation statistics, see Amy Fry, "Conventional Wisdom or Faulty Logic? The Recent Literature on Monograph Use and E-book Acquisition," *Library Philosophy and Practice* (August 29, 2015), http://digitalcommons.unl.edu/libphilprac/1307.

11. Paul Courant and Matthew Nelson, "On the Cost of Keeping a Book," in *The Idea of Order: Transforming Research Collections for 21st Century Scholarship* (Washington, DC: Council on Library and Information Resources, 2010), 81–105, https://www.clir.org/wp-content/uploads/sites/6/pub147.pdf.

12. See Jennifer Epstein, "A Win for the Stacks," *Inside Higher Ed* (November 13, 2009), http://www.insidehighered.com/news/2009/11/13/win-stacks; Sarah E. Bond, "After Uproar, University of Texas Decides Not to Relocate Its Fine Arts Library," *Hyperallergic* (April 10, 2018), https://hyperallergic.com/437093/ut-austin-fine-arts-library-saved/; and David Yaffe-Bellany and Jacob Stern, "Yale Students Aren't Ready to Close the Book on the School's Libraries Just Yet," *Washington Post* (April 21, 2019), https://www.washingtonpost.com/education/2019/04/21/yale-students-arent-ready-close-book-schools-libraries-just-yet.

13. Nicholson Baker, *Double Fold: Libraries and the Assault on Paper* (New York: Random House, 2001).

14. Robert Darnton's review, "The Great Book Massacre," in the *New York Review of Books* (April 26, 2001), took Nicholson Baker's arguments seriously and produced an interesting exchange in a later issue (March 14, 2002), with a response by Shirley K. Baker, then the president of the Association for Research Libraries. At that time, Baker assured readers that digitization has not, "as Darnton and Baker warn it might, produced 'another purge of paper.'" This was just before Google Books began, in 2004. See also Richard J. Cox, "Don't Fold Up: Responding to Nicholson Baker's *Double Fold*," *Archival Outlook* (May–June 2001): 8–14.

15. Spencer Acadia, "Books Be Gone! Reducing an Academic Library's Print Collection by Half to Meet Strategic Planning Initiatives and Participate in a Joint Library Resource-Sharing Facility," *Journal of Library Administration* 56, no. 2 (February 17, 2016): 144–57, https://doi.org/10.1080/01930826.2015.1105668.

16. David Woolwine, "Collection Development in the Humanities and Social Sciences in a Transitional Age: Deaccession of Print Items," *Library Philosophy and Practice* (2014): 1–40, 1, http://digitalcommons.unl.edu/libphilprac/1173/.

17. Robert H. Kieft and Lizanne Payne, "Collective Collection, Collective Action," *Collection Management* 37, nos. 3–4 (2012): 138, https://doi.org/10.1080/01462679.2012.685411.

18. Constance Malpas, *Cloud-Sourcing Research Collections: Managing Print in the Mass Digitized Library Environment* (Dublin, OH: OCLC Research, 2011), 64.

19. On this metaphor as applied to print collections management, see my "A Forest for the *Trees*: A Response to Jacob Nadal's 'Silvaculture in the Stacks,'" *Against the Grain* 27, no. 5 (November 1, 2015): 82–83.

20. Roger C. Schonfeld and Ross Housewright, "What to Withdraw: Print Collections Management in the Wake of Digitization," ITHAKA S+R research report (September 1, 2009), 2, https://sr.ithaka.org/publications/what-to-withdraw-print-collections-management-in-the-wake-of-digitization/.

21. Rebecca Lossin, "Against the Universal Library," *New Left Review* 107 (September–October 2017): 100–101.

22. Yet such a transition in librarianship has a longer twentieth-century history. Randolph G. Adams wrote of this split as far back as 1937, in an essay entitled "Librarians as Enemies of Books": "The librarian . . . is no longer a curator of books—he is an administrative official and a promoter of adult education. The modern American book-collector . . . is more likely to be a close student of bibliography who does not hesitate to write both popular

and learned articles on the subject. It may even be said that the collector is picking up the mantle of scholarship dropped by the librarian as the latter ascends into the heaven of efficiency. This is entirely proper, as the book-collector is often a man of feeling and sentiment, characteristics which are in danger of being trained out of the modern librarian" (*Library Quarterly* 7, no. 3 [July 1937]: 317–18).

23. See, for example, Susanne K. Clement, "From Collaborative Purchasing Towards Collaborative Discarding: The Evolution of the Shared Print Repository," *Collection Management* 37, nos. 3–4 (2012): 153–67.

24. Andrew Stauffer, "My Old Sweethearts: On Digitization and the Future of the Print Record," in *Debates in the Digital Humanities 2016*, ed. Matthew Gold (Minneapolis: University of Minnesota Press, 2016), 218–29.

25. Michael Garabedian, "Condition Considerations: An Inquiry into Recording Conditions in Consortial Collections for the Purpose of Selecting (and Deselecting) Shared Print Copies," *Proceedings of the Charleston Library Conference* (2014): 230.

26. Ian Bogus and Zach Maiorana, "Everything Not Saved Will Be Lost: Preservation in the Age of the Shared Print and Withdrawal Projects," *College and Research Libraries* 80, no. 7 (2019): 951.

27. Sara Amato et al., Eastern Academic Scholars' Trust Partnership for Shared Book Collections: Risk Research Working Group, June 2019 report, p. 6, https://eastlibraries.org /partnership-shared-book-collections.

28. Falconer Madan, "'The Duplicity of Duplicates' and 'A New Extension of Bibliography,'" *Library: Transactions of the Bibliographical Society* 12 (1911–13): 15.

29. Modern Language Association, "Statement on the Significance of Primary Records," *Profession* (1995): 28.

30. Susan Staves, "Traces of a Lost Woman," *Profession* (1995): 36–38, www.jstor.org /stable/25595548.

31. Jerome McGann, "The Gutenberg Variations," *RBM: A Journal of Rare Books, Manuscripts, and Cultural Heritage* 3, no. 1 (Spring 2002): 22. See also McGann's *The Beauty of Inflections: Literary Investigations in Historical Method and Theory* (Oxford: Oxford University Press, 1985) and *The Textual Condition* (Princeton: Princeton University Press, 1991).

32. Baker, *Double Fold*; Lossin, "Against the Universal Library," 102–5.

33. E. W. Walton has shown that students are torn by their own use of digital books over printed ones ("Why Undergraduate Students Choose to Use E-books," *Journal of Librarianship and Information Science* 46, no. 4 [2014]: 263–70).

34. For a full report on the project Book Traces @ UVA, see Kristin Jensen et al., "Book Traces @ UVA," a white paper available at https://libraopen.lib.virginia.edu/public_view /cv43nw88q.

35. I am thinking here of Sustainable Collections Services, the data-driven deselection arm of the OCLC, which "offers deselection decision-support tools to academic libraries. SCS tools enable carefully managed drawdown of low-use print monograph collections. . . . Our uniquely tailored reports combine local circulation and item data with WorldCat holdings, Hathi Trust Digital Library holdings, and authoritative title lists." Circulation data and the availability of digital versions of a book are primary factors in the "managed drawdown" of "low-use print" (OCLC, "Sustainable Collections Services," https://www.oclc.org/en /sustainable-collections.html).

36. A recent example of using quantitative methods for removing books is detailed in Cynthia Ehret Snyder, "Data-Driven Deselection: Multiple Point Data Using a Decision Support Tool in an Academic Library," *Collection Management* 39, no. 1 (2014): 17–31.

37. Representative is Brian Lavoie's 2016 remark on the OCLC blog: "Managing down print monograph collections by moving them into some form of shared stewardship has

been a matter of keen interest for academic libraries, as they seek to leverage new efficiencies while preserving the value-creating capacity of the legacy print investment" ("The Collective Perspective," *OCLC Next* [June 21, 2016], http://www.oclc.org/blog/main/the-collective -perspective/). For a 2013 overview of the collective collections movement and its attendant conversations, see the OCLC research report by Lorcan Dempsey et al., *Understanding the Collective Collection: Towards a System-Wide Perspective on Library Print Collections* (Dublin, OH: OCLC Research, 2013), https://www.oclc.org/research/publications/library/2013/2013 -09r.html. See also Rick Lugg, "The Remarkable Acceleration of Shared Print," *OCLC Next* (March 1, 2018), http://www.oclc.org/blog/main/the-remarkable-acceleration-of-shared-print/.

38. David F. Kohl, *Circulation, Interlibrary Loan, Patron Use, and Collection Management: A Handbook for Library Management* (Santa Barbara, CA: ABC-CLIO, 1986).

39. Marks of provenance help track copies in a complex system. Evan Anderson discusses "the need for additional marking of items identified in a shared print agreement," suggesting that inscriptions and marginalia could serve an organizational function in shared print programs ("A Marking Heuristic for Materials in a Shared Print Agreement," *Library Resources and Technical Services* 61, no. 1 [2017]: 4–12).

40. Paul Conway, "Preserving Imperfection: Assessing the Incidence of Digital Imaging Error in HathiTrust," *Digital Technology and Culture* 42, no. 1 (2013): 17–30, https://doi .org/10.1515/pdtc-2013-0003.

41. Kevin Seeber, "Legacy Systems" (June 15, 2018), https://kevinseeber.com/blog/legacy -systems/.

42. Jerome McGann, "On Creating a Usable Future," *Profession* (2011): 186.

43. Philip Larkin, "Church Going," in *The Complete Poems*, ed. Archie Burnett (New York: Farrar, Straus and Giroux, 2013), lines 47–53.

Envoi

1. Pierre Nora, "Between Memory and History: Les Lieux de Mémoire," *Representations* 26 (1989): 14.

Bibliography

Printed Books with Marginalia and Reader Interventions

Columbia University, New York, NY

Bertarelli, L. V. *L'Italie en un volume.* Paris: Hachette, 1932. Butler Library (noncirculating). DG416 .T6 1932g.

The Poetical Works of Thomas Moore. Buffalo, NY: George H. Derby and Co., 1852. Juliana Shields Haskell's copy. Butler Library (noncirculating). PR5054 .P6 1852g.

Harvard University, Cambridge, MA

Ingelow, Jean. *Songs of Seven.* Boston: Roberts Brothers, 1884. Florence McKeehan's copy. Widener Library. Hollis Number 005386446.

University of Louisville, Louisville, KY

Hopkins, Alphonso Alva. *Geraldine: A Souvenir of the St. Lawrence.* Boston: James R. Osgood, 1881. Esther Annie Brown's copy. Arthur Y. Ford donation. PS 1999 .H415G3 1881. Barcode: U005 00495339 4.

The Poetical Works of Winthrop Mackworth Praed. Ed. R. W. Griswold. New York: Henry Langley, 1844. Mary Cosby's copy. Ekstrom Library. PR5189 .P7 1884. Barcode: U005 01020990 7.

Simmons, James Wright. *The Greek Girl.* Boston, 1852. George Butler Griffin's copy. Ekstrom Library. PR 2839 .S4 c. 1. Barcode: U005 00498427 2.

University of Miami, Miami, FL

The Changed Cross and Other Religious Poems. 2nd ed. New York: Anson Randolph, 1872. Deering family copy. Richter Library.

The Waif: A Collection of Poems. Ed. Henry Wadsworth Longfellow. Cambridge, MA: J. Owen, 1845. Adams family copy. Richter Library.

University of Nevada, Las Vegas, NV

Moore, Thomas. *Literature, Art, and Song: Moore's Melodies and American Poems.* . . . Ed. Sir John Stevenson; illus. Daniel Maclise and William Riches. New York: International Publishing, 1872. Annie Wheeler's copy. Lied Library.

University of Virginia, Charlottesville, VA

The Complete Works of Sir Walter Scott. Vol. 7. New York, 1833. Ivy Stacks. PR5300 1833 v.7. Barcode: X004490675.

The Holy Bible. New York: Daniel D. Smith, 1820. Papers of the Pierrepont and Minor Families, 7286-c, Box 2, Albert and Shirley Small Special Collections Library.

The Holy Bible. Philadelphia: E. H. Butler and Co., 1853. Papers of the Pierrepont and Minor Families, 7286-c, Box 2, Albert and Shirley Small Special Collections Library.

The Illuminated Bible. New York: Harper and Brothers, 1846. Papers of the Pierrepont and Minor Families, 7286-c, Box 1, Albert and Shirley Small Special Collections Library.

Lady Morgan. *Florence Macarthy: An Irish Tale.* Philadelphia: M. Carey and Son, 1819. Alderman Library. PR 5059 .M3F5 1819a copy 2. Barcode: X030703492.

Letters of Hannah More to Zachary Macaulay. New York, 1860. Ivy Stacks Limited Circulation. PR3605 .M6 A8 1860. Barcode: X004884744.

Longfellow, Henry Wadsworth. *Poems and Ballads.* New York: Worthington Company, 1891. Jane Slaughter's copy. Alderman Library. PS 2252 .W6 1891. Barcode: X000754276.

Meredith, Owen. *Lucile.* Boston: Fields, Osgood and Co., 1869. Jennie Tayloe's copy. Alderman Library. PR 4954 . L7 1869. Barcode: X002650884.

Papers of the Gordon Family, 1812–1916. Albert and Shirley Small Special Collections Library. MSS 10089 (6 boxes).

Pendleton Family Papers, 1830–1929. Albert and Shirley Small Special Collections Library. Accession Number 415 (Box 1).

The Poetical Works of Mrs. Felicia Hemans. Philadelphia: Grigg & Elliot, 1839. Albert and Shirley Small Special Collections Library. PR4780 .A1 1839. Barcode: X030434848.

The Poetical Works of Mrs. Felicia Hemans. Philadelphia: Grigg & Elliot, 1843. Ellen Pierrepont Minor's copy. Alderman Library. PR 4780 .A1 1843. Barcode: X001269666.

Shakespeare, William. *The Dramatic Works of William Shakespeare.* Philadelphia: J. B. Lippincott, 1847. Alderman Library. PR2752 .J7 1847 copy 2.

———. *The Works of William Shakespeare.* New York: Redfield, 1853. Miriam Trowbridge's copy. Alderman Library. PR 2753 .C75 1853. Barcode: X000027697.

Tennyson, Alfred. *Henoch Arden naar het Engelsch.* Trans. S. J. van den Bergh. The Hague, 1869. Thomas Randolph Price's copy. Alderman Library. PR 5556 .A63 1869. Barcode: X030702646.

Thomas, Edith M. *Babes of the Year.* Illus. Maud Humphrey. New York: Frederick A. Stokes, 1898. Alderman Library. PS 3027.B3 1888. Barcode MX001597318.

Whittier, John Greenleaf. *The Whittier Year Book: Passages from the Verse and Prose of John Greenleaf Whittier.* Boston: Houghton Mifflin, 1895. Ivy Stacks. PS3253 .H62 1895. Barcode: X031424320.

Other Works Cited

Ablow, Rachel, ed. *The Feeling of Reading: Affective Experience and Victorian Literature.* Ann Arbor: University of Michigan Press, 2010.

Acadia, Spencer. "Books Be Gone! Reducing an Academic Library's Print Collection by Half to Meet Strategic Planning Initiatives and Participate in a Joint Library Resource-Sharing Facility." *Journal of Library Administration* 56, no. 2 (February 17, 2016): 144–57. https://doi.org/10.1080/01930826.2015.1105668.

Adams, Randolph G. "Librarians as Enemies of Books." *Library Quarterly* 7, no. 3 (July 1937): 317–31.

Ahmed, Sara. *The Cultural Politics of Emotion.* New York: Routledge, 2014.

Allan, David. *Commonplace Books and Reading in Georgian England*. Cambridge: Cambridge University Press, 2010. https://doi.org/10.1017/CBO9780511760518.

Altick, Richard Daniel. *The English Common Reader: A Social History of the Mass Reading Public, 1800–1900*. Chicago: University of Chicago Press, 1957.

Andersen, Jennifer, and Elizabeth Sauer, eds. *Books and Readers in Early Modern England: Material Studies*. Philadelphia: University of Pennsylvania Press, 2001.

Anderson, Evan. "A Marking Heuristic for Materials in a Shared Print Agreement." *Library Resources and Technical Services* 61, no. 1 (2017): 4–12.

"Annie Laurie." In *The Songs of Scotland, Ancient and Modern*, ed. Allan Cunningham, vol. 3, p. 256. London: John Taylor, 1825.

"Aster hybridus nanus." *Garden* 40 (December 26, 1891): 580.

Baker, Nicholson. "Discards." *New Yorker* (April 4, 1994): 64–86.

———. *Double Fold: Libraries and the Assault on Paper*. New York: Random House, 2001.

Baldwin, Charles Sears. "Thomas Randolph Price (March 18, 1839–May 7, 1903)." *Journal of English and Germanic Philology* 5, no. 2 (December 1903): 239–52, 255–59.

Behrendt, Stephen C. Review of *Felicia Hemans: Selected Poems, Letters, Reception Materials. Criticism* 44, no. 2 (2002): 217–20. https://doi.org/10.1353/crt.2002.0017.

Bendixen, Alfred, and Stephen Burt, eds. *The Cambridge History of American Poetry*. Cambridge: Cambridge University Press, 2014.

Benedict, Barbara M., et al. *Annotation in Eighteenth-Century Poetry*. Ed. Michael Edson. Bethlehem, PA: Lehigh University Press, 2017.

Benjamin, Walter. *Illuminations: Essays and Reflections*. Ed. Hannah Arendt. Trans. Harry Zohn. New York: Schocken, 1969.

———. *Walter Benjamin: Selected Writings*. Vol. 4, *1938–1940*. Ed. Howard Eiland and Michael W. Jennings. Cambridge, MA: Harvard University Press, 2003.

Bird, Amelia. *Walden Marginalia; or, The Contents of a Dozen Shanties*. Kingston, NY: Women's Studio Workshop, 2012.

Birkerts, Sven. *Changing the Subject: Art and Attention in the Internet Age*. Minneapolis: Graywolf Press, 2015.

———. *The Gutenberg Elegies: The Fate of Reading in an Electronic Age*. New York: Farrar, Straus and Giroux, 2006.

Blair, Kirstie. "'Thousands of Throbbing Hearts': Sentimentality and Community in Popular Victorian Poetry: Longfellow's *Evangeline* and Tennyson's *Enoch Arden*." *19: Interdisciplinary Studies in the Long Nineteenth Century* (April 1, 2007). https://doi.org/10.16995/ntn.455.

Bode, Katherine. *A World of Fiction: Digital Collections and the Future of Literary History*. Ann Arbor: University of Michigan Press, 2018.

Bogus, Ian, and Zach Maiorana. "Everything Not Saved Will Be Lost: Preservation in the Age of the Shared Print and Withdrawal Projects." *College and Research Libraries* 80, no. 7 (2019): 945–72.

Bond, Sarah E. "After Uproar, University of Texas Decides Not to Relocate Its Fine Arts Library." *Hyperallergic* (April 10, 2018). https://hyperallergic.com/437093/ut-austin-fine-arts-library-saved/.

Boym, Svetlana. *The Future of Nostalgia*. New York: Basic Books, 2002.

Brinkman, Bartholomew. *Poetic Modernism in the Culture of Mass Print*. Baltimore: Johns Hopkins University Press, 2016.

Brown, Sylvia, and John Considine. *Marginated: Seventeenth-Century Printed Books and the Traces of Their Readers*. Edmonton: University of Alberta Press, 2010.

Browning, Elizabeth Barrett. *Selected Writings*. Ed. Josie Billington and Philip Davis. Oxford: Oxford University Press, 2014.

Browning, Robert. *Robert Browning's Poetry*. Ed. James F. Loucks and Andrew M. Stauffer. New York: W. W. Norton, 2007.

Bryant, William Cullen, and Oliver Bell Bunce, eds. *Picturesque America; or, The Land We Live In. A Delineation by Pen and Pencil of the Mountains, Rivers, Lakes, Forests, Water-Falls, Shores, Cañons, Valleys, Cities, and Other Picturesque Features of Our Country, With Illustrations on Steel and Wood*. New York: D. Appleton, 1872. http://archive.org/details /picturesqueameri01bryauoft.

Butler, Joseph. *Bishop Butler's Analogy of Religion*. Ed. G. R. Crooks. New York: Harper and Brothers, 1852. Mary Belle Miller's copy. Formerly held by the University of Virginia. BT1100. B9 1852. Barcode: X001140350.

Byron, George Gordon, Lord. *The Complete Poetical Works*. Ed. Jerome J. McGann. 7 vols. Oxford: Clarendon Press, 1980–93.

Calhoun, Charles C. *Longfellow: A Rediscovered Life*. Boston: Beacon Press, 2005.

Calhoun, Joshua. "The Word Made Flax: Cheap Bibles, Textual Corruption, and the Poetics of Paper." *PMLA* 126, no. 2 (March 2011): 327–44. https://doi.org/10.1632/pmla.2011.126 .2.327.

Carr, Nicholas. *The Shallows: What the Internet Is Doing to Our Brains*. New York: W. W. Norton, 2011.

Casper, Scott E., et al. *A History of the Book in America*. Vol. 3, *The Industrial Book, 1840–1880*. Chapel Hill: University of North Carolina Press, 2007.

Castillo Deball, Mariana. *Interlude: The Reader's Traces*. Maastricht: Jan van Eyck Academie, 2005.

Chandler, James. *An Archaeology of Sympathy: The Sentimental Mode in Literature and Cinema*. Chicago: University of Chicago Press, 2013.

"Charles Deering." *Wikipedia* (June 15, 2018). https://en.wikipedia.org/wiki/Charles _Deering.

Clement, Susanne K. "From Collaborative Purchasing Towards Collaborative Discarding: The Evolution of the Shared Print Repository." *Collection Management* 37, nos. 3–4 (2012): 153–67. https://doi.org/10.1080/01462679.2012.685413.

Coffin, Mary A. "Pressed Flowers and Their Associations." *Ladies' Companion: A Monthly Magazine Devoted to Literature and the Fine Arts* (August 1841): 203–5.

Cohen, Michael C. "Album Verse and the Poetics of Scribal Circulation." In *A History of Nineteenth-Century American Women's Poetry*, ed. Jennifer Putzi and Alexandra Socarides, 68–86. Cambridge: Cambridge University Press, 2016. https://doi.org/10.1017 /9781316018767.005.

———. "Reading the Nineteenth Century." *American Literary History* 26, no. 2 (Summer 2014): 406–17.

———. *The Social Lives of Poems in Nineteenth-Century America*. Philadelphia: University of Pennsylvania Press, 2015.

Coleman, Donald Cuthbert. *The British Paper Industry, 1495–1860: A Study in Industrial Growth*. Oxford: Clarendon Press, 1958.

Coleridge, Samuel Taylor. *Coleridge's Poetry and Prose*. Ed. Nicholas Halmi et al. New York: W. W. Norton, 2003.

———. *The Collected Works of Samuel Taylor Coleridge*. Vol. 16, *Poetical Works, Part 1*. Ed. J. C. C. Mays. Princeton: Princeton University Press, 2001.

Colley, Anne C. *Nostalgia and Recollection in Victorian Culture*. New York: Palgrave Macmillan, 1998.

Collins, Billy. *Sailing Alone Around the Room: New and Selected Poems*. New York: Penguin, 2002.

Conway, Paul. "Preserving Imperfection: Assessing the Incidence of Digital Imaging Error in HathiTrust." In *Digital Technology and Culture* 42, no. 1 (2013): 17–30. https://doi.org/10.1515/pdtc-2013-0003.

Cook, Eliza. *The Poems of Eliza Cook*. New York: Leavitt & Co., 1850.

Courant, Paul, and Matthew Nelson. "On the Cost of Keeping a Book." In *The Idea of Order: Transforming Research Collections for 21st Century Scholarship*, 81–105. Washington, DC: Council on Library and Information Resources, 2010. https://www.clir.org/wp-content/uploads/sites/6/pub147.pdf.

Cox, Richard J. "Don't Fold Up: Responding to Nicholson Baker's *Double Fold*." *Archival Outlook* (May–June 2001): 8–14.

Crain, Patricia. *Reading Children: Literacy, Property, and the Dilemmas of Childhood in Nineteenth-Century America*. Philadelphia: University of Pennsylvania Press, 2016.

Culler, Jonathan. *Theory of the Lyric*. Cambridge, MA: Harvard University Press, 2017.

Dahlström, Mats. "A Book of One's Own: Examples of Library Book Marginalia." In *The History of Reading*, vol. 3, *Methods, Strategies, Tactics*, ed. Rosalind Crone and Shafquat Towheed, 115–31. New York: Palgrave Macmillan, 2011.

Dain, Phyllis. "Scholarship, Higher Education, and Libraries in the United States: Historical Questions and Quests." In *Libraries and Scholarly Communication in the United States: The Historical Dimension*, ed. Phyllis Dain and John Y. Cole, 1–44. New York: Greenwood Press, 1990.

Dames, Nicholas. "Seventies Throwback Fiction." *N+1* (December 10, 2014). https://nplusonemag.com/issue-21/reviews/seventies-throwback-fiction/.

Darnton, Robert. "The Great Book Massacre." *New York Review of Books* (April 26, 2001): 16–19.

"Deaths." *United States Army and Navy Journal* 58, pt. 1 (February 26, 1921): 718.

Dempsey, Lorcan, et al. *Understanding the Collective Collection: Towards a System-Wide Perspective on Library Print Collections*. Dublin, OH: OCLC Research, 2013. http://www.oclc.org/content/dam/research/publications/library/2013/2013-09intro.pdf.

Derrida, Jacques. *Archive Fever*. Chicago: University of Chicago Press, 1996.

Dickinson, Cindy. "Creating a World of Books, Friends, and Flowers: Gift Books and Inscriptions, 1825–60." *Winterthur Portfolio* 31, no. 1 (Spring 1996): 53–66.

Dickinson, Emily. *The Poems of Emily Dickinson*. Variorum ed. 3 vols. Cambridge, MA: Belknap Press of Harvard University Press, 1999.

Du Bois, W. E. B. *The Souls of Black Folk*. Ed. Brent Hayes Edwards. Oxford: Oxford University Press, 2009.

Duke, Walter Garland. *Henry Duke, Councilor: His Descendants and Connections Comprising Partial Records of Many Allied Families*. Richmond, VA: Dietz Press, 1949.

Dunn, D. Elwood. "The Episcopal Church in Liberia Under Experimental Liberian Leadership: 1884–1916." *Anglican and Episcopal History* 58, no. 1 (March 1989): 3–36.

Edelman, Hendrik, and G. Marvin Tatum Jr. "The Development of Collections in American University Libraries." *College and Research Libraries* 37, no. 3 (May 1976): 222–45.

Edwards, Brent Hayes. "The Taste of the Archive." *Callaloo* 35, no. 4 (Fall 2012): 944–72. https://doi.org/10.1353/cal.2013.0002.

Eliot, George. *The Mill on the Floss*. Ed. Oliver Lovesey. Peterborough, ON: Broadview Press, 2007.

Eliot, Simon. "Bookselling by the Backdoor: Circulating Libraries, Booksellers and Book Clubs, 1870–1906." In *A Genius for Letters: Bookselling from the Sixteenth to the Twentieth Century*, ed. M. Harris and R. Myers, 145–66. New Castle, DE: Oak Knoll, 1995.

Elliott, Brian P. "'Nothing Beside Remains': Empty Icons and Elegiac Ekphrasis in Felicia Hemans." *Studies in Romanticism* 51, no. 1 (2012): 25–40.

Emerson, Ralph Waldo. "Self-Reliance." In *The Essential Writings of Ralph Waldo Emerson*, 132–53. New York: Modern Library, 2000.

The Encyclopedia of Louisville. Ed. John E. Kleber. Lexington: University Press of Kentucky, 2001.

Epstein, Jennifer. "A Win for the Stacks." *Inside Higher Ed* (November 13, 2009). http://www.insidehighered.com/news/2009/11/13/win-stacks.

Eulalie. *Buds, Blossoms, and Leaves: Poems*. Cincinnati, OH: Moore, Wilstach and Keys, 1854.

"Extensive Robbery—Ten Thousand Dollars Worth of Opium Stolen." *Daily Dispatch* 35, no. 63 (September 11, 1868): 3.

Favret, Mary A. "The Pathos of Reading." *PMLA* 130, no. 5 (October 2015): 1318–31. https://doi.org/10.1632/pmla.2015.130.5.1318.

Feldman, Paula R. "Endurance and Forgetting: What the Evidence Suggests." In *Romanticism and Women Poets: Opening the Doors of Reception*, ed. Harriet Kramer Linkin and Stephen C. Behrendt, 15–21. Lexington: University Press of Kentucky, 1999.

———. "Women, Literary Annuals, and the Evidence of Inscriptions." *Keats-Shelley Journal* 55 (2006): 54–62.

Felski, Rita. *The Uses of Literature*. Oxford: Wiley-Blackwell, 2008.

Ferris, Ina, and Paul Keen, eds. *Bookish Histories: Books, Literature, and Commercial Modernity, 1700–1900*. New York: Palgrave Macmillan, 2009.

Flora and Thalia, or Gems of Flowers and Poetry: Being an Alphabetical Arrangement of Flowers, with Appropriate Poetical Illustrations, Embellished with Coloured Plates. Philadelphia: Carey, Lea, and Blanchard, 1836. https://doi.org/10.5962/bhl.title.7069.

Foucault, Michel. *Power*. Ed. James D. Faubion. Trans. Robert Hurley. New York: New Press, 2001.

François, Anne-Lise. "Ungiving Time: Reading Lyric by the Light of the Anthropocene." In *Anthropocene Reading: Literary History in Geologic Times*, ed. Tobias Menely and Jesse Oak Taylor, 239–58. State College: Pennsylvania State University Press, 2017.

Fried, Michael. *Absorption and Theatricality: Painting and Beholder in the Age of Diderot*. Chicago: University of Chicago Press, 1980.

Fry, Amy. "Conventional Wisdom or Faulty Logic? The Recent Literature on Monograph Use and E-book Acquisition." *Library Philosophy and Practice* (August 29, 2015). http://digitalcommons.unl.edu/libphilprac/1307.

Gallagher, Catherine, and Stephen Greenblatt. *Practicing New Historicism*. Chicago: University of Chicago Press, 2001.

Garabedian, Michael. "Condition Considerations: An Inquiry into Recording Conditions in Consortial Collections for the Purpose of Selecting (and Deselecting) Shared Print Copies." *Proceedings of the Charleston Library Conference* (2014): 230–35.

Gettelman, Debra. "Reading Ahead in George Eliot." *Novel: A Forum on Fiction* 39, no. 1 (Fall 2005): 25–47.

Gigante, Denise. *The Keats Brothers: The Life of John and George*. Cambridge, MA: Harvard University Press, 2013.

Gillespie, Alexandra, and Deidre Lynch, eds. *The Unfinished Book*. Oxford: Oxford University Press, forthcoming 2020.

Gitelman, Lisa. *Paper Knowledge: Towards a Media History of Documents*. Durham, NC: Duke University Press, 2014.

Grafton, Anthony. "Is the History of Reading a Marginal Enterprise? Guillaume Budé and His Books." *Papers of the Bibliographical Society of America* 91, no. 2 (1997): 139–57.

Greenblatt, Stephen. *Shakespearean Negotiations: The Circulation of Social Energy in Renaissance England*. Berkeley: University of California Press, 1988.

Griffin, Clementina de Forest. "A Sketch of the Life of George Butler Griffin." *Annual Publication of the Historical Society of Southern California* 14, no. 2 (January 1, 1929): 208–13. https://doi.org/10.2307/41168836.

Griffin, Meredith. "High-Yield, Low-Risk Deselection in an Academic Library." International Federation of Library Associations World Library and Information Conference (2016). http://library.ifla.org/1571/.

Gruber-Garvey, Ellen. "Scissoring and Scrapbooks: Nineteenth-Century Reading, Re-Making and Re-Circulating." In *New Media, 1740–1915*, ed. Lisa Gitelman and Geoffrey B. Pingree. Cambridge, MA: MIT Press, 2003.

Hackel, Heidi Brayman. *Reading Material in Early Modern England: Print, Gender, and Literacy.* Cambridge: Cambridge University Press, 2009.

Halbwachs, Maurice. *On Collective Memory.* Trans. Lewis A. Coser. Chicago: University of Chicago Press, 1992.

Halpern, Faye. *Sentimental Readers: The Rise, Fall, and Revival of a Disparaged Rhetoric.* Iowa City: University of Iowa Press, 2013.

Halsey, Katie, and William R. Owens, eds. *Evidence from the British Isles: C. 1750–1950.* Vol. 2, *The History of Reading.* New York: Palgrave Macmillan, 2011.

Harding, Anthony. "Felicia Hemans and the Effacement of Woman." In *Romantic Women Writers: Voices and Countervoices*, ed. Paula R. Feldman and Theresa M. Kelley, 138–49. Hanover, NH: University Press of New England, 1995.

Hardy, Thomas. *Wessex Poems and Other Verses.* New York: Harper and Brothers, 1898.

Harris, Katherine D. *Forget Me Not: The Rise of the British Literary Annual, 1823–1835.* Athens: Ohio University Press, 2015.

Harris, Neal. "Special Collections and Academic Scholarship: A Tangled Relationship." In *Libraries and Scholarly Communication in the United States: The Historical Dimension*, ed. Phyllis Dain and John Y. Cole, 64–70. New York: Greenwood Press, 1990.

"Heartsease." *London Magazine* 10 (September 1824): 308.

Hemans, Felicia. *Felicia Hemans: Selected Poems, Letters, Reception Materials.* Ed. Susan J. Wolfson. Princeton: Princeton University Press, 2001.

———. *Felicia Hemans: Selected Poems, Prose and Letters.* Ed. Gary Kelly. Peterborough, ON: Broadview Press, 2002.

———. *The Poetical Works of Mrs. Felicia Hemans; Complete in One Volume.* Philadelphia: Grigg & Elliot, 1836.

———. *The Poetical Works of Mrs. Felicia Hemans; Complete in One Volume.* Philadelphia: Grigg & Elliot, 1839.

Higham, John. "The Matrix of Speculation." *Bulletin of the American Academy of Arts and Sciences* 33, no. 5 (February 1980): 9–29.

Hills, Richard Leslie. *Papermaking in Britain, 1488–1988: A Short History.* London: Athlone Press, 1988.

Hopkins, Gerard Manley. *Gerard Manley Hopkins: The Major Works.* Ed. Catherine Phillips. Oxford: Oxford University Press, 2009.

Housman, A. E. *A Shropshire Lad.* London: Kegan Paul, 1896.

Houston, Natalie, and Neal Audenaert. "VisualPage: Towards Large Scale Analysis of Nineteenth-Centusry Print Culture." *2013 IEEE International Conference on Big Data* (October 2013): 9–16.

Howe, Julia Ward. *Passion Flowers.* Boston: Ticknor, Reed, and Fields, 1854.

Hunter, Dard. *Papermaking: The History and Technique of an Ancient Craft.* New York: Dover Publications, 2011.

Ingelow, Jean. *Songs of Seven.* Boston: Roberts Brothers, 1881. https://catalog.hathitrust.org/Record/009578364.

———. *Songs of Seven.* Boston: Roberts Brothers, 1884. http://hdl.handle.net/2027/hvd.hn3jza.

Iser, Wolfgang. *The Implied Reader: Patterns of Communication in Prose Fiction from Bunyan to Beckett.* Baltimore: Johns Hopkins University Press, 1978.

———. "The Reading Process: A Phenomenological Approach." *New Literary History* 3, no. 2 (1972): 279–99. https://doi.org/10.2307/468316.

Jackson, Heather. *Marginalia: Readers Writing in Books*. New Haven, CT: Yale University Press, 2001.

———. *Romantic Readers: The Evidence of Marginalia*. New Haven, CT: Yale University Press, 2005.

Jackson, Virginia. *Dickinson's Misery: A Theory of Lyric Reading*. Princeton: Princeton University Press, 2005.

Jensen, Kristin, Kara McClurken, Andrew Stauffer, Jennifer Roper, Ivey Glendon, and Christine Ruotolo. "Book Traces @ UVA." Report. University of Virginia (July 26, 2017). https://libraopen.lib.virginia.edu/public_view/cv43nw88q.

Johnson, Wendy Dasler. *Antebellum American Women's Poetry: A Rhetoric of Sentiment*. Carbondale: Southern Illinois University Press, 2016.

Johnston, Josiah Stoddard. *Memorial History of Louisville from Its First Settlement to the Year 1896*. Vol. 2. Chicago: American Biographical Publishing Company, 1896. http://archive.org/details/memorialhistoryo02john.

Kafka, Ben. *The Demon of Writing: Powers and Failures of Paperwork*. New York: Zone Books, 2012.

Keats, John. *Complete Poems*. Ed. Jack Stillinger. Cambridge, MA: Belknap Press, 1991.

———. "Lines Supposed to Have Been Addressed to Fanny Brawne ['This Living Hand']." In *The Poetical Works of John Keats*, ed. H. B. Forman, 6th ed. London: printed for Reeves and Turner, 1898.

Keller, René Schneider, and Benno Volk. Dublin, OH: OCLC Research, 2012. https://doi.org/10.1515/9783110312812.180.

Kelley, Theresa M. *Clandestine Marriage: Botany and Romantic Culture*. Baltimore: Johns Hopkins University Press, 2012.

Kelly, Gary. "Introduction." In *Felicia Hemans: Selected Poems, Prose and Letters*, 15–85. Peterborough, ON: Broadview Press, 2002.

Kete, Mary Louise. *Sentimental Collaborations: Mourning and Middle-Class Identity in Nineteenth-Century America*. Durham, NC: Duke University Press, 2000.

Khalip, Jacques, and Forest Pyle, eds. *Constellations of a Contemporary Romanticism*. New York: Fordham University Press, 2016.

Kieft, Robert H., and Andrew Stauffer. "Curating Collective Collections—A Forest for the Trees: A Response to Jacob Nadal's 'Silvaculture in the Stacks.'" *Against the Grain* 27, no. 5 (November 1, 2015). https://doi.org/10.7771/2380-176X.7207.

Kieft, Robert H., and Lizanne Payne. "Collective Collection, Collective Action." *Collection Management* 37, nos. 3–4 (2012): 137–52. https://doi.org/10.1080/01462679.2012.685411.

King, Amy M. *Bloom: The Botanical Vernacular in the English Novel*. Oxford: Oxford University Press, 2003.

Kleber, John E., ed. *The Kentucky Encyclopedia*. Lexington: University Press of Kentucky, 1992.

Knapp, Emma Benedict, and Shepherd Knapp. *Hic Habitat Felicitas: A Volume of Recollections and Letters*. Boston: W. B. Clarke, 1910. https://catalog.hathitrust.org/Record/005777267.

Knight, Leah, Micheline White, and Elizabeth Sauer, eds. *Women's Bookscapes in Early Modern Britain: Reading, Ownership, Circulation*. Ann Arbor: University of Michigan Press, 2018.

Kohl, David F. *Circulation, Interlibrary Loan, Patron Use, and Collection Management: A Handbook for Library Management*. Santa Barbara, CA: ABC-CLIO, 1986.

Kooistra, Lorraine Janzen. *Poetry, Pictures, and Popular Publishing: The Illustrated Gift Book and Victorian Visual Culture, 1855–1875*. Athens: Ohio University Press, 2011.

Koops, Matthias. *Historical Account of the Substance Which Have Been Used to Describe Events, and to Convey Ideas from the Earliest Date to the Invention of Paper.* 2nd ed. London: Jacques and Co., 1801. http://archive.org/details/historicalaccoun00koop.

Kulp, George B. *Families of the Wyoming Valley: Biographical, Genealogical, and Historical. Sketches of the Bench and Bar of Luzerne County, Pennsylvania.* Wilkes-Barre, PA: E. B. Yordy, 1885. https://catalog.hathitrust.org/Record/100770587.

Lamb, Charles. "Detached Thoughts on Books and Reading." *London Magazine* 6 (July 1822): 33–36.

Landon, Letitia E. "The Basque Girl and Henri Quatre." *Literary Gazette and Journal of the Belle Lettres* (October 12, 1822): 648–49.

———. "Emily," *Finden's Gallery of the Graces*, n.p. London: Charles Tilt, 1834.

———. "The Lost Pleiad." In *"The Venetian Bracelet," "The Lost Pleiad," "A History of the Lyre" and Other Poems*, 51–84. London: Longman, Rees, Orme, Brown, and Green, 1829.

———. "The Michaelmas Daisy." *Literary Gazette* (March 18, 1820): 190.

———. "Sonnets for Pictures." *New Monthly Magazine* 47 (1838): 175.

———. "The Violet." In *Flora and Thalia, or Gems of Flowers and Poetry: Being an Alphabetical Arrangement of Flowers, with Appropriate Poetical Illustrations, Embellished with Coloured Plates*, 124. Philadelphia: Carey, Lea, and Blanchard, 1836.

———. "The Wandering Thought." In *The Amulet: A Christian and Literary Rembrancer*, ed. S. C. Hall, 172–75. London: Frederick Westley and A. H. Davis, 1834.

The Language and Poetry of Flowers. London: George Routledge and Sons, 1860.

Larkin, Philip. *The Complete Poems.* Ed. Archie Burnett. New York: Farrar, Straus and Giroux, 2013.

Latané, David E. "Who Counts? Popularity, Modern Recovery, and the Early Nineteenth-Century Woman Poet." In *Teaching British Women Writers 1750–1900*, ed. Jeanne Moskal and Shannon R. Wooden, 205–23. New York: Peter Lang, 2005.

Lavoie, Brian. "The Collective Perspective." *OCLC Next* (June 21, 2016). http://www.oclc.org/blog/main/the-collective-perspective/.

Learned, Walter. "On the Fly-Leaf of a Book of Old Plays." In *Ballads of Books*, ed. Brander Matthews, 93–94. New York: George J. Coombes, 1887.

Lee, Hermione. *Virginia Woolf.* London: Vintage, 1999.

Lerer, Seth. "Devotion and Defacement: Reading Children's Marginalia." *Representations* 118, no. 1 (2012): 126–53. https://doi.org/10.1525/rep.2012.118.1.126.

The Life and Age of Woman. Barre, MA: A. Alden, ca. 1835.

Life of Henry Wadsworth Longfellow. Ed. Samuel Longfellow. Vol. 2. Boston: Ticknor and Co., 1886. http://hdl.handle.net/2027/uc1.b4826204.

"Lines Written in a Copy of Lalla Rookh, Presented to _____." In *The Keepsake*, 140. London: Thomas Davison, 1828.

Liu, Alan. "Local Transcendence: Cultural Criticism, Postmodernism, and the Romanticism of Detail." *Representations* 32, no. 1 (1990): 75–113. https://doi.org/10.2307/2928796.

———. "The Power of Formalism: The New Historicism." *ELH* 56, no. 4 (Winter 1989): 721–71.

Livingstone, Eric. "The Textuality of Pleasure." *New Literary History* 37, no. 3 (Summer 2006): 655–72.

Loeffelholz, Mary. *From School to Salon: Reading Nineteenth-Century American Women's Poetry.* Princeton: Princeton University Press, 2004.

Longfellow, Henry Wadsworth. *Poems and Ballads.* New York: Worthington Company, 1891.

———. *The Seaside and the Fireside.* Boston: Ticknor, Reed, and Fields, 1850.

———. *The Waif: A Collection of Poems.* Cambridge, MA: J. Owen, 1845.

Lootens, Tricia. "Hemans and Home: Victorianism, Feminine 'Internal Enemies,' and the Domestication of National Identity." *PMLA* 109, no. 2 (1994): 238–53. https://doi.org/10.2307/463119.

Lossin, Rebecca. "Against the Universal Library." *New Left Review* 107 (September–October 2017): 99–114.

Lugg, Rick. "The Remarkable Acceleration of Shared Print." *OCLC Next* (March 1, 2018). http://www.oclc.org/blog/main/the-remarkable-acceleration-of-shared-print/.

Lundeen, Kathleen. "'When Life Becomes Art'—on Hemans's 'Image in Lava.'" *Romanticism on the Net*, nos. 29–30 (2003). https://doi.org/10.7202/007716ar.

Lupton, Christina. *Knowing Books: The Consciousness of Mediation in Eighteenth-Century Britain*. Philadelphia: University of Pennsylvania Press, 2011.

———. *Reading and the Making of Time in the Eighteenth Century*. Baltimore: Johns Hopkins University Press, 2018.

Lupton, Deborah. *The Quantified Self: Social Media and the Accounting of Everyday Life*. Cambridge, UK: Polity, 2016.

Lutz, Deborah. "The Dead Are Still Among Us: Victorian Secular Relics, Hair Jewelry, and Death Culture." *Victorian Literature and Culture* 39, no. 1 (2011): 127–42. https://doi.org/10.1017/S1060150310000306.

Lynch, Deidre Shauna. *Loving Literature: A Cultural History*. Chicago: University of Chicago Press, 2015.

———. "Paper Slips: Album, Archiving, Accident." *Studies in Romanticism* 57, no. 1 (Spring 2018): 87–119.

M. Joblin and Co. *Louisville Past and Present*. Louisville, KY: John P. Morton and Co., 1875. http://archive.org/details/LouisvillePastAndPresent.

Madan, Falconer. "'The Duplicity of Duplicates' and 'A New Extension of Bibliography.'" *Library: Transactions of the Bibliographical Society* 12 (1911–13): 15–24.

Malpas, Constance. *Cloud-Sourcing Research Collections: Managing Print in the Mass Digitized Library Environment*. Dublin, OH: OCLC Research, 2011.

Mansfield, Kerry. *Expired*. San Francisco: Modernbook Editions, 2017.

McAllister, Alex D., and Allan Scherlen. "Weeding with Wisdom: Tuning Deselection of Print Monographs in Book-Reliant Disciplines." *Collection Management* 42, no. 2 (April 3, 2017): 76–91. https://doi.org/10.1080/01462679.2017.1299657.

McCabe, W. Gordon. "Graduates of West Point Serving in the CSA Army." *Southern Historical Society Papers* 30 (1902): 34–76.

McDowell, Kathleen. "Toward a History of Children as Readers, 1890–1930." *Book History* 12, no. 1 (2009): 240–65. https://doi.org/10.1353/bh.0.0021.

McGann, Jerome. *The Beauty of Inflections: Literary Investigations in Historical Method and Theory*. Oxford: Oxford University Press, 1985.

———. "The Gutenberg Variations." *RBM: A Journal of Rare Books, Manuscripts, and Cultural Heritage* 3, no. 1 (Spring 2002): 15–31.

———. "On Creating a Usable Future." *Profession* (2011): 182–95.

———. "Philology in a New Key." *Critical Inquiry* 39, no. 2 (2013): 327–46.

———. *The Poetics of Sensibility: A Revolution in Literary Style*. Oxford: Oxford University Press, 1998.

———. "Private Enigmas and Critical Functions, with Particular Reference to the Writing of Charles Bernstein." *New Literary History* 22, no. 2 (1991): 441–64.

———. *The Textual Condition*. Princeton: Princeton University Press, 1991.

———. "The Way We Live Now, What Is to Be Done?" *Electronic Book Review* (January 3, 2007). https://electronicbookreview.com/essay/the-way-we-live-now-what-is-to-be-done/.

McGill, Meredith L. *American Literature and the Culture of Reprinting, 1834–1853*. Philadelphia: University of Pennsylvania Press, 2007.

McKitterick, David, ed. *The Cambridge History of the Book in Britain*. Vol. 6, *1830–1914*. Cambridge: Cambridge University Press, 2014.

———. *The Invention of Rare Books: Private Interest and Public Memory, 1600–1840*. Cambridge: Cambridge University Press, 2018.

McLaughlin, Kevin. *Paperwork: Fiction and Mass Mediacy in the Paper Age*. Philadelphia: University of Pennsylvania Press, 2011.

Mead, Rebecca. "The Scourge of 'Relatability.'" *New Yorker* (August 1, 2014). https://www.newyorker.com/culture/cultural-comment/scourge-relatability.

Modern Language Association. "Statement on the Significance of Primary Records." *Profession* (1995): 27–28.

Moffat, Abbot Low. *The Pierreponts, 1802–1962: The American Forebears and the Descendants of Hezekiah Beers Pierpont and Anna Maria Constable*. Washington, DC: Privately printed, 1962.

Moine, Fabienne. *Women Poets in the Victorian Era: Cultural Practices and Nature Poetry*. New York: Routledge, 2016.

Mole, Tom. *What the Victorians Made of Romanticism: Material Artifacts, Cultural Practices, and Reception History*. Princeton: Princeton University Press, 2017.

Moore, Thomas. *The Poetical Works of Thomas Moore, Collected by Himself*. 10 vols. London: Longmans, 1840–41.

Morrogh, Mary J. "Poetry and the Evidence of Nineteenth-Century Reading." MA thesis. University of Virginia, 2017. https://doi.org/10.18130/V3B941.

Multigraph Collective. *Interacting with Print: Elements of Reading in the Era of Print Saturation*. Chicago: University of Chicago Press, 2018.

Myers, Robin, Michael Harris, and Giles Mandelbrote, eds. *Owners, Annotators, and the Signs of Reading*. New Castle, DE / London: Oak Knoll / British Library, 2005.

Nichols, Stephen G., and Abby Smith. "The Evidence in Hand: Report of the Task Force on the Artifact in Library Collections." *Council on Library and Information Resources* (November 2001). https://clir.wordpress.clir.org/wp-content/uploads/sites/6/pub103_57d70f7019307.pdf.

Nora, Pierre. "Between Memory and History: Les Lieux de Mémoire." *Representations* 26, no. 1 (1989): 7–24. https://doi.org/10.2307/2928520.

Nunberg, Geoffrey. "Google's Book Search: A Disaster for Scholars." *Chronicle of Higher Education* (August 31, 2009). https://www.chronicle.com/article/Googles-Book-Search-A/48245.

Oliva, Victor T. "Deselection of Print Monographs in the Humanities and Social Sciences in the Digital Age." *Collection Building* 35, no. 2 (2016): 37–47.

O'Neill, Michael. "A Deeper and Richer Music: Felicia Hemans in Dialogue with Wordsworth, Byron, and Shelley." *Charles Lamb Bulletin* 145 (2009): 3–12.

Orgel, Stephen. *The Reader in the Book: A Study of Spaces and Traces*. Oxford: Oxford University Press, 2018.

Osgood, Charles G. "Library Notes and Queries." *Princeton University Library Chronicle* 2, no. 3 (April 1941): 111–16.

Osman, Sharifah. "'Mightier Than Death, Untamable by Fate': Felicia Hemans's Byronic Heroines and the Sorority of the Domestic Affections." *Romanticism on the Net: An Electronic Journal Devoted to Romantic Studies* 43 (August 2006). https://doi.org/10.7202/013590ar.

Owens, Irene. "Stories Told but Yet Unfinished: Challenges Facing African-American Libraries and Special Collections in Historically Black Colleges and Universities." *Journal of Library Administration* 33, nos. 3 and 4 (April 2001): 165–81.

Pater, Walter. *The Renaissance: Studies in Art and Poetry, the 1893 Text*, ed. Donald L. Hill. Berkeley: University of California Press, 1980.

Phillips, Alfred A., ed. *The Bouquet for 1847*. New York: Nafis & Cornish, 1847. https://catalog.hathitrust.org/Record/008884337.

Pierrepont, Henry Evelyn. *Historical Sketch of the Fulton Ferry, and Its Associated Ferries*. Brooklyn: Eagle Job and Book Printing Department, 1879.

Pinch, Adela. *Strange Fits of Passion: Epistemologies of Emotion, Hume to Austen*. Stanford, CA: Stanford University Press, 1996.

Piper, Andrew. *Book Was There: Reading in Electronic Times*. Chicago: University of Chicago Press, 2013.

———. *Dreaming in Books: The Making of the Bibliographic Imagination in the Romantic Age*. Chicago: University of Chicago Press, 2013.

———. *Enumerations: Data and Literary Study*. Chicago: University of Chicago Press, 2018.

Plotz, John. "Out of Circulation: For and Against Book Collection." *Southwest Review* 84, no. 4 (1999): 462–78.

———. Review of *Practicing New Historicism*. *Modern Language Quarterly* 62, no. 3 (September 2001): 285–90. https://doi.org/10.1215/00267929-62-3-285.

Plotz, Judith. *Romanticism and the Vocation of Childhood*. New York: Palgrave Macmillan, 2001.

Poe, Edgar Allan. "The Raven." In *The Collected Works of Edgar Allan Poe*, vol. 1, *Poems*, ed. T. O. Mabbott. Cambridge, MA: Harvard University Press, 1998.

Porter, Dahlia. "Specimen Poetics: Botany, Reanimation, and the Romantic Collection." *Representations* 139, no. 1 (Summer 2017): 60–94.

Porter, Theodore M. *Trust in Numbers*. Princeton: Princeton University Press, 1996.

Potter's American Monthly 11, no. 83 (November 1878). https://catalog.hathitrust.org/Record/006062074.

Poulet, George. "Phenomenology of Reading." *New Literary History* 1, no. 1 (1969): 53–68. https://doi.org/10.2307/468372.

"Presentation of the Thomas Price Memorial Library." *University of Virginia Bulletin*, New Series, 5, no. 1 (January 1905): 1–17.

Price, Leah. *How to Do Things with Books in Victorian Britain*. Princeton: Princeton University Press, 2012.

———. "Reading: The State of the Discipline." *Book History* 7 (2004): 303–20.

Price, Thomas. "The Breakers Broken." *Southern Magazine* 8 (1871): 564.

Rathjen, Jamie. "Book Find: The Partridges Live On | Book Traces @ UVA." https://booktraces.library.virginia.edu/book-find-the-partridges-live-on/.

Raven, James. *The Business of Books: Booksellers and the English Book Trade, 1450–1850*. New Haven, CT: Yale University Press, 2007.

Renker, Elizabeth. "The 'Genteel Tradition' and Its Discontents." In *The Cambridge History of American Poetry*, ed. Alfred Bendixen and Stephen Burt, 403–24. Cambridge: Cambridge University Press, 2014. https://doi.org/10.1017/CHO9780511762284.021.

Richards, Eliza. "Outsourcing 'The Raven': Retroactive Origins." *Victorian Poetry* 43, no. 2 (Summer 2005): 205–21.

Robson, Catherine. *Heart Beats: Everyday Life and the Memorized Poem*. Princeton: Princeton University Press, 2015.

Rohrbach, Emily. *Modernity's Mist: British Romanticism and the Poetics of Anticipation*. New York: Fordham University Press, 2015.

Ross, Marlon B. *The Contours of Masculine Desire: Romanticism and the Rise of Women's Poetry*. Oxford: Oxford University Press, 1990.

Rudy, Kathryn M. *Postcards on Parchment: The Social Lives of Medieval Books.* New Haven, CT: Yale University Press, 2015.

Sachs, Jonathan. *The Poetics of Decline in British Romanticism.* Cambridge: Cambridge University Press, 2018.

———. "Slow Time." *PMLA* 134, no. 2 (March 2019): 315–31.

Sánchez-Eppler, Karen. *Dependent States: The Child's Part in Nineteenth-Century American Culture.* Chicago: University of Chicago Press, 2005.

———. "In the Archives of Childhood." In *The Children's Table: Childhood Studies and the Humanities,* ed. Anne Mae Duane, 213–37. Athens: University of Georgia Press, 2013.

Scott, Walter Dill, and Robert B. Harshe. *Charles Deering, 1852–1927: An Appreciation.* Boston: Privately printed, 1929.

Seaton, Beverly. *The Language of Flowers: A History.* Charlottesville: University of Virginia Press, 2012.

Seeber, Kevin. "Legacy Systems" (June 15, 2018). https://kevinseeber.com/blog/legacy-systems/.

Senchyne, Jonathan. "Vibrant Material Textuality: New Materialism, Book History, and the Archive in Paper." *Studies in Romanticism* 57, no. 1 (Spring 2018): 67–85.

"Service Weddings." *United States Army and Navy Journal and Gazette* (May 24, 1902): 951.

Shelley, Percy Bysshe. "Ozymandias." In *Shelley's Poetry and Prose,* ed. Donald Reiman and Neil Fraistat, 109–10. New York: W. W. Norton, 2002.

Sherman, William H. *Used Books: Marking Readers in Renaissance England.* Philadelphia: University of Pennsylvania Press, 2009.

Shore, Daniel. *Cyberformalism: Histories of Linguistic Forms in the Digital Archive.* Baltimore: Johns Hopkins University Press, 2018.

Silverman, Gillian. *Bodies and Books: Reading and the Fantasy of Communion in Nineteenth-Century America.* Philadelphia: University of Pennsylvania Press, 2012.

Simmons, J. W. *The Greek Girl: A Tale in Two Cantos.* Boston: James Munroe and Company, 1852.

———. *An Inquiry into the Moral Character of Lord Byron.* London: Ibotson and Palmer, 1826.

Simpson, David. *Wordsworth, Commodification, and Social Concern: The Poetics of Modernity.* Cambridge: Cambridge University Press, 2009.

Slaughter, Katherine E. "Jane Chapman Slaughter: Virginia's Daughter of the Modern Era." *Central Virginia Heritage* 18, no. 2 (Spring 2001).

Smith, Leanne E. "Clark, Emily Tapscott (ca. 1890–1953)." *Encyclopedia Virginia* (September 11, 2018). https://www.encyclopediavirginia.org/Clark_Emily_Tapscott_ca_1890 -1953.

Snyder, Cynthia Ehret. "Data-Driven Deselection: Multiple Point Data Using a Decision Support Tool in an Academic Library." *Collection Management* 39, no. 1 (2014): 17–31. https://doi.org/10.1080/01462679.2013.866607.

Spacks, Patricia Meyer. *On Rereading.* Cambridge, MA: Belknap Press, 2011.

Spiro, Lisa. "Reading with a Tender Rapture: 'Reveries of a Bachelor' and the Rhetoric of Detached Intimacy." *Book History* 6 (2003): 57–93.

Stanton, Frank L. "Annetta Jones—Her Book." *Current Opinion* 10 (August 1892): 126–27.

———. "A Little Book." *Current Opinion* 10 (August 1892): 383.

Stauffer, Andrew. "The Date-Stamped Book." In *The Unfinished Book,* ed. Alexandra Gillespie and Deidre Shauna Lynch, 397–411. Oxford: Oxford University Press, 2020.

———. "Hemans by the Book." *European Romantic Review* 22, no. 3 (2011): 373–80. https://doi.org/10.1080/10509585.2011.564461.

———. "My Old Sweethearts: On Digitization and the Future of the Print Record." In *Debates in the Digital Humanities 2016*, ed. Matthew K. Gold, 216–29. Minneapolis: University of Minnesota Press, 2016.

———. "The Nineteenth-Century Archive in the Digital Age." *European Romantic Review* 23, no. 3 (June 2012): 335–41. https://doi.org/10.1080/10509585.2012.674264.

———. "Ruins of Paper: Dickens and the Necropolitan Library." *Romanticism and Victorianism on the Net* 47 (August 2007). https://doi.org/10.7202/016700ar.

Staves, Susan. "Traces of a Lost Woman." *Profession* (1995): 36–38. www.jstor.org/stable/25595548.

St. Clair, William. *The Reading Nation in the Romantic Period.* Cambridge: Cambridge University Press, 2004.

Steedman, Carolyn. *Past Tenses: Essays on Writing, Autobiography and History.* London: Rivers Oram Press, 1992.

Stevenson, R. L. *A Child's Garden of Verses.* Illus. Jesse Wilcox Smith. New York: Scribners, 1905.

Stewart, Susan. *On Longing: Narratives of the Miniature, the Gigantic, the Souvenir, the Collection.* Durham, NC: Duke University Press, 1993.

"Sustainable Collections Services." OCLC. https://www.oclc.org/en/sustainable-collections.html.

Sweet, Nanora, and Julie Melnyk, eds. *Felicia Hemans: Reimagining Poetry in the Nineteenth Century.* New York: Palgrave Macmillan, 2001.

Swinburne, Algernon Charles. "Ave atque Vale." In *The Poems of Algernon Charles Swinburne,* 6 vols., 3:54. London: Chatto & Windus, 1904.

Syme, Alison. "Pressed Flowers: Burne-Jones, *The Romaunt of the Rose,* and the Kelmscott Chaucer." *Journal of Pre-Raphaelite Studies* 28 (Fall 2019): 42–70.

Tanner, Henry. *The Louisville Directory and Business Advertiser for 1861.* Louisville, KY: Louisville Directory, Printing and Binding Establishment, 1861.

Taylor, Andrew. *Textual Situations: Three Medieval Manuscripts and Their Readers.* Philadelphia: University of Pennsylvania Press, 2002.

Taylor, Bayard. *Poet's Journal.* London: Ticknor and Fields, 1863.

———. "The Song of the Camp." *Southern Literary Messenger* (August 1856): 156.

Tennyson, Alfred, Lord. "Locksley Hall." In *The Poems of Tennyson*, ed. Christopher B. Ricks, 697. London: Longmans, 1969.

———. "Ring Out, Wild Bells, to the Wild Sky." *In Memoriam (1850).* Ed. Matthew Rowlinson, 122–23. Peterborough, ON: Broadview Press, 2014.

———. *The Song of the Brook.* Troy, NY: Nims and Knight, 1886.

———. *Tennyson: A Selected Edition.* Ed. Christopher Ricks. Rev. ed. London: Routledge, 2007.

Transactions of the Medical Association of Georgia: Forty-Fourth Annual Session. Atlanta: Medical Association of Georgia, 1893.

Tucker, Herbert F. "House Arrest: The Domestication of English Poetry in the 1820s." *New Literary History* 25, no. 3 (1994): 521–48. https://doi.org/10.2307/469465.

———. "Over Worked, Worked Over: A Poetics of Fatigue." In *The Feeling of Reading: Affective Experience and Victorian Literature*, ed. Rachel Ablow, 114–30. Ann Arbor: University of Michigan Press, 2010.

Underwood, Ted. "A Genealogy of Distant Reading." *Digital Humanities Quarterly* 11, no. 2 (June 27, 2017). http://www.digitalhumanities.org/dhq/vol/11/2/000317/000317.html.

———. "Why Literary Time Is Measured in Minutes." *ELH* 85, no. 2 (June 6, 2018): 341–65. https://doi.org/10.1353/elh.2018.0013.

Vincent, David. *Literacy and Popular Culture: England 1750–1914*. Cambridge: Cambridge University Press, 1993.

Walker, Cheryl. *The Nightingale's Burden: Women Poets and American Culture Before 1900*. Bloomington: Indiana University Press, 1983.

Walt Whitman Archive. Ed. Kenneth M. Price and Ed Folsom. https://whitmanarchive.org/.

Walton, E. W. "Why Undergraduate Students Choose to Use E-books." *Journal of Librarianship and Information Science* 46, no. 4 (2014): 263–70.

Warhol, Robyn R. *Having a Good Cry: Effeminate Feelings and Pop-Culture Forms*. Columbus: Ohio State University Press, 2003.

Weedon, Alexis. *Victorian Publishing: The Economics of Book Production for a Mass Market 1836–1916*. Aldershot, UK: Ashgate, 2003.

Weeks, Lyman Horace. *A History of Paper-Manufacturing in the United States, 1690–1916*. New York: Lockwood Trade Journal Company, 1916.

Weiner, Sharon Gray. "The History of Academic Libraries in the United States: A Review of the Literature." *Library Philosophy and Practice* 7, no. 2 (Spring 2005). http://www.webpages.uidaho.edu/~mbolin/weiner.htm.

Wellmon, Chad. *Organizing Enlightenment: Information Overload and the Invention of the Modern Research University*. Baltimore: Johns Hopkins University Press, 2015.

Whitman, Walt. "So Long!" In *Leaves of Grass*, 451–56. Boston: Thayer and Eldridge, 1860.

Williams, Abigail. *The Social Life of Books: Reading Together in the Eighteenth-Century Home*. New Haven, CT: Yale University Press, 2017.

Williams, Margery. *The Velveteen Rabbit; or, How Toys Become Real*. Illus. William Nicholson. New York: Doubleday, Doran, and Co., 1922.

Wilson, Krissy. *The Art of Google Books*. http://theartofgooglebooks.tumblr.com.

Wimsatt, W. K. *The Verbal Icon: Studies in the Meaning of Poetry*. Lexington: University Press of Kentucky, 1954.

Winnicott, D. W. *Playing and Reality*. 1971. New York: Routledge Classics, 2005.

Wolfson, Susan J., ed. *Felicia Hemans: Selected Poems, Letters, Reception Materials*. Princeton: Princeton University Press, 2001.

———. "Felicia Hemans and the Revolving Doors of Reception." In *Romanticism and Women Poets: Opening the Doors of Reception*, ed. Harriet Kramer Linkin and Stephen C. Behrendt, 214–41. Lexington: University Press of Kentucky, 1999.

———. "'Something Must Be Done': Shelley, Hemans, and the Flash of Revolutionary Female Violence." In *Fellow Romantics: Male and Female British Writers, 1790–1835*, ed. Beth Lau, 199–222. Surrey, UK: Ashgate, 2009.

Woolwine, David. "Collection Development in the Humanities and Social Sciences in a Transitional Age: Deaccession of Print Items." *Library Philosophy and Practice* (2014): 1–40. http://digitalcommons.unl.edu/libphilprac/1173.

Wordsworth, William. *Ode on Immortality, and Lines on Tintern Abbey*. London: Cassell and Company, 1885. https://catalog.hathitrust.org/Record/005238556.

———. *William Wordsworth: The Major Works Including "The Prelude."* Ed. Stephen Gill. Oxford: Oxford University Press, 2008.

———. *Wordsworth's Poetry and Prose*. Ed. Nicholas Halmi. New York: W. W. Norton, 2013.

Yaffe-Bellany, David, and Jacob Stern. "Yale Students Aren't Ready to Close the Book on the School's Libraries Just Yet." *Washington Post* (April 21, 2019). https://www.washingtonpost.com/education/2019/04/21/yale-students-arent-ready-close-book-schools-libraries-just-yet.

Yeats, William Butler. *The Countess Kathleen and Various Legends and Lyrics*. Ed. John T. Nettleship. London: T. F. Unwin, 1892.

Zwerger, Mark R., et al. *The Osborn*. Charleston, SC: Arcadia Publishing, 2007.

Zytaruk, Maria. "Caught in the Archive: Unruly Objects at the Foundling Hospital." *Studies in Romanticism* 57, no. 1 (Spring 2018): 39–65.

———. "Preserved in Print: Victorian Books with Mounted Natural History Specimens." *Victorian Studies* 60, no. 2 (Winter 2018): 185–200.

Index

Acknowledgments

Book Traces has been a collaborative project from its beginnings and would not exist without the support, guidance, and plain hard work of many people to whom I owe a debt of immense gratitude. Thanks first to my students at the University of Virginia, the ones who surfaced this topic and pursued it with me for a number of years, as seekers, researchers, cataloguers, early readers, advisors, editors, and enthusiasts: Sarah Storti (who found the first book and set everything in motion), Samuel Lemley, Jackie Morrogh, James Rathjen, and Maggie Whalen, along with Emma Alpern, Kirsten Andersen, Jared Jones, Julia Shrenk, Lingerr Senghor, and Elizabeth Sutherland.

My colleagues in the UVa English Department have been a great resource throughout the years during which this project has been growing, and I want to thank all of them for the ongoing collegiality they offer and the high intellectual bar they set. I owe particularly large debts to some for their help with the writing of this book and the crafting of its arguments: Steve Arata, Ian Baucom, Anna Brickhouse, Bruce Holsinger, Jerry McGann, John Parker, Jim Seitz, and Chip Tucker. It is a great privilege and daily joy to be among their company. In the cases of Jerry and Chip, my career-long reliance on their generous influence will be obvious to anyone reading these pages.

At a key stage in its development, this book received extensive editorial advice from three of my favorite colleagues: Deidre Lynch, Jonathan Mulrooney, and Jonathan Sachs. The pages here are shot through with their brilliant interventions. Via Jonathan Sachs, the Interacting with Print Group in Montreal became a center of gravity for my work, with Andrew Piper and Tom Mole leading an extraordinary collaborative community of book historians, including Mark Algee-Hewitt, Angela Borchert, David Brewer, Thora Brylowe, Julia Carlson, Brian Cowan, Susan Dalton, Marie-Claude Felton, Michael Gamer, Paul Keen, Michelle Levy, Michael Macovski, Nick Mason, Nikola von Merveldt, Dahlia Porter, Diana Solomon, Richard Taws, and Chad Wellmon. The intellectual range and bonhomie of this group were an inspiration.

Dependent on library circulating collections, *Book Traces* has flourished because of the interest and investments made by many institutions and the generous people who work there. In every case, local faculty and librarians were crucial collaborators, arranging for stack searches with students and giving me a platform for the project. Particular thanks to Pete Capuano and Liz Lorang at the University of Nebraska; Alison Chapman at the University of Victoria; Carol Chiodo at Yale University; Lauren Coats and John Miles at Louisiana State University; Christopher Decker at University of Nevada at Las Vegas; Amy Earhart at Texas A&M University; Paula Feldman at the University of South Carolina; Ann Houston, Terese Heidenwolf, and Diane Shaw at Lafayette College; Ewan Jones at the University of Cambridge; Casie LaGette at the University of Georgia; Jill Ehnenn at Appalachian State University; Annie Johnson at Lehigh University; Jonathan Mulrooney and Mark Shelton at the College of the Holy Cross; Teresa Mangum and Amy Chen at the University of Iowa; Michelle Levy at Simon Fraser University; Deborah Lutz and Rob Detmering at the University of Louisville; Walt McGough at Brandeis University; Deborah Morse and Kim Wheatley at the College of William and Mary; Karla Neilsen and Alex Gil at Columbia University; Patricia Nugent and Sarah Allison at Loyola University New Orleans; Christopher Ohge at the University of Maine; Michael Pickard at Millsaps College; Leah Price at Rutgers University; Erin Schreiner at the New York Society Library; Amanda Licastro and Cheryl Wilson at Stevenson University; and Jay Sylvestre at the University of Miami. Many others at these institutions, including a lot of wonderful students I worked with along the way, were also active and inspiring contributors, and they have my collective thanks.

Support for the Book Traces effort was provided by the Council for Library Information Resources (CLIR) via a Cataloguing Hidden Collections grant (2015–17), which allowed us to do a large-scale survey of the pre-1923 imprints in the Alderman Library circulating collections at Virginia. A strategic planning grant from the Andrew W. Mellon Foundation (2019–20) allowed us to develop the project and scale it up. A number of the books discussed here were found thanks to those efforts. I want to convey gratitude and admiration for project manager Kristin Jensen, my co-investigator on our Mellon grant, an imaginative colleague, wise counselor, and leader of many fruitful searches in the library stacks; to Kara McClurken, my co-investigator on the CLIR grant, who sustained the work at Virginia; and to our prime collaborator Chris Ruotolo. Their engaged and indefatigable work on the project has been crucial. I am also indebted to other members of the University of Virginia library staff whose intellectual labor and support were key to this project: Jean Cooper, Cynthia Davis, Christina Deane, Lou Foster, Ivey Glendon, Jeff Hill, Holly Robertson, Jennifer Roper, Molly Schwartzburg, and Rob Smith, and, at an early stage, Nicole Bouche. Special thanks to John Unsworth for his support and guidance throughout.

Other librarians, archivists, and academic policy leaders have been key to *Book Traces*, and I want to single out the following who were paricularly sustaining: Greg Eow, Michael Furlough, Molly Hardy, Chuck Henry, Athena Jackson, Robert Kieft, Jacob Nadal, Karla Neilsen, Lizanne Payne, Alice Schreyer, Susan Stearns, and Doug Way. For lending their wisdom to these conversations as part of the Future of the Print Record Working Group, I also want to thank Dan Cohen, Seth Denbo, Kathleen Fitzpatrick, Michael Hancher, Elliott Shore, and Steve Wheatley.

My writing and thinking were generously supported by a Pine Tree Fellowship in the Advanced Research Collaborative (ARC) at the City University of New York Graduate Center in 2013–14. Many thanks to Sylvia Tannenbaum, whose support funded the fellowship, and to Don Robotham, Matt Gold, and the ARC community for their advice and support during that fantastic year in New York, a transformative one for the project.

For the wisdom and encouragement they provided, my warm thanks to the following scholars: Halina Adams, Tom Augst, Michael Cohen, Pat Crain, Lindsey Eckert, Ari Epstein, John Garcia, Sarah Gardner, Anthony Grafton, Austin Graham, Peter Graham, Barbara Heritage, Mary Louise Kete, Devoney Looser, Christina Lupton, Meredith McGill, Bethany Nowviskie, Leah Price, Michelle Taylor, and Marion Thain. Joe Wallace did a first-rate job of improving the prose, spotting errors, and pushing the book toward consistency and completion. Special gratitude for friendship and advice through it all to Zahr Said, Michael St. Clair, and Jim Wamsley.

Thanks to Jerry Singerman, my editor at the University of Pennsylvania Press, for his unflagging sponsorship of the book and his trenchant advice that shaped its arguments and presentation. My two anonymous readers at the press were also extremely important in determining the final shape of things, and I appreciate their helpful suggestions that came from analyses of the manuscript as incisive as they were generous. My copy editor Christine Dahlin sharpened my prose, clarified my arguments, and made sure that everything tallied, and Erica Ginsburg, Managing Editor at the press, made many welcome adjustments and guided this volume to publication with a steady hand. They both have my sincere gratitude; any remaining errors are my own.

An earlier version of Chapter 1 appeared as "An Image in Lava: Annotation, Sentiment, and the Traces of Nineteenth-Century Reading," *PMLA* (2019), and some of its examples had been first presented in "Hemans by the Book," *European Romantic Review* (2011). Chapter 5 on library policy developments has a few parts adapted from another *European Romantic Review* piece, "The Nineteenth Century Archive in the Digital Age" (2012), and a shorter, different version of the chapter will be published in a volume of essays on libraries edited by Jason Camlot, *The Promise of Paradise: The Changing Meaning of Libraries.* Several paragraphs from Chapter 3 appeared in my article "Poetry, Romanticism, and the Practice of Nineteenth-Century Books," *Nineteenth-Century Contexts* (2012), and some examples from that chapter also appear in the "Marking" chapter of Multigraph Collective's *Interacting with Print* (University of Chicago Press, 2018). My thanks to these venues for publishing my work and for granting permission for its reuse here.

I began this book with an epigraph from Yeats, in which Fergus marvels at the "great webs of sorrow" hidden in those little bags of dreams we sometimes call books, and I'll end with him as well. In *Pictures of the Gone World* (City Lights, 1955), Lawrence Ferlinghetti writes that reading Yeats makes him think of "midsummer New York / and of myself back then / reading that copy I found / on the Thirdavenue El":

Reading Yeats I do not think
                            of Arcady
and of its woods which Yeats thought dead
                            I think instead
    of all the gone faces
        getting off at midtown places
    with their hats and their jobs
    and of that lost book I had
        with its blue cover and its white inside
    where a pencilhand had written
                    HORSEMAN, PASS BY!

A good part of *Book Traces* was written in New York City, when I was living with Megan O'Donnell on Bleecker Street, close to Third Avenue, where Ferlinghetti's elevated subway once ran. In the copy of Ferlinghetti's *Pictures of the Gone World* that I found then at a nearby bookstore, I made a discovery of my own: a clipped printing of Yeats's "When You Are Old" used as a bookmark by a former reader—itself a little book trace, a picture of a Gonne world. That copy—also "gone" (like Ferlinghetti's world) in the Beat sense (i.e., amazing and cool)—seems an apt and serendipitous emblem for the layers of memory, material, and marking that I have traversed in writing this book and these acknowledgments. I could not have done it without the love and support of my partner, Megan, my children,

Layth and Farah, and my parents, Libby and George, all of whom have sustained me and believed in me through the years and whom I will love even beyond when I am "old and grey and full of sleep." I promise I will annotate their personal copies with even more well-deserved sentimental traces. "Cast your mind on other days," says Yeats in "Under Ben Bulben," from which Ferlinghetti's marginalian quotes in his pencilhand. All of the people named here, and others, friends and companions who colored the fabric of my days as this book was being written, make heeding that directive a joy.